CLASSICAL
RHETORIC &
MEDIEVAL
HISTORIOGRAPHY

CLASSICAL RHETORIC & MEDIEVAL HISTORIOGRAPHY

Edited by

ERNST BREISACH

STUDIES IN MEDIEVAL CULTURE XIX
MEDIEVAL INSTITUTE PUBLICATIONS
WESTERN MICHIGAN UNIVERSITY
KALAMAZOO, MI — 1985

Library of Congress Cataloging in Publication Data
Main entry under title:

Classical rhetoric and medieval historiography.

(Studies in medieval culture ; 19)
1. Rhetoric, Medieval—Addresses, essays, lectures.
2. Historiography—History—Addresses, essays, lectures.
I. Breisach, Ernst. II. Title: Medieval historiography.
III. Series.
CB351.S83 vol. 19 [PN183] 940.1'7 s [907'.2] 85-3055
0-918720-56-7
0-918720-57-5 (pbk)

Cover design by Pamela Rups
Printed in the United States of America

CONTENTS

INTRODUCTION

Unlike modern scholars, medieval historians were not overly genre-conscious, although they could have learned from Isidore of Seville about the late classical categories of history writing— *historia, chronica, annales*, and *calendaria*—and how these were distinguished by the scope and fullness of their accounts. Eventually, in the High Middle Ages, the problem of genres resurfaced, prompted most often by the perceived differences between *historia* and *chronica*—two genres for which scope alone proved insufficient as the distinguishing criterion. What provoked attention was the manner in which the story of the past was told: bare in the *chronica*; elaborate, even interpretive, in the *historia*. Thus the issue of the exact role of language in the historical narrative was once more joined and continued to be raised, especially in the context of rhetoric, as late as the debates over the *ars historica* in the sixteenth and seventeenth centuries. Afterwards, as the new spirit of the sciences and of rationalist philosophy moved discussions of historical truth into the proximity of epistemology, debates on the issue lost some of their fervor and popularity and became detached from the close link with rhetoric. History began to aspire to depicting reality devoid of all distortions by eloquence or didactics, and, thus, nineteenth century historians with all their loving attention to the finding, editing, and publishing of medieval source material, did not conceive of rhetoric as a proper instrument for the appreciation and evaluation of that material. Their concern with the *wie es eigentlich gewesen ist* led to a sorting of the wheat (the facts in the modern sense) from piles of chaff (the "distorted" material) in which rhetoric appeared as a purely negative feature, an obstacle on the way to truth.

About a century ago, however, the intellectual climate began

1

to change in a direction favorable to the understanding, if not the appreciation, of rhetoric. The perennial struggle for historical truth became even more arduous when waves of doubt began to erode all traditional supports for an absolute truth, and scholars commenced to perceive the narratives of history as constructs of human perception rather than as mirror images of reality. That perception bridged (or, as critics would say, ignored) the gulf between a partially known and knowable reality of interconnected phenomena and its perceptual mastery in language. As a consequence, language increasingly came to be seen as the key to understanding the complex connections between human perception and a puzzling external reality until, for some critics and philosophers, reality was just about absorbed into the language act.

Such a situation was bound to recall to modern minds the ancient and medieval enterprise of rhetoric which always had insisted that, inasmuch as language in many ways did shape if not constitute reality, language and reality were intricately connected. Yet, even with the recent radical tilt towards language in the relationship between reality and language, the problem of historical discourse has remained unresolved, as witnessed by the recent discussions in analytical philosophy, narrativist theory, and structuralist thought.

Favored by that new climate, there has occurred, since 1945, a remarkable renaissance of rhetorical studies in the wider context of the investigations of the relationship between language and reality. That interest has been running counter to the increasingly deprecating use of the term "rhetoric" by the mass media, equating it with dissimulation, and the relative neglect of rhetoric by modern communication theory. During the last three decades, the study of rhetoric in the Middle Ages and the Renaissance has flourished. Many publications have traced the development of rhetoric and its influence on a wide variety of language acts during these periods. Yet, historical writing was not a favored object of scrutiny among the many studies of rhetoric's influence on medieval literature, education, and preaching. This situation prompted a few scholars to call more attention to the work being done and yet to be done that demonstrates the links between the rhetoric of the ancient period and the historiography of the Middle Ages and the Renaissance. Beginning in 1978 they organized a number of sessions on the topic within the framework of the Medieval Congresses at Kalamazoo. There, the authors of the essays in this volume and other scholars presented results of their research for scholarly discussion, and presented here is a selection of works by participants in those sessions.

Nancy Partner's essay explores in a wide-ranging manner the issue of the connection between language and reality. Her analysis of the relationship between logic and rhetoric in the twelfth century provides the starting point for an extensive intellectual journey exploring typical ways in which human experience is expressed in language by writers of even the most recent period. Proust and modern theoreticians of language help her to illumine what she considers the impossible task medieval historians faced in depicting *invisibilia* and how startlingly continuous the language-reality argument is.

Roger Ray and John Ward share John of Salisbury as the focus of their investigations, and they proceed along similar lines. Gervase's bafflement over the differences between the *historici* and *chronici*—their eloquent and their bare accounts—triggers Roger Ray's inquiry into the historical narrative as a language form. For Ray, rhetoric emerges as the crucial and positive element in constructing a verisimilar discourse about the amibiguity of human existence. Ward also starts with the investigation of language as the mediator between the immediacy of life and the narrative, but he stresses the danger that rhetoric, the clever art of persuasion, might seduce the historical narrator into giving inauthentic accounts. Aiming at recovering the core of facts, Ward sees in the study of rhetoric the means to delineate the elements of interpretation, selection, and truth-seeking in medieval historical narratives.

The greater and more conscious use of rhetoric in the 1500s and the 1600s is reflected in Donald J. Wilcox's essay, where the major point is a comparison between the depicting of events in medieval historical narratives and in Machiavelli's work. The issue is less whether the narrative in general is *verum* or *verax* than what the narrative reveals about the changing image of reality. Wilcox argues for a sharp difference between the abstract, *a priori* procedure of medieval historians, who saw events succeed each other in a line leading "from-to," and Machiavelli's attempt to show the knotting of many interconnected forces in noteworthy events. Language forms reflect thought models.

This collection of essays neither aims nor pretends to be a comprehensive treatment of the questions raised by the interconnections between rhetoric and historical narratives. The four

3

scholars, however, deal with issues that demonstrate the crucial importance of these interconnections for an understanding of historical writing in the Middle Ages and the Renaissance. Together with the well-known works by Jerome Siegel, Nancy Struever, and other scholars, the collection will help fortify the strength of interest and inquiry directed toward rhetoric's symbiosis with historiography in centuries past. It illustrates an approach to explanation that pushes the explanatory limits beyond the realm of pure *Ideengeschichte* (history of ideas) and the positivism of facts and yet stays well within modern analytical thought.

Ernst Breisach
Western Michigan University

THE NEW CORNIFICIUS: MEDIEVAL HISTORY AND THE ARTIFICE OF WORDS

NANCY F. PARTNER

Traditional Rhetoric and Medieval Historical Writing

> I would openly identify Cornificius and call him by his own name, I would reveal to the public his bloated gluttony, puffed-up pride, obscene mouth, rapacious greed, irresponsible conduct, loathsome habits (which nauseate all about him), foul lust, dissipated appearance, evil life, and ill repute, were it not that I am restrained by reverence for his Christian name. . . . I have thought it better to be lenient.

> In the judgement of Cornificius (if a false opinion can be called a judgement), there is no point in studying the rules of eloquence, which is a gift that is either conceded or denied to each individual by nature. . . . Finally [Cornificius argues], what can eloquence and philosophy possibly have in common? The former relates to language, but the latter seeks after, investigates, applies itself to learning the ways of wisdom. . . . Clearly the rules of eloquence confer neither wisdom nor love of wisdom. . . . Philosophy (or wisdom, its object) is concerned not with words, but with facts.[1]

There is a noticeable tendency, surfacing at various times and places in history, for discourse on the role and importance of language in human affairs to become a bit overwrought. Socrates and Plato accused the Sophists of fostering a cynical moral bankruptcy in susceptible youth by teaching them to talk well, thereby beginning the quarrel between the philosophers and the rhetors, acts and words, truth and seeming, real and fictive, inner and

5

outer—a dispute which, so long as words can persuade and pun, will never end. Augustine, whose matured intricate style was the effective expressive instrument of his spiritual life, remembered his parent's self-sacrifice to finance his education with astonishing ingratitude and, in deep, obscure connection, positively blamed them for neglecting to control his adolescent sexuality. By the time John of Salisbury studied at Paris and Chartres, the beauties of language were no longer a danger to salvation, and it is odd to note the persistent themes of corruption and sex with the argument reversed. Nothing quite like that hot tone had been a part of European discourse on language since Jerome's soul fought the seduction of Cicero and the young Benedict stepped back from the abyss of sin by dropping out of school. John's abuse ("obscene mouth," "loathsome habits," "foul lust") of a man, whoever Cornificius was, who thought that eloquence made a trivial and superficial study, testifies to the return of civilization in the twelfth century.

But just as in Plato's time, those who win the arguments do not always have their way. Young men, who should have been learning to define the Good and the Beautiful, flocked to the teachers who promised them what they wanted—verbal resource and elegance. So in twelfth-century Europe, although John could not see "how anything could be more generally useful: more helpful in acquiring wealth, more reliable in winning favor, more suited for gaining fame, than eloquence,"[2] students increasingly wanted logic. There was not much opposition. As the center and focus of higher education, the systematic acquisition of the skills of persuasive speech had long since disappeared (Augustine's *De doctrina Christiana* must be one of the last books written in the West which could assume the existence of professional rhetors offering the old course of study), and eloquence had largely become a textbook subject. John himself had had the advantage of studying with Bernard of Chartres, who adapted Quintilian's methods for his own students and clearly made literary language a live pursuit, but Bernard was exceptional.[3] And, by 1159 when he completed the *Metalogicon*, so was John in his insistence on an equal place in the *Trivium* for literary studies along with Aristotelian logic.

Prescriptive or technical rhetoric, as it was known to medieval students through Isidore of Seville's epitome and the few classical texts which were themselves only handbooks or digests meant to accompany a course of exercises, was easily subordinated to the uses of dialectical reasoning. Boethius had already done just that with his work, *De topicis differentiis*, which was intended as an ancillary study on the correct analysis of terms for use in syllogistic constructions; Cicero's book on invention (especially with later commentaries) lent itself to the same uses.[4] The traditional, theoretical use of rhetorical art for argument in courts of law, carefully (or quixotically) preserved in all the classical handbooks long after jury trials were defunct, gave textbook rhetoric the general tone of formal disputation, distinct from dialectic in that it dealt only with particular cases and probable argument or enthymeme, whereas dialectic was concerned with general propositions and demonstrative reasoning. Nonetheless, the bare possibility that rhetoric could be largely removed from its broad literary uses to become limited to the classification of terms for correct predicate ascription in syllogistic argument would not (even with Boethius' influence) have diminished it to that technical use during the high Middle Ages had there not already been an overwhelming attraction to the study of logic.

Even so, it is one thing to understand (following Richard McKeon's classic essay on the subject[5]) how rhetoric was subsumed into logic as the part concerned with probable argumentation, and quite another to understand why there should have been so strong an attraction on the part of so many generations of students (few of whom became professional academics) to a subject of so little obvious charm as Aristotelian logic. The most persuasive explanation has to be Richard Southern's intuitive vision of formal logic as the triumph of medieval "humanism" (in the sense of the tendency to stress "dignity, order, reason, and intelligibility . . . in human experience"), the confident extension of human reason over all the phenomena of the world, bringing definition, understanding, and control where there had been only chaos, confusion, and helplessness.[6] We sort experience now into explanatory categories, assigning provisional causes for incomplete or odd information with such off-hand competence that we can only sometimes, in imagination, feel a baffled impuissance before the familiar but imponderable. The timeless erotic still holds occasions for cultural relapse and consequent longings for order: all his knowledge of literature did not help Proust's Marcel decipher his first experience with love:

> Faced with the thoughts, the actions of a woman whom
> we love, we are as completely at a loss as the world's

first natural philosophers must have been, face to face
with the phenomena of nature. . . . Or, worse still, we
are like a person in whose mind the law of causality
barely exists, a person who would be incapable, therefore, of establishing a connection between one phenomenon and another and to whose eyes the spectacle of
the world would appear as unstable as a dream. Of course
I made efforts to emerge from this incoherence, to find
reasons for things.[7]

Recapitulating with Marcel, in his wretchedness, a telescoped
version of cultural development (incomplete however—he never
understands Gilberte), we perhaps grasp for a moment the excitement of a promised relief from inadequacy and incoherence,
the promise of entry into a world susceptible of analysis, and
security. Southern's interpretation of the dominant influence of
formal logic in the high Middle Ages assumes that whatever was
present in striking and admirable degrees, some vital sense of
causality, of intuitive, automatic connections between things, was
absent from the mental culture in equally striking degrees.

Many of us, modern students of medieval writing, would
gladly give the victory back to John. Aristotelian logic may have
restored a sense of mental competence to thousands of medieval
students, but it takes a strenuous act of imagination to see it in
that light. It is far clearer to us that traditional rhetoric, especially
as conveyed by the intelligence of Cicero, Quintilian, and the *Ad
Herennium* author, with its delineation of strategies of argument,
narrative logic, and use of evidence, all in recognizable human
terms, implies and supports a high degree of rational, human
competence.

Cornificius' advice to do what comes naturally might be all
very well for innately gifted talkers and writers, but it offers precious little guidance for later, often puzzled, readers. John's approach, which stresses continuity with an older literary culture,
gives some hope to scholars that they can reconstruct some of
the mental framework within which literature was produced and
so understand it. Aristotle's *Categories* do not help us read the
kinds of literature that were deeply intertwined with the traditions
and standards of eloquence—epic and lyric poetry, panegyric and
hagiography, romance and history. But the desire of scholars for
a set of analytical instruments for dissecting texts is not the sole
reason to consider keeping rhetoric at the center of the study of

medieval culture. John of Salisbury may have despaired of the coming generation of logic-babblers, but rhetoric was too solidly entrenched in the very conception of literature to be dispensed with entirely. Pushed from the center of intellectual formation, it held firmly elsewhere.

Truncated, epitomized and dessicated, culturally displaced, and badly taught, rhetoric was yet antiquity's domineering gift from the grave. Rhetoric had been for centuries the center and organizing focus of the cultivated mind. From it proceeded poetry and literary prose, the discourse of law courts, public eulogies and propaganda, and sheer virtuosic display for entertainment. It offered rules and procedures for making literature: techniques for finding material, strategies for arranging it well, endless variety of possible diction, and an analytical vocabulary sufficient for discussing both itself and all literature. What could possibly replace this wealth? Even the mature, self-critical, and puritanical Augustine of the *Doctrina Christiana* would not banish those resources from Christian life, only discipline them.[8] There cannot be any fundamental question of the survival of technical rhetoric into the Middle Ages. As a subject in itself, medieval rhetoric is on secure ground and, in recent years, in exceptionally capable scholarly hands.[9]

The trickier questions arise in attempts to use rhetoric to discern in various kinds of medieval literature the preconceptions, models, and intentional techniques of their authors. Everyone who has attempted it knows too well that the relationship between prescriptive theory and specific text, so clear and indubitable in Virgil, Juvenal, or Livy, is nowhere near so apparent in any case from Gregory of Tours and later authors.

History makes an irresistible and exasperating test case. Suspended, as a genre, somewhere between epic (as Quintilian saw it) and laundry lists (as many medieval monks practiced it), history was deeply imbedded in the art of eloquence: "What class of orator and how great a master of language is qualified to write history?" is the question that opens the discussion of historical writing in Cicero's *De oratore*.[10] The mild objection that the rhetoric texts offer no specific directions for that kind of writing is dismissed with the sensible observation that since history is only a specific application of the inclusive art of language, it requires no special training. Once the prospective historian had mastered the essentials, that is, the high degree of "fluency and diversity of diction" necessary for history, and had determined to be honest

9

and "make bold to tell the whole truth," everything else followed quite naturally: chronological arrangement, important actions and their results, depiction of character, motive, accident and intention, a pleasurable unexaggerated style. History was a difficult art whose difficulties were encompassed entirely in the normal course of rhetorical education; like many other special arts, "when the hardest portions of each have been taught, the rest, through being either easier or just like the former, call for no teaching."[11] Cicero's assumptions about the historian's education and art were quite traditional in his own day and continued unchallenged in theory and only partially modified in practice until quite recently.

The argument from tradition and authority is reinforced for modern tastes by a genuine rational impetus as well. We know very well that Cicero's off-hand confidence merely avoided many problems specific to the art of history even as practiced in his time and that these problems were made incalculably more complex by the opening of history to the new preoccupations, new classes of actor and event, the extended, immaterial reality of medieval Christian life. Yet history remained fixed, perhaps more than other genres, in its classical status as a minor form of eloquence; the continuity of rhetoric as a part of education helped to ensure that. If there were no analyzed models of historical procedure, no schools or masters of history, no rigorous standards for evidence, documents, witnesses—in fact, nothing but the feeble, reiterated, traditional assertion by the historian that he is an honest man and intends to tell the truth—then how perfectly tempting, and sensible, to look to the books we know the historians as schoolboys did study and see what in them could have influenced historical writing. At least the rhetorical manuals deal with the social world, the *saeculum*, and so does history (even if medieval historians wander from it); they teach how to select and arrange evidence into lines of probable connection (even though medieval historians rarely did that); the closeness of rhetoric to logic and law brings into play natural reason whose suitable object is human life (even if medieval historians did not wholly accept that). The historical understanding, as most modern historians accept it, is deliberative rhetoric made retrospective. The example from the *Ad Herennium* for debate—in the Italic war, the senate deliberates whether or not to grant citizenship to the Allies—requires only minor adjustment to become a modern consideration of that decision and its consequences for the Roman state.[12]

10

In any case, any demonstrable influence of rhetoric on medieval historical writing seems to introduce an element of rational inquiry and critical judgement. It seems to save it from total irrationality and slackness and makes it seem at least an honest, if humble, precursor of modern critical history. From that point of view, an argument can be made that influence from classical rhetoric was one channel for self-sufficient reason into medieval historical thought. This is precisely the argument made by Nancy Struever about the effect of intensified interest in rhetoric on historical conceptions in Renaissance Italy.[13]

Some of the streams of continuity are reasonably direct. Classical history favored near-contemporary subjects, eye-witness evidence, or good testimony, a plausible, coherent narrative full of convincing detail arranged in the narrative-speech-narrative rhythm, explanation of events based on the moral character and intelligence of the active agents, and (*pace* Cicero) as much fictional invention as seemed necessary to create the desired effects. (It is not at all clear that Cicero intended his stricture about historians telling only the truth to apply to anything beyond moral considerations—assigning praise and blame without servility or malice. Plausible fictions for the sake of fullness and narrative continuity probably were considered morally neutral and aesthetically imperative.)

Even in classical antiquity, the influence of rhetoric on history was mostly casual and semi-direct, because then, as later, history was not taught as a genre of prose composition with its own techniques and methods. As Cicero makes clear, it was discussed a bit, but that is to approach the subject very much from the outside and after the fact. There were no historians who were not something else first and more importantly. But in antiquity, rhetoric dominated intellectual and literary life: it was not *taught* in higher education, it *was* higher education. Rhetoric supplied not merely a method of composition and oration but a world of expectations, perceptions, values, ends, means, effects—in short, everything that makes up a mental life. History absorbed some of its dominant concerns, especially persuasiveness, *gravitas*, order, and a special kind of verisimilitude with a flexible link to verifiable accuracy. Classical history was rhetorical in the sense that all literary and intellectual effort was rhetorical.

Certain traditions inherited by medieval history include the prologue, use of speeches, character sketches in classical format, moral action as a causal agent, and an inclination to write about

11

war. Christian history could not be confined to contemporary politics, but classical standards of evidence remained untouched, indeed reached a strangely pure fulfillment, however the chronological span lengthened and subjects changed. The necessary documentary evidence for past events was assimilated to testimony (as Eusebius had introduced it), and the authors of written evidence were evaluated for moral soundness. (The charters and records of gifts copied into monastic chronicles could be literally called as witness in civil suits.) Words that sounded like first-hand witness satisfied the rhetorical imperative of plausibility; such is Felix's eye-witness account of the death of Guthlac, taken from Bede's death of Cuthbert, identical with an earlier, anonymous account. A good cause could produce almost anything in the way of testimony—like Eadmer's forged saints' lives for Canterbury. Like the song that goes, "I danced with a man, who danced with a girl, who danced with the Prince of Wales," the point was to get close enough to see for yourself or, more commonly, to give that impression. (In an odd way, visions of the Other World fulfilled classical requirements for evidence remarkably well.)

The harder question turns on how thoroughly, consciously, and purposefully historians used the rhetorical knowledge available to them. It is not especially helpful to students of medieval culture to work out in much detail that knowledge of the *Ad Herennium* suggested to an historian that he begin with an exordium and end with a conclusion (which, in any case, many neglected to do). If the object is to understand medieval minds and medieval practices, then tracking the rhetorical figures in historical writing is only rewarding if the use of those devices was more than superficial, if the categories and means of argument offered by prescriptive rhetoric actually appear to have helped a medieval historian work out an intelligible sense of life. It is not enough for *us* to notice that much of judicial rhetoric was obviously appropriate for historical thought and writing when the question is whether medieval historians noticed it and whether, given their own post-classical view of the world and its forces, they really saw the connection at all.

The very thing that made rhetoric so useful for all serious medieval literature could have been exactly what prevented its deeper application to the problems of historical argument and presentation—the fact of history as literature. The idea, so indubitable, that serious history was "high" literature, with all the stylistic demands that that implied, would necessarily turn the

12

author's fullest attention to the tropes and figures and, perhaps, distract him from the somewhat less obviously useful aspects of evidence and argument. Cicero never mentions evidence. He describes the development of history from bare notation to high art solely in terms of verbal ornament:

> A similar style of writing [to the Pontifical Chronicles] has been adopted by many who, without any rhetorical ornament, have left behind them bare records of dates, personalities, places and events . . . it is only of late decoration of that sort has been brought into this country. . . .

One of the speakers remarks on "how great a responsibility the orator has in historical writing. I rather think that for fluency and diversity of diction it comes first."[14] Quintilian had little to say on the subject except that history was like epic, only in prose. The *Ad Herennium* is silent. After Herodotus who, honest man that he was, tells us that he asked questions and heard stories and will repeat what he heard, most historians, ancient and medieval, suppress ignorance and fill in gaps, as the books had taught them.

Both Tacitus and Bede wrote history and on rhetoric; their respective rhetorical books are as revealing as their histories. Tacitus' *Dialogue on Oratory* is a leisurely, good-humored vignette from the social life of men like himself: in a morning of visits, a group of friends considers the best use to which an educated man should put his skill with language—a public life of clients, applause, protégés, money, or a retired life of dignified leisure and elegant literary pursuits. The debate is more than a bit artificial because the two lives blend easily, as Tacitus' career reveals; the same developed skill in expression supported the full range of activity favored by upper-class men. Bede's work on rhetoric was equally characteristic of his career: it was a text on tropes and figures for the use of the boys he taught in his monastery. One can certainly find a variety of rhetorical figures in his historical writing, but the vital, fluid continuity between an elaborate, prolonged education in literary expression and the writing produced by the graduates, initiates really, of that education, which Tacitus displayed in every line he wrote, is gone, Even for the learned Bede, rhetoric was a textbook artifact of a distant age and culture; the clues to his history lie elsewhere. Tacitus' friends chatting about life and letters reveal the unstrained congruity of learned discourse with a complete underlying society. Tacitus' book on rhetoric and his histories merge as they reflect a single world, seen from a unified point. Auerbach's beautiful analysis of the revolt of the Germanic legions in Tacitus' *Annals* acknowledges the power of rhetorical history, its integrated, dramatic effect, and its intellectual limits as well.[15]

The speakers in the *Dialogue* draw a distinction between the structure and the ornamentation of a building (much later, a central idea for Ruskin, for similar reasons) which is analogous to the structure of a literary work, its narration and argument as distinct from its verbal ornament. The ability to create a sound structure is taken much for granted; taste and original genius play over the surface. No one of this company has a kind word for simple chroniclers.[16] Like the aesthetic standards they share, the lives of the friends in the *Dialogue* are founded on the social, economic, and political conditions of cultivated upper-class life, taken entirely for granted, over which individual taste can seek expression within the canons of elegance and suitability. Literature and life share the same world.

The element in Bede's history which compels admiration is its triumph over chaos: a triumph in perpetual, uneasy risk until the end of the book, so deeply moving, when the beauty of the author's character and courageous, high vision of spiritual and political unity, so far from achieved, assure us (already thinking of Northmen) that some triumphs, those of intelligence and nobility of spirit, do endure. That steady focus, the principle of selection and emphasis which asserts its clear purpose over the violence and disorder of the world and makes history out of raw experience, did not proceed from Bede's literary education or from his experience of eighth-century Northumbria. His ability to create a coherent world was his own deeply personal and deeply religious achievement. The difference between the worlds of Gregory of Tours and of Bede has more to do with Gregory and Bede than the advance of civilization from the sixth to the eighth centuries.[17] Bede's book on rhetoric was a dutiful homage, a minor weapon for the battle of the *milites Christi* against gross ignorance. The ornaments of words that Bede taught the boys, given, like himself, to a fortress against the world, had to be superimposed on a social, economic, and intellectual life which shared nothing with the culture which had found its natural expression in the beauty of transposed words.

14

> See now, I have carefully investigated and truthfully de-
> scribed what God's ordinance providently revealed in
> the duke's last days. I neither compose a fictitious trag-
> edy for the sake of gain, nor entertain cackling parasites
> with a wordy comedy, but truly record events of differ-
> ent kinds for studious readers.[18]

Not tragedy or comedy but history, Orderic Vitalis rather querulously insisted toward the middle of his history of the abbey of St. Evroulx, and Normandy, and England. He had learned (from Quintilian perhaps) where to place his work on the tradi-tional rhetorical spectrum which ranged from tragedy which was fictional and improbable, through comedy which was fictional but plausible, to history which was true and plausible.[19] Orderic's history is punctuated, at the beginnings and ends of books, with retorts, self-justifications, and mysterious attacks on unnamed critics who apparently were dissatisfied with his book for obscure reasons; it is hinted that some of his readers, or auditors, wanted more meaning, more morals to the story, more uplift.[20] It is pos-sible, of course, that they were simply bored. He might have done better to study tragedy and comedy more closely. In his more peevish moments, Orderic is the classical truth-teller, sadly com-pelled to record all the sordid iniquity of the age, even though his frivolous readers prefer lowbrow marvels and happy endings. It is hard to infer what exactly was found lacking in his history by contemporaries; reading it now does not produce an impression of unrelieved moral gloom. In fact, the mass of his material, ar-ranged with evident difficulty into chronological sequence, un-controllably shapeless, tends to drown out any particular impression. Orderic's relation to his sources is a watery one, with the overwhelmed author swimming hard to stay on top. His orig-inal choice of subject, the history of his monastery, was inade-quate to contain his materials or his ambitions, but as subject opened upon subject, he never redesigned the enterprise. His history, like that of so many of his contemporaries, is full of good things—but the structure of the edifice, which Tacitus' friends found so boring to discuss, is hopelessly lost.[21]

We may never discover exactly what Orderic's readers found lacking in his history, but it is always the paratactic arrangement of medieval historical narrative that is at the heart of everything we find most difficult about it and which ultimately defies under-standing. Compared with the narratives of antiquity which served as models, medieval narrative seems terribly slack and fallen-off from any aesthetic or intellectual standard. Of all the forms of literary prose, history would seem to depend most on coherent narrative structure for its larger effects. The reader's sense of conviction is a response to apt selection of materials and the relations in which they are set forth: sufficient fullness without pointless digression; intelligible sequence; descriptions made probable with respect to known facts of person, time, and place; and inferences which move in reasonable lines of argument. None of this requires the study of formal logic—it is all enthymeme and belonged to the rhetorical fields of *narratio* and *argumentum*.[22] The *Ad Herennium* author recognized that a scrupulous recitation of actual fact could still lack plausibility if the *narratio* were ineptly constructed;[23] convincing narrative of fact required the same care as ficton.

But when Cicero mentioned the "hard parts" of eloquence from which all kinds of literature proceed, he was probably thinking more about diction and expressive ornament than structure. In educational practice in antiquity, narrative was the ground bass over which the sequence of exercises played their increasingly elaborate motifs. Whatever else it did or failed to do in antiquity, rhetorical training—not the handbooks and texts which must have been about as interesting to read then as they are now, but the whole extended course of exercises written, corrected, and sometimes recited under the direction of a teacher—made men fluent and clever. It may not have made them honest or good or wise, original, profound, or witty—but it did make them capable with words. The "secret" lay in all those little boys re-telling Aesop's fables in their own words and explaining what the fox and the crow really meant, and then composing a few words for Achilles at the funeral of Patrocles, and going on to tell the story of Hannibal crossing the Alps—in reverse order.[24] This practice made fluent and coherent speakers and writers. In the Renaissance, something very similar may have worked again to the same purpose. Quintilian gives the whole of Book 7 of the *Institutes* to a thorough and penetrating discussion of the problems and techniques of prose structure; he describes the very interior process of thinking through an array of ideas, making calculations of selection and suppression for the sake of an intended effect. And he admits that this skill cannot be taught by rule.

The difficulties in reading medieval histories are nearly all narrative. The plausibility of historical narrative is not a function of abstract truth and falsity, or even verifiability (our current rhetorical strategy, largely a matter of shared conventions, is a strategy even when the parts "work"), certainly not of any fixed standard for reality (in Bede's time miracles were plausible), but of the telling, the connections and sequences of things. Almost nothing medieval historians tell us is plausible, even when we know it is true.[25] Where had verisimilitude gone? It had gone the way of narrative.

One can only speculate on the causes for this absence of explanatory form. Perhaps in an intellectual world where so many ultimate truths were known, yet so much of secular and natural life was mysterious and uncontrollable, the ability to discern the "argument," which involves the alignment of discreet entities with one another in a manner that invokes the verifying presence of some generally accepted principle, was nearly lost. The significance of single events was often, of course, a subject for comment, but the events in which historians found meaning, linking heaven and earth in a vertical cut (in Auerbach's classic formulation) were almost always *out* of the ordinary: marvels, wonders, surprises. It is already apparent in Eusebius' history that the infinitely expanded scope of a human history that begins with the Beginning, and includes all the facets of ultimate truth that touch human life, threatened to dissolve literary coherence. Heaven and earth cannot be given equal attention in one book. (Even Milton only managed by confining himself to a time when earth had a limited population and very little history.)

Rhetorical history, ancient and medieval, was exemplary history; writers of antiquity could be just as moralizing as later writers, could distort and invent for the sake of a lesson. But there is a difference between the kinds of good and evil which interested writers in antiquity and in medieval times. The classical virtues of the ancestors were civic, domestic, and ethical, with the effect of guiding and stabilizing social and political life; their vices were also social (ambition, demagoguery, treason, luxury, corruption of youth and women) and took their toll in the social spheres of life. The punishment of evil, when punishment occurred, was the revenge of justice; more often, harm was seen to be inflicted on the *res publica* or on smaller human associations—class, family, or friends. History, as a literary genre, could accommodate this better than the demands of Christian virtue and sin, which break through human habits and values and are addressed to God, not our ancestors, for a standard. Furthermore, it is in God's power to reward and punish: sometimes He does and sometimes not, or only after great delay. His mysterious ways, to which so many medieval historians resigned themselves, are hard to record "historically"; divine mystery disrupts chronology and distorts it, and opens the question of why apparent vice and virtue do not receive clear and immediate justice. Pagan writers simply did not face that problem; the punishment in classical history is the falling away from the standards of "our ancestors": for Periclean Athens or Republican Rome, the sin, in a way, *is* the punishment, and the punishment is seen in the sin. The Christian scheme is harder to satisfy, at least in literature which is supposed to be exemplary, once the citizen had become a pilgrim. Parataxis seems to have been the stylistic expression of a generalized inability, or humble reluctance, to order experience.

There is a way of seeing paratactic prose as a conscious alternative to linear structure, ruled by its own aesthetic. This attractive, sophisticated hypothesis (which conjures up a funny, sympathetic "club" of people like Matthew Paris, Donald Barthelme, Gregory of Tours, and Eisenstein) requires that we assume a world of writers and readers who found in juxtaposition their primary clue to meaning. Like practiced viewers of films whose central "statement" works from calculated montage, these imagined past readers easily filled in gaps, "read" the significance of contiguous images, made form out of the presented elements of artistic experience. This is part of the argument of Robert Alter's brilliantly persuasive book, *The Art of Biblical Narrative*, although, I think, the least persuasive part.[26] One quickly sees how motif repetition and thematic words work in biblical prose and how variations on conventional scenes "register" as subtle variations in meaning; but even Alter's resource and knowledge really cannot make parataxis, except in select cases, seem like a technique which is "there," as opposed to an artistic and intellectual vacancy. The narratives that Alter examines are also very early prose and were the cumulative, experimental solutions to the challenge of recording the religious-historical experience of Israel. One cannot help but wonder how, once the world had seen Thucydides, Cicero, Livy, Tacitus, and Jerome, it could return to Genesis—except, perhaps, through a fall.

Analogies with the visual arts have an immediate suggestiveness, but do not stand close inspection. The fact that Eisenstein consciously and artfully used paratactic images to convey historical ideas does not make a similar case for writers and readers of prose in earlier times.[27] (Or even always for film—the screening of *Happy Bar-Mitzvah, Bernie!* in *The Apprenticeship of Duddy Kravitz* can be soberly instructive.)[28] It is doubtful that paratactic construction, however consciously contrived, is an appropriate instrument to convey history as it was developed by Herodotus, Thucydides, and all who followed from them. The interconnected sequences of event—meaning that seems inherent in the conflux of experience, the consciousness of time—demand the sinewy connectedness of linear prose. Medieval histories, too, often leave us feeling that the best parts have been left on the cutting room floor.

When John of Salisbury wrote history, his particular subject was the papal curia during 1148 to 1152, the years when he was able to observe it first-hand, the ideal classical historian's situation. In the *Prologue* he places himself latest in a distinguished line of historians beginning with the historical books of the Hebrew Bible, through Luke, Eusebius, Bede, to Hugh of St. Victor and Sigebert of Gembloux, an intellectual genealogy whose stem is the "single purpose: to relate noteworthy matters, so that the invisible things of God may be clearly seen by the things that are done. . . ."[29]

He promises *figura*, the highest endeavour of Christian history: the exegetical "reading" of the living world regarded as God's book in which higher levels of meaning hover over the "letter" of personalities and events, to be discovered by the same techniques as were applied to Scripture. The great model for *figura*, richly varied in detail yet unified in ultimate meaning, was the relation of the Old Testament to the New.[30] The history of Israel held both its own reality and that of Christ and the Church, some of it to be fulfilled in time, some in eternity. This was the final, purifying use of classical rhetoric whose tropes and figures found their own conversion in unlocking the letter to reveal the allegorical meanings of the spirit. Augustine, disdainful of rhetors and the carnal eloquence of careerists like his younger self, yet explained in patient detail in the *Doctrina Christiana* how the invisible things were to be discovered through the visible signs, quoting Paul from *Romans* 1.20, as so many later writers and especially historians were to do: "so that the 'invisible things' of God 'being understood by the things that are made' may be seen. . . ."[31] The method for unveiling the invisible things involved distinguishing the literal from the figurative signs of Scrip-

19

ture and "reading" the figures correctly. Although Augustine notoriously disapproved of attempts to decipher God's intentions in events (most adamantly in the *Civitas Dei*, less so in the *Doctrina*), he had to regard the *saeculum* as God's work: "Although human institutions of the past are described in historical narration, history itself is not to be classed as a human institution; for those things which are past and cannot be revoked belong to the order of time, whose creator and administrator is God."[32] The rhetoric of tropes and figures was thus central to the serious purpose of exegesis: that is the part of rhetoric Bede chose for his book, and that is the part usefully consulted in reading his history.[33]

There is no end to the resonance of tropological exegesis through medieval culture. The repeated and elaborated explanations of the theory by theologians, poets, and historians leave no doubt that the levels of meaning from literal to spiritual were recognized as a correct mimesis of the universe. The first major event of John of Salisbury's history was the papal council at Rheims in 1148. The council culminated in a visible sign of great significance: while Pope Eugenius was celebrating mass, a careless assistant spilled the consecrated wine on the rug before the altar: great consternation. The piece of carpet was cut out and put among the "other relics" (not, one imagines, in a very conspicuous place). Penance was imposed on the offending cupbearer. Yet, serious people regarded the accident as significant, "and indeed this belief did not err."[34] Indeed, the tremendous disasters that befell the crusading armies in the East in that very same year produced *figura* in quite correct form. (As usual, it makes the narrative lurch awkwardly forward.)

That is the auspicious beginning, and also the end, of figurative history in John's book; the rest is very interesting and exceptionally well-presented, but the "invisible things of God" remain in their usual obscurity under, above, behind, or immanent in the visible life of the curia. The foreground and middle ground of the history are fully occupied with human ambitions, jealousies, well- and ill-meaning purposes and cross-purposes; "Indeed," admits John at one point, "I am at a loss to explain why many of Eugenius' judgements were so easily revoked. . . ."[35] The literal level of our text, the text that is our life, is hard enough to explain in its own terms, as John understood, and the invisible things will have to wait for another writer.

The reading of events for Christian meaning, high purpose

20

though it set out to be, tended in the direction of the reading of tea leaves in a cup:

> In the year of our Lord 1095, the third indiction, on Wednesday, 4 April, the twenty-fifth day of the moon, countless witnesses in France saw a great shower of stars thick enough to have passed for hail but for its brightness. Many held the view that the stars had fallen so that the Scripture might be fulfilled, which says that some day the stars will fall from Heaven.[36]

Well, yes. . . . And most of the attempts of medieval historians at the higher exegesis were on that same level—history, to abuse Augustine's famous metaphor, was a nut which did not readily give up its kernel.

The only medieval "historian" to record both the literal and the allegorical levels of experience simultaneously and successfully was Dante, who freely created the literal reality of his story to correspond perfectly with what he knew to be the eternal truth of the soul's pilgrimage to God.[37] For historians of the intractable "given" of literal experience, the letter tended to remain very opaque and the spirit very elusive. When both levels of reality are fixed by the limits of experience and doctrine respectively, something (vitality, plausibility, coherence) will always be lost in the attempt to align them in the relations necessary to *figura*, or allegory; the resources of classical rhetoric are not fully adequate (for writer or reader) to the task. Still, the partial failure, partial success of medieval historians does not have to condemn us (any more than it did them) to a world in which the letter of experience is all inert clay and the spirit of meaning a disconnected and arbitrary shadow. We are only taught how much finer and more supple must be the instruments that expose the connective filaments that join the direct with the hidden truths of life.

> . . . already at Combray I used to fix before my mind for its attention some image which had compelled me to look at it, a cloud, a triangle, a church spire, a flower, a stone, because I had the feeling that perhaps beneath these signs there lay something of a quite different kind which I must try to discover, some thought which they translated after the fashion of those hieroglyphic characters which at first one might suppose to represent only material objects. No doubt the process of decipherment

21

was difficult, but only by accomplishing it could one arrive at whatever truth there was to read.[38]

Rhetoric Reconsidered: The New Rhetorics and the Art of History

You have become regular speech-goers, and as for action, you merely listen to accounts of it. . . . Any novelty in an argument deceives you at once, but when the argument is tried and proved you become unwilling to follow it; you look with suspicion on what is normal and are the slaves of every paradox that comes your way. The chief wish of each one of you is to be able to make a speech himself. . . . What you are looking for all the time is something that is, I should say, outside the range of ordinary experience, and yet you cannot think straight about the facts of life that are before you. You are simply victims of your own pleasure in listening, and are more like an audience sitting at the feet of a professional lecturer than a parliament discussing matters of state.[39]

Anti-rhetoric developed alongside, commenting on, rhetoric in classical Greece. Cleon's demagogic debunking of eloquence, using the techniques of persuasion to undermine his audience's trust in language and their own ability to assess it (and thereby urge them on to a brutal act), contains all of Cornificius' objections, and far worse. Cleon's opposite number was Pericles, whose eulogy for the first dead of the war praised Athenians who, unlike the Spartans, "do not think that there is an incompatibility between words and deeds." Athenians are not afraid of words, and they go bravely into battle knowing "the meaning of what is sweet in life and of what is terrible . . . undeterred to meet what is to come."[40] But this strength depends upon the stability of words that distinguish "what is sweet" from "what is terrible," and in the plague year at Athens, the fragility of language as well as life was horribly exposed when religion and law lost their force and honor was turned inside out. Cleon's speech, coming not long after, increases the sense of disarray and confusion that afflicts Athenian policy and allows us to feel some of Thucydides' complicated ambivalence over the central place of speech in Athenian public life.

Suspicion of words has a long history. The sense that language, treacherously feeding a taste for odd pleasures and spurious achievements, left its jaded votaries incompetent in the face of facts and action belonged to one stream of anti-rhetoric, while a parallel channel directed disapproval towards the direct connection of words with feeling and their flexible connection with truth, morality, even reality (consider the variations on Francesca's complaint: ". . . that book was a pander. . ."). Magic and prayer revolve at opposed equidistant points about the invocatory power of words, so that deploring the one while urging the other always involved some sleight of hand. Everyday's rote sneer by journalist or student at "mere rhetoric" (the stuff that allegedly disguises the "real" motives of politicians, oil companies, espionage agencies—with pathetic inadequacy since everyone can "see through" it) reminds us that Cleon had touched something permanent and troubling in human reaction to the most human gift.[41]

Among the genres of serious literature, history (calmly centered between the excesses of the mind and the flesh) continued longest in unself-conscious and serene oblivion to the treason within—which is, that it is made of words. By the eighteenth century, for all its new subject matters and new philosophy, history was still openly rhetorical: "If a speech be well drawn up, I read it with pleasure, by whomsoever it may be made—and probably with much greater, if the production of Mr. Hume or Mr. Robertson, than if the genuine words of Caractacus, Agricola, or Alfred the Great,"[42] and was still enjoyed as such, according to the testimony of one of Jane Austen's characters. Austen's tolerant history reader was certainly unaware of the contempt history was beginning to provoke in those who, following Newton or Descartes, wanted a model for knowledge which allowed only clear, demonstrable, and certain constructs.[43] Mr. Hume's histories could give her no hint of any radical dissatisfaction with the accepted standards for knowledge of the world. Even among historians of most "advanced" opinion, in the works of Hume, Gibbon, or Voltaire, the voice of the author, personal and opinionated, confidently tells us outright or guides us by the traditional verbal manoeuvres of tone and style toward what we should think about Agricola or Alfred or the Petrine Succession.

Modernity, in the form of professionalism, university chairs, and the systematic paraphernalia of a learned discipline, captured history fairly late. No sooner had it settled into its new dignities than Science (or whatever non-scientists took that to be) invaded the learned world and, as logic had done long before, won the war with words. Serious history formally broke off relations with imaginative literature (an unreliable ally—the trophies always went to Virgil, Dante, Milton and that lot), stripped historical language of its decorations, and aligned itself in a secondary but honorable position behind cool, lucid, exact Science.[44] History was admitted, even by its own practitioners, to be the least "scientific" of all the disciplines contending for that title, but it had been distracted and corrupted for centuries by bad associates, and needed time to reform and cleanse itself.

As usual after one of its defeats by a force of superior mentality, traditional rhetoric held on in some strategic, if comic, citadels. One of them can be seen through the exam question which Marcel, feeling quite superior himself, listens to the girls at Balbec discuss: "Sophocles, from the Shades, writes to Racine to console him for the failure of *Athalie*"—they wondered especially about the proper form of salutation.[45] Shades indeed, of the Speech in Character.

Historians, however, no longer composed speeches. Fustel de Coulanges is reputed to have pronounced at his lectures that it was not he who spoke, but History speaking through him—an important proclamation, not about method but about style. Whatever was intended by that statement, it describes, with a pure grandeur of self-effacement equal, in its way, to classical *gravitas*, an abdication on the part of the historian—of speech. It was an announcement of great portent for history. For the most part, what has come to characterize "serious" modern historical writing and distinguish it from "popular" history is the absence of any marked stylistic character.[46] Unable to create a language as proper to itself as mathematics is to the "hard" sciences, historians have tended to try to make their language express some of the vaguer, affective qualities of scientific knowledge—impersonal neutrality, equability of tone, absence of ornament. The ideal, composite description of this manner is "transparency." History, as much as possible, is to speak *through* the neutral, undistorting medium of the historian. In his essay, "Rhetoric and History," Hayden White has acutely and cogently examined the implications of this style, one which is taught, certainly encouraged, in graduate schools; it is the mark of professionalism in that it carries implicit claims to dispassion, disinterest, and factualness.[47] In the iconographic setting of the scholarly monograph— the formal composition of acknowledgements to teachers, colleagues, granting agencies, foreign librarians, and spouse; introduction; footnotes; appendices; bibliography; index—the transparent style suggests to the most cursory browser a complete, sustaining world of personal credentials and reliable, science-like learning, a first impression designed to make the prospective reader benevolent, receptive, and malleable, just as Cicero advised.

Confidence in the totality and ultimate unity of the greater historical enterprise is gone. Individual historians cannot now think of themselves as dedicated shapers of mosaic bits, all separately worked by the same pure "scientific" methods which will all someday soon fall into place, revealing patterns of permanent, even predictive, truth. Reasons ranging from ideology through the expanding universe of historical subjects and techniques make that illusion unsustainable.[48] But historians generally find it quite easy to ignore the history-as-science debate, which has gone stale anyway, and have rather cheerfully accepted the fragmentation and cross-purpose movements of the modern discipline (none of which hinders professional careers). The current theoretical debate is back to history-as-literature, and that, too, is cheerfully ignored by practical historians who know that they do very well without it (unless they want to press an article on *History and Theory*). And so historians continue to *know* in a fuzzy, resolute way that historical writing must be "clear" above all, because it must not impede the reader's view of the History apprehended "through" it.[49]

Of course, like countless others in their plight who are always the last to know, the trusting must inevitably be undeceived by knowing onlookers exasperated by the sight of so much determined naïveté. There have recently been many eager to perform this office; among the most effective are the group of philosophers and literary critics whose essays are collected in *The Writing of History: Literary Form and Historical Understanding*, a book whose cumulative effect is to compel at least one realization: the historians who thought they had escaped the wayward dangers of language by taking Cleon's advice seriously, leaving the theater of words to confront the facts *tout court*, had backed, all unknowing, right onto the stage.[50] With Hayden White's precise recognition that the transparent style *is* a style, with its own freight of rhetorical, persuasive gestures and postures, the way is cleared of ingenuous (or disingenuous, no matter) disclaimers of artistry and open to re-acknowledging history's lineage as a species of high literary effort.

I have no intention of trying here to survey the full range of modern theoretical discussion which bears on the role of language in creating the body of knowledge and literature called history. I do, however, wish to sketch in some of the serious implications which language theory holds for history, from the radical, enclosed epistemology proposed by some structuralist and semiotic critics, through moderating variants on those ideas, and current reconsiderations of rhetoric as a source for the vocabulary of historiographical theory. I am quite aware that, as a medieval historian (a profession the mere naming of which, as W. H. Auden knew, is capable of extinguishing all conversation), I may be accused of having slipped into a looking-glass world and wandered dazzled among the wilful talkers who, like Humpty Dumpty, make words mean exactly what they want. My defense is simply that, *as* a medieval historian, I must be even more aware than others that the longest tradition of serious thought about history is precisely about language. The tradition that begins with the rhetors and continues through Augustine to those who thought about biblical exegesis and tried to understand human life with exegetical techniques is a continuous meditation on the relation of language to reality.

Ever since Augustine said that everything is either a thing or a sign, and things can be signs as well, there has been a semiotics of history.[51] The entire complex of intricate relations between the visible and the invisible, which we vaguely call the "critical method" of history, is our modern, secular version of discerning the *invisibilia* through the things that are seen, now called "evidence." Current philosophical and literary discussion extends and refines those concerns. New subject matters, new sources of evidence, and new techniques for assembling and evaluating evidence cannot replace serious consideration of how history is made from its only visible components—words. Even those who think that a perversely wrong-headed statement might enjoy condemning it systematically. I should add that elaborated description of the many fundamental elements common to history and fiction, such as narrative, argument or plot, imagery and figurative language, seems to me unnecessary: that history and naturalistic fiction share the same strategies of language as modes of realism (whether the reality described is regarded as actuality or verisimilitude) and thus can be subjected to the same kinds of analysis, also seems widely accepted,[52] although many would object that such literary analysis could not be exhaustive in the case of history. The interesting questions now are concerned with matters of greater refinement of critical technique and harder examination of underlying premises.

Assumptions about language and its relation to anything other than itself cover a spectrum beginning at the extreme realist end (the most familiar) at which language *refers* to a real universe outside itself: language names things perceptible to the senses and furnishes sounds which, by convention, indicate concepts created by the mind (or apprehended, in the case of Platonists). This referential language can be checked for reliability: if I insist that "the cat is on the mat," then any anglophone hearer, understanding what objects cats and mats are, and the temporal and spatial relations indicated by "is" and "on," can go and see where the cat really is.

The extreme other end of the spectrum is where the action is. To begin *in medias res*: reviewing Cynthia Ozick's recent book of stories, Leslie Epstein complained that the plausibility and emotional force of the fiction were undermined by the intrusion of improbable, supernatural incidents and unlikely emotions into the fictional world. The author replied:

> One longs to cry out: Leslie Epstein! Why do you willfully seek to bind imagination, to dictate where it may or may not turn?
> One of the oldest and profoundest tales is precisely about the unraveling of a resolution rightly demanded. Abraham has just bound Isaac for an offering, and we are set up for recognizable human feelings: . . . Instead, something quirky happens, breaking all the rules of probability and necessity. An angel . . . puts a ram in a thicket. Isaac lives. . . Plausibility, foreseeable emotions, reasonable presumptions, above all the sanity and focus of the narrative—everything has been shattered, scattered, stunned and shunned by an act of the liberating imagination. The story has taken a jarring turn, and the world is reborn free of human sacrifice and—as a model for all stories ever afterward—freed from the bondage of pious expectation.
> Leslie Epstein! Undo your blasphemy! Revoke your impertinence! If God himself allowed the First Plot to walk away from its script for the sake of an original thought, who are you to insist on the binding, hand and foot, of narrative freedom?[53]

27

Epstein's "blasphemy" was to suggest that fiction which is not fable, myth, epic, or fantasy, but which offers the reader a recognizable world, loses something, some vital connection to the reader, when it violates those limits of plausibility which contain the physical world and the inner lives of the sane. His criticism was based on a conception of language which is ultimately referential, which affirms the existence of a shared and knowable external world; it is a conception which can legitimately subject realistic fiction to a standard which measures it, however freely and sensitively, against the external world. Literary language here is mimesis.

Ozick's reply is quite correctly based on the Hebrew Bible (even if her reading of Abraham and Isaac is a bit capricious).[54] God made the world with words: word and act perfectly united in purest creation, for the word which made the world could refer to nothing but itself, there being nothing prior or external to it. Ozick's conception of literary language is based on the Logos, the word as creative power, and every act of literary creation re-enacts Genesis and recreates the world. Within this God-like conception of art, demands that the fictional world conform to any pattern of expectation external to itself may well be deemed "blasphemy." It is quite clear that Epstein and Ozick, from their opposite ends of the spectrum, are not speaking the same language.

It is not at all clear whether Cynthia Ozick considers herself a structuralist writer (although, given His penchant for dualities—light and dark, sea and land—and for calling things into being, a strong case can be made for God), but she is a very candid and forthright example of the artistic consequences of the structuralist position on language.

The complex web of thought which takes language as a primary model—as point of departure and point of return—grouped, with increasing imprecision, under the term "structuralism," touches every area of humanistic concern: linguistics itself, literature and criticism, all social sciences, and philosophy. Emerging, or converging, as it has from the anthropology of Levi-Strauss, the linguistic theory of Saussure, and a long development of French literary criticism whose best-known exponent is Roland Barthes, the structuralist program is not at all unified in its premises or implications, except in its demand that every human discipline be thought through again in terms of language and that the model of language be one of an enclosed, self-sufficient system of signs whose meaning is expressed in their patterns of relation to one

28

another within the language system.[55] This model accepts as "language" any form of expression or behavior which conveys meaning through patterns which can be "read" (here Levi-Strauss' influence is dominant, and psychoanalytic theory which reads behavior and imagery is also a sympathetic discipline). Further, language in the conventional sense is regarded as a system of acoustic units of meaning humanly created to signify concepts: the terms *signifiant* for sign, and *signifié* for the thing signified, have become unfortunately modish among some writers of English. Semiotics, the study of signs and what they signify, and how, plays a major role in discussing all expressive language, and the meaning of meaning, or signification. The structuralist concept of the sign and its connection to what it signifies involves a deliberate rejection of language as symbol, a term which turns attention from the verbal sign to a referent "outside" in the real world. Linguistic structuralism attempts to reconcile us to the fact that we can never get *through* language by means of which we apprehend reality, *to* a reality free of language.

This understanding of language as a created system radically severed from any necessary, or at least easily negotiated, relation to a reality outside itself involves a severe ambiguity of knowledge. Language here *is* reality, a pattern running parallel to the real universe which it must recreate wholly (not symbolize or name in a one-to-one relation of reference) in order that we may know anything.[56] Structuralism involves full recognition of everything about language that so worried and disgusted the debunkers of language from Plato through Cornificius and on, but it embraces *that* as the field of inquiry and as the defining human gift. It is dealing with many of the same ancient issues of the relation of language to reality, but in easier acceptance of the idea that since we know the world through language, the world we know *is*, in some sense, language. The ancient suspicion of words has become, in certain quarters, celebration—and for the same reasons. Reality itself is thus rendered ambiguous and uncertain, since the ultimate referent of the system of signs may well underlie the system but is not attached to it at any particular point. Verification, in the sense of moving from statement to single referent and back, is not easily possible in a structuralist universe, although other standards, for intelligible pattern and significant structure, still apply. The thing signified becomes far more a thing created than a thing found, and the whole of reality far more dependent on the human mind and less an independent, stable existence. The epistemological dilemma of structuralism, however, has not distracted or deceived any of its major exponents into solipsism. Whether ultimate reality is taken to correspond in parallel system, or harmonize through some innate disposition of the mind, or distantly underpin the language of the mind, it is always assumed to exist. Like Isaac Singer's comment about free will: "We have to believe in it; we have no choice."

The great value in the structuralist program is that it focuses attention on the articulated structures through which experience, in itself formless and meaningless, is organized. There can be here no simple assumption of the independent existence of anything language purports to describe, and that difficulty leads to a rigorous standard of analysis of the thing signified, most especially in those cases for which real existence is claimed. This consequence, of an unrelenting degree of difficulty, falls most heavily, and against the most resistence, on non-fictional literature and, of course, on life itself. Serious readers of fiction know that the separation of language from external reality, the dissolution of the connecting system of reference and the consequent dissolution of certain knowledge, indeed the threat of final human disconnection, are not the inventions of decadent intellectuals determined to make things hard for the rest of unsuspecting humanity. Projected into broadly moral terms, the dislocation of experience lived from experience felt and understood, the terrible loss of life in our endless series of delayed reactions, the felt impossibility of impressing our sense of life through the invisible, impermeable membranes which enclose other lives, other worlds, and the necessity of doing so if we are to live at all, was all, long before the formulations of structuralist thought, much of the subject of modern fiction. It is all present to the mature Marcel walking again in the Bois de Boulogne:

> I wished to hold before my bodily eyes, to see whether they were indeed as charming as they appeared to the eyes of memory, little women's hats, so low-crowned as to seem no more than garlands. All the hats now were immense, covered with all manner of fruits and flowers and birds. In place of the beautiful dresses in which Mm. Swan walked like a queen, Graeco-Saxon tunics, pleated à la Tanagra. . . . And seeing all these new components of the spectacle, I had no longer a belief to infuse into them to give them consistency, unity and life; they passed before me in a desultory, haphazard, mean-

> ingless fashion, containing in themselves no beauty which
> my eyes might have tried, as in the old days, to re-create.
> They were just women, in whose elegance I had no faith,
> and whose clothes seemed to me unimportant.

And elsewhere:

> The evidence of the senses is also an operation of the
> mind in which conviction creates the facts.[57]

The charm of the little garland hats, so blankly missing from
the new large ones, was all in Marcel's conception of such beauty
and in the society which had formed and informed his vision when
he first began to notice the speaking elegance of clothing. This
realization about the nature of perception extends far beyond
hats, engulfing all aesthetic perception and all social and personal
expression. The forms of fashion change quickly and thus expose
in figured relief larger truths about experience and meaning which
are too deep-set and pervasive for direct observation, for the
organizing forms with which the mind addresses experience are
the very structures of the mind.

Language as Logos, the belief which infuses consistency,
unity, and life into life, can seem to be the theoretical basis for
discrediting a literature of mimesis (Auerbach's reputation is in
temporary decline), but the truth is that the two are suspended
in peaceful antinomy in fiction. The fiction always is the artifact
of words, complete and whole in itself, and it also connects with,
involves, penetrates, enlivens reality. It makes reality real. The
successful work of art effortlessly accomplishes the theoretically
impossible; complaints of faulty mimesis invariably point to a
failure of the verbal structure.

Henry James, who took a deeply serious view of the reality
of fiction—"If there are exact sciences, there are also exact
arts . . ."[58]—insisted that the author who exposed the artifice,
stepped visibly onto the stage, pen in hand, was committing a
"betrayal of a sacred office" and, by showing his work to be only
a story, was shamefacedly making it "only a joke."[59] (The fact
that some contemporary novelists assert the reality of the fiction
and the "sacred office" of the author by precisely those means
does not change the essential point.) James insisted that the integrity of fiction demanded that it be presented as history:

31

> . . . to insist on the fact that as the picture is reality, so
> the novel is history. That is the only general description
> (which does it justice) that we may give of the novel.
> But history also is allowed to represent life; it is not,
> any more than painting, expected to apologize.

Fiction must speak with "the tone of the historian."[60] In James'
discussion, fiction and history inhabit the same real world and
are constructed from the same plastic element—mimetic language—that is why "the novel is history."

But what can "the tone of the historian" be when the history
is a novel? Everything—from the ancient literary connections of
history to the most recent linguistic theory—points again to the
idea that history is a literary form, most closely allied with the
novel. Structuralist critics tend to be very impatient with distinctions of genre, adopting Barthes' category of *écriture* which includes all serious literature; for them, the intelligible structures
of language can be examined equally well in works of fiction and
non-fiction. But this approach, like that of Henry James, works
to the advantage of fiction and the confusion of history. In claiming for fiction "the tone of the historian," James was claiming a
share of confidence, serenity, seriousness, and self-importance—
qualities that now radiate every kind of insensitivity and foolish
naïveté and provoke contempt:

> Literary artists and historians are apparently much fur-
> ther apart both in their conception and their practice of
> literature than they have been in the past. Indeed, the
> historian who conceives of literature . . . as "style" or
> as a means of adorning otherwise simple propositions—
> may bring history close to literature (in Barthe's desig-
> nation): but he will be further than ever from the con-
> cerns of the contemporary literary artist.[61]

History, so near and so far from fiction, is the recalcitrant case,
insisting on an accessible, prior reality and a language which refers to it. As for history as *écriture*, a creation of significant language, historians for the most part are having none of it. The
impatience and irritation this arouses in sophisticated critics is
understandable; but then so is the exasperated question: "What,
after all this fuss, is the tone of the historian supposed to be?"
No one yet has suggested a very satisfying answer.

If even a part of what many critics assert to be intrinsic and inevitable to all highly developed literature is true, then historical writing cannot exempt itself as a special case. For if the assumption of simple, referential language for present experience turns out to be surprisingly tricky, such an assumption about descriptions of things no one can claim to see or hear is philosophically silly. History, after all, is the ultimate self-involved discourse because it demands that the reader accept its claim to a level of referential, verifiable truth approriate to "the cat is on the mat" statements, in a world presently containing no such cats and no such mats. Admittedly, it feels odd to think this way about sober studies of constitutional history, feudalism, or canon law, but, in fact, this is as far as fictional realism can go. And so, one feels, something had better be said for history before it is taken away, signing frantically, to be deconstructed by the literary gnostics. Appalling as the prospect is, historians have to take a stand on the epistemological status of language.

The two main avenues of structuralist influence in history are the social sciences and language theory.[62] While structuralist anthropology and sociology make an awkward mesh with traditional history because of the non-chronological, non-causal, generalizing character of the method, still, for essentially descriptive studies of a society at a particular time, the traditional historian may very well choose to be a "structuralist" of a sort without ultimately sacrificing the concepts of causal sequence and temporal development. There is, in fact, considerable encouragement here for historians (of which I am one) who are attracted to analytical description: studies which make a cross-cut section in order to expose the plane pattern plain, and attempt to see things, *sub specie eternitatis*, for a moment wholly in their moment. Serious, self-conscious fiction is entirely helpful in this enterprise, as are psychoanalytical theory and all essentially formalist approaches to human experience and creation.

The case of linguistic structuralism, à la Barthes and his disciples, is the much harder one (and even more interesting, or irritating, according to taste). The structures sought in this approach are those of language itself (one may even say, of thought itself), and all literature, from this point of view, is the product or creation of those structures, which may be created anew by each author. History, so regarded, becomes a form of discourse characterized by certain verb tenses, narrative strategies, authorial pronoun stances, and other verbal devices combined to create the surface structure, the artifact made of words, which is history. The relation of the historical text to other, previously existing texts is an elaborated verbal structure, a crucial part of which consists in naming the previous artifacts "evidence" and indicating, through various modes and verbal constructions, a special relation between the present text, "history," and previous, "evidence." The model holds equally for non-verbal "evidence." This form of discourse is based on some unprovable epistemological assumptions concerning an entire, once existing but irrecoverable world of persons and events to which certain texts stand in the relation called "evidence." (This relation supplies the definition of the term, "evidence.") Once the causal assumption about the relation between the irrecoverable past and existing "evidence," and between "evidence" and history texts, is seriously questioned, then history as discourse remains, but only as one more mode of specialized literature—one whose genre characteristics are the self-imposed limitations of evidence-text structures and various narrative strategies. The evidence-text structure and the verbal modes of creating it have much the same ontological status as the Alexandrine line, or the heroic couplet—entirely "real" by any philosophical definition (excluding Anselm's), but with no indubitable claim to external reality. In other words, history as a mode of thought and writing claiming a specially close relationship to a past, external, real world is dissolved and reconstituted from its own elements as a literature whose special, voluntarily assumed constraints give it the panache of high artifice. "The tone of the historian" would have to be, at the very least, a highly self-conscious one.

This proposed change in western culture (itself, according to Barthes, merely another structure—there is a political subtext to his ideas), so chillingly depressing to most historians, so apparently exhilarating to non-historian structuralists and related critics, suggests that the historian's task is not to reconstruct or explain the past but positively to create it, in responsible, creative freedom, acknowledging the ultimate self-enclosed "game" conditions of the discipline, (now called "art"), finding in that freedom that he is the author of the totality of his work—signs, system, and all. Historian as *homo ludens*: history as re-creation.

When I was a graduate student I used to like posing the question: "What if you (that is, I—no one else was listening) were to discover that everything everyone accepts as authentic evidence of the Middle Ages is really the work of a single, mad, incredibly skillful nineteenth-century forger?" I would answer myself: "I would go on just as before, nothing changed." I always had a feeling for the thin air of extreme artifice. Now that I discover that my exercise in decadence is a defensible philosophic position, I find it loses much of its attraction. It is not that a heightened and self-conscious awareness of the God-like powers of language (to make a world and name everything in it, for a start) holds any threat. Nothing can be more human, more rational and poetic; and historians (if there ever were any such) who think history is something (i.e., some "thing") that you "write up" from pieces of "thing" recorded on cards and in notebooks, live a reductive intellectual life. But to concede that language speaks in its own "language" chiefly about itself must inexorably cut its connection to any past reality and freeze history to death. There is no exhilaration in that, because there is no source of energy. It is a question to which some writers of fiction may be indifferent (in fact, the anaesthetic tone is characteristic of much post-modern writing). But for historians, mimesis is life, and we must argue that the same epistemology which confirms the high probability of the existence of, and our knowledge of, the external world applies also, albeit with diminished force, to the past. We have to assume that the testimony of others is "evidence," partly because we have to begin everything somewhere, and this is where history begins, and partly because the consequence of doing otherwise is the loss not merely of history but of the independent reality of anything not present to the senses, which does not leave much of the world.

To those who are attracted to history as high artifice, this may seem a poor, shuffling evasion: Johnson again kicking the Berkeleian rock (although Berkeley never denied that what appear to be rocks always appear to behave as such appearances have always appeared to do). The "real" world we inhabit daily is a world of probable sequences, of prediction based on repetition, and the verifying connivance of others. Closed-circle theories do have a certain elegance; more elegance, perhaps, than reality requires. In life, and in realist literature, we inhabit the middle distance between extreme consciousness of consciousness, and naive realism. The middle ground is the field of comprehensible things, the mental place where the multifarious elements registered by the senses come into focus, or rather are grouped and organized by the mind into things with names according to our ideas of what things are. We cannot restore to history the confident ability to represent life, to be the present picture of the real past, as James was generously prepared to allow—in fact, history can never attain the same intense and indubitable reality of successful fiction which is experience in its only possible expression—but the force of mimesis can be retained without overly naive assumptions about language.

There are some guides to the most useful landmarks of the middle distance. E. H. Gombrich's *Art and Illusion* is a beautifully articulated exposition of how the mind works with schemata (its own and those presented by an artist) in the *active* process of making crude experience into pictorial representation.[63] The analogy between visual and verbal language is kept distinctly present in his historical account of the emergence of representational art in the West.

> There is no neutral naturalism. The artist, no less than the writer, needs a vocabulary before he can embark on a "copy" of reality. . . . Everything points to the conclusion that the phrase, the "language of art," is more than a loose metaphor, that even to describe the visible world in images we need a developed system of schemata.[64]

His speculations on the possible relations between Homeric narrative and the appearance and development of means for mimesis in Greek art is equally suggestive for history and its resources of language. The historian's schemata, in Gombrich's useful term, are the verbal constructs which allow him to recognize significant constructs from the partial, assembled evidence he has, through a process of projection, followed by "correction, adjustments, adaptations to means, to probe reality and to wrestle with the particular."[65]

In *Mimesis*, Erich Auerbach analyzes the same effect with respect to narrative that Gombrich discusses in terms of the visual arts: the ways in which the artist manipulates his medium so as to enlist the audience in creating a convincing illusion of the world. Both concentrate on the expectations, what is believed, the schemata of formulas with which we resolve the ambiguity of experience into meaning, as the key element in understanding how a thing of canvas and paint, or of words, can persuade us it is a representation of reality. The expectations we have of the visual world which allow us to "see" space, movement, depth, and figures in a painting correspond to the basic figures of thought in language, the transferred or extended meanings of words which allow us to "discover" the intelligible meaning of the past.

The idea of the historian projecting onto his evidence pre-existing formulas of meaning may make some historians uncomfortable. A truism of sound modern interpretive technique is the injunction to avoid anachronism, which usually means refraining from passing judgement on past institutions and political and social behavior by measuring them against current favored models. Thus, the aware, conscientious student is to clear his mind of bias (first, by becoming conscious of its existence) and presumably allow the dispositions inherent in past societies to impress themselves on him as he immerses himself in evidence. For all the obvious common sense of this approach, it does not answer all the problems of encountering (in imagination, always) the past or offer any intelligible account of it. Once we make honest efforts to shed gross bias and suspend inappropriate formulas, we have only grappled with the most superficial, accessible layer of possible schemata. We still need, more than ever, schemata of expectation to "see" any "past" at all in the texts and artifacts we regard as "evidence." We are never passive or neutral in the search for history in its distant and indeterminate debris.

Conceiving of the historical imagination in this way (whether one inclines toward "creation" or unreconstructed "reconstruction"), the historian's direct experience with what he regards as evidence is organized by certain formulas of language which describe the evidence in units which are comprehensible and humanly significant. Thus, the historian's middle distance is the realm of metaphor, metonomy, synecdoche, and irony—the figures which express his sense of those historical constructs which seem to have integral existence, and to resonate in sympathy with enduring human concerns—the Renaissance, Roman Imperial government, the Western Frontier, and events like the battle of Gettysburg, the defeat of Harold in 1066, and such social elements as death and burial, marriage, class, and crime. As intellectual constructs, with form and meaning, these are all like medieval monies of account—the shillings, pounds, and marks which were special assemblages of silver pennies.

It is here that the historian works, creating the significant objects (Barthes' *signifiés* again) of historical discourse by making the elemental figures of language act on, organize, and reform the similar elements he has analyzed from the evidence—this is language acting on and recreating itself (again, using "language" in the large sense in which visual art and social life have "language" or intelligible, expressive pattern) assuredly, but it is not a hopeless house of mirrors for all that. The mind reflects on itself as it uses language and, even though we think in the language we think about, that is not adequate reason to despair of reference as a disciplining exercise of historical language. Reference is the intelligible pattern of connection between the present text, *history*, and the prior texts, *evidence*. What the historian creates is the significant, intelligible structure of history from language which both refers and creates. The *signifié* (whose absence from the work, and perhaps the consciousness, of naive realist historians is so deplored by some critics) is the historical construct—the thing that resonates. Only hats infused with an idea, of elegance or its opposite, are historical hats. The historical construct is not a reconstruction—the past as experience is irrecoverable—and that is nothing to be mourned or regretted: the past was merely experience; in the present we make history.

It should be evident how it is that traditional rhetoric, having been kicked out the metaphorical door, has managed to come back in the ironical window. In his *Literary Language and its Public*, Auerbach acknowledged his debt to Vico, whose struggle to fuse poetic theory with an epistemology of history inspired his own method, and many others have come to recognize the brilliance of Vico's understanding of the tropes as modes of perception.[66] Cleared of assumptions and aesthetic standards based on the political and social conditions of antiquity, rhetoric remains the most satisfactory repository of seemingly permanent truths about the strategies of language, and offers a vocabulary, long shared and still vital, for how we think in language, about language, about reality.

Rhetoric has been making a modest, dignified "comeback" as an object of study in itself, as a positive instrument for understanding a large variety of literary genres which developed under its influence and, most recently and ingeniously, as the analytical vocabulary of non-technical reasoning which can be used to analyze the structure of thought in works of the non-scientific, scholarly disciplines. The name of Kenneth Burke is most closely associated with serious reconsideration of rhetoric as a philosophical instrument, especially the consideration of the major figures of speech (the Master Tropes) as basic modes of thought; his work is essential to historians who think seriously about the process by which evidence becomes history.[67] Burke's disciple, Richard Lanham, is, in many ways, an even more useful teacher of language, and not only because his writing is witty and more immediately understandable. In his *Style: An Anti-Textbook* and in *The Motives of Eloquence*, Lanham examines the meaning and implications of mimesis and its opposite in terms that are precise and applicable to social and political life, the interior sense of self, as well as the aesthetics of texts.[68] Lanham reads language to see the form of the world and the self implied by its forms. His work is especially interesting to those who find traditional rhetoric still alive and suggestive, although too over-burdened with the social and literary forms of antiquity to address post-antique texts. Lanham's replacement of the classical vertical hierarchy of style with a horizontal spectrum running from the "transparent" language and "serious" reality of representation, at one end, to the "opaque" language of self-conscious, "rhetorical" reality at the other where style is all, is one of the few genuinely useful critical instruments to come from the theorists of language which can be applied to pre-modern writing.[69]

All of these matters of intelligibility and language apply equally to the writing and reading of history, and I had hoped to lead the patient reader (and I admit that the reader who has come this far has been patient, or perhaps impatient) back to the consideration of rhetoric in relation to medieval historical writing by a route that felt rather more inevitable and less like the ascent of Mt. Ventoux. The lesson, however, from a book within a book within a book, applies to every attempt to understand what experience offers: only the poetic structure of the mind enables us to "see" what we see.

> An image presented to us by life brings with it, in a single moment, sensations which are in fact multiple and heterogeneous. The sight, for instance, of the binding of a book once read may weave into the characters of its title the moonlight of a distant summer night. . . . An hour is not merely an hour, it is a vase full of scents and sounds and projects and climaxes, and what we call reality is a certain connection between these immediate sensations and the memories which envelop us simultaneously with them . . . a unique connection which the writer has to rediscover in order to link forever in his phrase the two sets of phenomena which reality joins together. He can describe a scene by describing one

39

after another the innumerable objects which at a given
moment were present at a particular place, but truth
will be attained by him only when he takes two different
objects, states the connection between them—a connection analogous in the world of art to the unique connection which in the world of science is provided by the
law of causality . . . truth—and life, too—can be attained by us only when, by comparing a quality common
to two sensations, we succeed in extracting their common essence and in reuniting them to each other, liberated from the contingencies of time, within a
metaphor.[70]

New Rhetoric and Medieval Historical Writing

Thanks to this boon of peace, men governed themselves
in accordance with laws and justice, devising by skill
and study every kind of argument for use in the courts,
so that when anyone was attacked he could defend himself by the strength and eloquence of rhetoric, or when
he was attacking, he might ensnare his enemy, who would
be deceived by the wealth of his oratory. Rhetoric was
now used both by the educated and by those who were
naturally talented, for there were many illiterate people,
endowed by nature herself with the gift of eloquence
and rational methods of inference and argument, whom
those who were trained and skilled in the rhetorical art
were not able to resist or refute.[71]

Cornificius apparently thought that training in rhetoric, with its
emphasis on words as the objects and elements of thought, was
guilty of the dissociation of truth from expression. ("Clearly the
rules of eloquence confer neither wisdom nor love of
wisdom. . . .") So it is curious to note that Galbert, notary of
Bruges and historian, as he continues his remarks on justice and
eloquence in Flanders, accuses the unlearnedly eloquent, those
endowed with eloquence by nature (the only true source, according to Cornificius) of the perverted use of it in predatory lawsuits.

. . . because these by their deceits brought action in the
courts against the faithful and the lambs of God, who
were less wary, God, who sees all from on high, did not
fail to chastise the deceivers so that He might reach by
scourges those whom He had endowed with the gift of

40

eloquence for their salvation because they had used this
gift for their own perdition.

Provoked by this vulpine use of His gift, God sent His own signs
to those who could read them—an eclipse of the sun in August
of 1124. When that warning did not bring correction, famine was
inflicted on the land.[72]

These passages and remarks which occur, a bit puzzlingly,
at the very beginning of Galbert's history of the murder of Count
Charles of Flanders, speak to a contemporary sense that language, like arrows and swords, was capable of acting dangerously
unhinged from wisdom, justice, truth, and fact, that there was no
reliable way of keeping it honest, and the Justice beyond the grave
would have to make reparations to the innocent bamboozled on
earth.

I will provisionally juxtapose with Galbert John of Salisbury's carefully fair remarks about Bernard of Clairvaux when
the abbot tried to organize a papal denunciation of Gilbert of
Poitiers. John describes Bernard as "a man of the greatest eloquence and highest repute"[73] whose zeal to attack learned men
aroused "various opinions"; John's account reveals the extreme
bitterness that marked every phase of this episode. Gilbert aroused
suspicion because his compendious reading and ready speech
gave him an unanswerable answer to every accusation, and so his
adversaries accused him of hiding reprehensible opinions beneath
the "obscurity of words" because, John thought, they simply
could not understand him.[74] Bernard, in John's memorable
description,

> was so saturated in the Holy Scriptures that he could
> fully expound every subject in the words of the prophets
> and apostles. For he had made their speech his own,
> and could hardly converse or preach or write a letter
> except in the language of scripture.[75]

John hints tactfully at the range of emotional reaction Bernard
aroused, much of it hostile and deeply suspicious of his motives.

Both of these fragments from twelfth-century historical writing turn in obvious yet oblique ways on language as an intellectual
and emotional axis. In the conflict between Gilbert and Bernard,
the disputed point of doctrine (never perfectly clear even, or especially, to those involved in the case) fades before the clash of

styles which cuts out the steady center from truth, leaving both sides to the combat accusing each other of hiding something ugly under an armour of words. Galbert tells us that Count Charles forced men to lay aside conventional weapons, compelling them to rely on words, which then ravaged justice in their own way. We still badly need an adequate critical vocabulary to discuss these matters, a vocabulary about human discourse continuous with, but not contained by, classical rhetoric. As I argued before, the straightforward approach of applying the categories and terms of traditional rhetoric to medieval historical writing looks superficially promising but runs quickly into blank walls. Yet the large area of inherited and consciously cultivated knowledge of eloquence cannot be ignored.

Unlike contemporary historians who would have to greet their status as rhetoricians much as Moliere's gentleman learned that all his life he had been speaking prose without knowing it, medieval writers knew they were supposed to be eloquent, and they had some idea of how to go about it. The odd dislocations of narrative cannot be explained easily. The possibilities of intentional parataxis only arise when parataxis is the normal procedure to which all writers resort and some few manipulate to better purpose. Linear, interlinked narrative is the language of chronology, the system of signs (pointed use of relative pronouns, adverbs, conditional syntax) by which discourse creates the sense of events interlinked in time. Its absence can only have been the gross symptom of a web of factors, including the tendency to search for meaning above or after, rather than in, events; the breakdown of the classical hierarchy of high and low subject matters and the failure, or humble reluctance, to find another principle of limitation; or simply inadequate training in writing narrative. The emphasis on the duty to distribute praise and blame may have encouraged historians to gloss over the effort of deciding just how to tell (in both senses) what happened, and concentrate on the "interesting" parts—as dilemmas of moral conflict and distinctions of guilt and innocence. Many of the standard rhetorical exercises are anecdotes in which bizarre circumstances combine to bring one virtue into conflict with another and make judgement of morality, honor, and law nearly impossible. That was what intrigued lawyers, rhetors, and historians in antiquity, and informed the moral drama of John of Salisbury's protracted account of the conflict between Bernard and Gilbert.

The attraction of rhetoric currently is that it defends the

soundness and utility of non-demonstrative reasoning against the encroaching influence of scientific or demonstrative procedures. This is much the same position held by rhetoric in antiquity when it defended the same things against the claims of philosophy. Ancient philosophy and modern science each claim to be the way people ought to think, even if they sloppily do not, and rhetoric replies that philosophy (or science) is an enclosed mode of discourse adapted to specific intellectual occasions and not to be imposed upon all the varieties of explanation, judgement, assessment, and description that intelligent life demands. It is and always has been an odd quarrel. Modern historians are in the thick of it, but it is hard to see how medieval historians can be placed in any conscious relation to the problem at all. Still, if one agrees with Hayden White that historical reasoning is the reasoning of enthymeme, is probable and not demonstrative, and, as a form of discourse in prose, captures its specific forms of argument in the figures described by traditional rhetoric, then every generation of historians must still supply the forming perception, the vision that connects things and "discovers" subjects (or *signifiés*) in the figures, sometimes by isolating and "seeing" them for the first time, sometimes by seeing old objects in new juxtapositions; and every historian does these things more or less well or badly. To say that a medieval writer of history, when he is writing at his most "medieval" pitch—choppy and paratactic, until his narrative resembles the flickering strobe light of a mad disco club—elevated and didactic, seeing trivial and silly divine purposes in commonplace events—is really using a new Christian rhetoric based on the classical tropes enhanced by Christian *figura*, is to explain something, but not a great deal.

But when confronted with the increasingly abstruse and intimidating body of thought about literary language, perception, and creation in relation to the non-fiction "fiction" which is history, what is the student of medieval history writing to do? Frankly, the texts in question seem to sink beneath the weight of such critical complication. Medieval history is not great history measured against the Greek and Roman past, or against the future; it is not great literature measured against the literature of its own age. It is merely very, very interesting. It is "wonderful" in the Jamesian tone of combined respect and amusement.

The necessary combination of tradition with new insight might well begin with Richard Lanham's suggestion for a horizontal spectrum (to replace the classical vertical hierarchy) of styles,

running from the "transparent" self-effacing style which presents
the "serious" self in continuous, close alignment with an external, stable reality, through gradations toward the aggressively self-
conscious styles of the "rhetorical" self, whose language repeatedly creates and recreates a dramatic self in a world theater whose
sets are constantly shifting.[76] This spectrum, from "serious" to
"rhetorical," plots shifts in the relation of writer to reality to
reader which can be described in a largely traditonal, rhetorical
vocabulary of style, but with much greater sensitivity to attitudes
and apprehensions before the powers of language.

A potent addition to this spectrum, which describes the
working of imagination on raw experience, is Gombrich's discussion of the ways in which the mind (of artist or observer) presents
and adapts schematic forms to the desired ends of expression,
whether representational ("serious" in Lanham's terms), or openly
schematic ("rhetorical"). It is interesting to think over the literary
analogue to Gombrich's remark about medieval and later art: "To
the Middle Ages, the schema is the image; to the postmedieval
artist, it is the starting point for corrections, adjustments, adaptations, the means to probe reality and to wrestle with the
particular."[77] The fundamental schemata for the ordering of experience into language are what Quintilian, Vico, Kenneth Burke,
and Proust acknowledged in the major figures (Burke's Master
Tropes)—metaphor, synecdoche, metonymy, irony.

Armed with this reliquary-hilted rapier, the new rhetor might,
for example, reconsider Auerbach's appraisal of the late-antique
mannerist style of Sidonius Apollinaris, a style he found "spooky"
for its playfulness which denies as it describes the doom of the
author's class and culture. Sidonius's expression "has become
hopelessly cut off from reality. . . . His art resembles a difficult
game which consists in capturing the truth and even the concrete
reality of things in a mesh of rhetorical figures; amazingly often
it is successful. . . . But it is a game for the initiate. . . ."[78] The
neo-rhetor would see Sidonius as a true *homo rhetoricus* (as Lanham sees Ovid) who creates a world of words over which he
reigns, barbarians or no. His high artificiality is a triumph and
holds its own realism in its illusions; the "difficult game" is here
the "truth" asserted, under fifth-century circumstances, with a
special courage. One is reminded, a little, of Ronald Firbank.

Something more of the secret of the compelling quality of
Bede's historical vision is opened by considering the "noblest
synecdoche, the perfect paradigm or prototype for all lesser

usages," the identity of microcosm and macrocosm. To continue quoting Burke:

> In such doctrines, where the individual is treated as a replica of the universe, and vice versa, we have the ideal synecdoche, since microcosm is related to macrocosm as part to whole, and either the whole can represent the part or the part can represent the whole. . . . One could thus look through the remotest astronomical distances to the "truth within.". . .[79]

Bede's organizing schema presents the Roman mission to England as a microcosm of the advent of the Gospel to mankind, and the constant, hovering presence of the model of the universally true story verifies the totality of Bede's history, while specific episodes—the metaphor of the sparrow flying out of the storm into the hall, the allegorical visions—move in epicycles on the parallel orbits of the small and great worlds. The effect is of an intelligible whole which is clearer and somehow more "present" than the parts that apparently compose it, which, in turn, are free to convey their own particular significant realities. Bede's history is a divine comedy in much the same mode as Dante's, with the difference that the literal history of the traveller's journey through the actual Other World, in the *Divine Comedy*, stands in the relation of the whole to the microcosmic part which is the movement of each Christian soul through sin toward God.

Richard of Devizes, whose characteristic trope is irony, is a writer who responds with alacrity to questions about his relation to language. The reader of his chronicle is more aware of the voice that addresses him than of any information it conveys, and that voice has neither a fixed point of reference nor a consistent response to the world it remarks upon—except that of assertive personality. The chameleon voice whose tone is sceptical, rarely outraged, quizzical, rather, and playful, plays its trickiest games with the reader who looks for a "serious" identity in the febrile, elegant persona who conducts him from one dramatic scene to the next, adjusting costume each time. The introductory passages of the chronicle, in which Richard offers his book about the vain world to Robert, prior of Winchester who had recently left to become a Carthusian monk, are the *homo rhetoricus'* Baedeker to the "serious" world: he finds it solemn and very silly. Each special arrangement of strict Carthusian life is fixed by a gaze of intent superficiality:

> . . . I saw something that I would not see anywhere else,
> something that I could not believe. . . .
> in each of your cells there is only one door, which
> you are allowed to open as you like, but through which
> you may not go out, except in such a way that one foot
> always stays short of the threshold and inside the cell.
> A brother may go out with one foot wherever he wants
> to, provided that the other foot stays inside the cell.
> There must be some great and profound mystery. . . .[80]

Of all the new orders, the Carthusians were the most literal-minded about poverty, obedience, and removal from the world; Richard's *faux naif* wit, itself a parody of literal-mindedness, describes them as all letter, no leaven. The Benedictines had learned to interpret the letter of the *Rule* with a certain rhetorical largeness. Richard and his onetime superior and friend, Robert, no longer speak the same language.

It can be argued that the steady, external touchstone of Richard's "real" self is traditional Benedictine monasticism about which he is defensive and touchy in the way of many loyal, "unreformed" black monks of his time, the late twelfth century. The passage in which he describes their traditional way of life touches us with its sincerity of tone, its balanced and harmonious vision. He speaks of ". . . the monks who, not through a vicar but with their own mouths, praised the Lord, who lived and walked in the Lord's house in harmony all the days of their lives. . . ."[81] But the very being of the rhetorical man is to be what the occasion demands, and if modest sincerity—then, modest sincerity. For if we insist too strongly on choosing only one of the many selves Richard presents to us as the "real" one, the moral center (through no textual evidence, but only because we "know" what he had to be), then we are much at a loss to cope with most of his book.

His bravura tour guide to the English towns is a catalogue of comic horrors starting with London's sexual delights ("Actors, jesters, smooth-skinned lads, Moors, flatterers, pretty boys, effeminates. . . ."), through every variant of bad climate ("Bath, placed or, rather dumped . . . in an exceedingly heavy air and sulphureous vapour. . . . Ely stinks perpetually. . . ."), repulsive populace ("York is full of Scotsmen, filthy and treacherous. . . . At Bristol there is no-one who is not or has not been a soapmaker. . . ."), and boredom, until Winchester, a civilized and prosperous place.[82] They have only one vice there: they lie about everything. Other than that, they are perfectly truthful. All of this, including the equivocal joke about Winchester (and what kind of joke about the entire book?), Richard, monk of Winchester, puts in the mouth of a French Jew who offers it as advice to a Christian boy on his way to England, along with a letter of recommendation to a Jew of Winchester. Then Richard switches to third-person narration to continue the odd story of how the boy disappeared and the Winchester Jews were accused of murdering him, but all is cast in the form of a parody of a popular child-martyr tale. In Richard's story, the accusation was gibbering and overwrought, the evidence almost non-existent, the judges venal, ". . . and the matter was dropped."[83] Not only does the entire episode, from the French Jew's advice to the child-martyr episode, have no moral at all (Richard is *not* a medieval protoliberal), it has no certain author, in terms interior to the text. The voice impersonating the French Jew is as convincing as the voice of the steadfast Benedictine. Richard shifts, chameleon-like, from one persona to the next—prompter, actor, and director of a theatrical world of gesture.

Richard's history moves in dramatic scenes, with concrete but exaggerated detail, short bursts of pointed dialogue, and asides from the narrator. It has an odd, detached emotional effect. We seem to be reading history but are constantly off balance because the historian refuses to take seriously the business of history. He is one writer for whom parataxis works well, emphasizing the sense of life as play, or *a* play about venality and ambition. Speech is central to all events: when a great man, Ranulf Glanvill, was ruined, he became so dull that he could no longer win a lawsuit.[84] Unlikely persons speak in classical tags, often from the satirists, with a histrionic flair for timing their lines—a device which fixes our attention on words and gives the action an affectless excitement. Speech frequently *is* the event: at the scene of his ultimate before failure to hold the power Richard I had entrusted in him before leaving on crusade, the chancellor, William Longchamp, recognizes that his enemies have outmanoeuvred him, but he has an elegant reply when the accusations finally end: "Am I always to be only a listener, and shall I never answer?"[85] (The rhythmic elegance gets lost in translation.) A gift from Richard, from Juvenal. Everyone, in Richard's history, in his world of words, has an answer.

As Lanham asks of Ovid (one of Richard's favorites), "Is there no central principle in the poem? Does anything persist in this poem of endlessly changing tones, motifs, spoofs, and reassertions? *Only the style.*"[86]

Geoffrey of Monmouth is another historian who plays elaborate jokes and is impenetrable to serious questions;[87] serious contemporary readers were either credulous or, in the single case of William of Newburgh, furious at Geoffrey's lies and popularity. The surface of his work is all incantations, archaic names, and ceremony, from Merlin's prophesies to Arthur's courteous knights and ladies who dressed, armour and clothes and all, in a single color (a visual sign describing what kind of rhetorical world they inhabit). William of Newburgh's humorless scholarly attack in which he opposes probability and chronology to Geoffrey's exotic world is an opposition, not of true against false history, but of external against self-contained reality, of referent against rhetorical language.

For classical and modern historians, serious reality is located outside the self, in nature and society. Classical rhetoric and history were closely allied in the task of organizing the surface of experience for a dignified, intelligible, interesting presentation of life as lived by men who were political actors. For medieval historians, although they clung to the old clichés, the whole purpose of history became an anti-rhetorical effort to penetrate the surface of experience, (especially human contrivance, that most volatile and uncertain surface) to the stable center of Divine purpose. Serious reality was no longer on earth at all, but only in the immaterial realm which alone gave meaning to human history, and could be traced in microcosm in the individual soul. This ultimately unworkable program made for a great deal of unsatisfying historical writing, because it confused the relation of language to serious reality, while rhetorical language and dramatic or play reality continued in effortless union (for those few writers who responded to that impulse). Serious intentions were no longer satisfied by a stable point of view or self controlling its expression; the language that attempts to reach for the *invisibilia* tends to overreach itself, in figure, allusion, allegory, until it approximates the language of play and theater. Bernard of Clairvaux spoke in Scripture just as Richard of Devizes spoke in Satire, which may point to the reason so many of his contemporaries found something hard to believe about Bernard (perhaps the something "spooky" that Auerbach felt about Sidonius).

After his single gesture in the direction of the *invisibilia dei*, John of Salisbury wrote his history in a low-keyed, transparent style, a language of simple reference to the earthbound world. When Orderic Vitalis insisted that he did not write comedy, or tragedy, but history, he was consciously abjuring fiction and, less consciously, meaning. He clearly was determined to connect his history with the true meaning immanent in, and higher than, human affairs, and he seems to have been sincerely content to record and wait for the figure in the carpet to appear, which it never did. Note his interesting contempt for Robert of Neubourg, "a man of great eloquence, but his arm is slow to act and he has won more by his tongue than by his lance."[88] Orderic, and William of Newburgh, and other sincere Christian historians tended to wait for meaning to appear, reluctant to impose it or stage-manage it; hence, the shambling, slack quality of their writing which lacks the skeletal control of informing figures or the larger tropes of meaning. The *homo rhetoricus*, who creates his world without compunction, always has the advantage.

It is interesting how many medieval historians comment uneasily on the victories of words in court; increasingly, of course, the ordeal and trial by battle (true semiotic expression) gave way before sworn testimony and argument, and yet all that rational elaboration of justice did not, as Galbert unhappily noted, satisfy Justice. Lanham discusses the debate at the beginning of Ovid's *Metamorphoses* between Ajax and Ulysses over the armor of Achilles; Ajax and Ulysses had been, for centuries, the very types of honest acton and vulpine wit. Ulysses, or rather, Eloquence, wins: Ovid looks on, indifferent.[89] Galbert of Bruges could not look without protest on wit that outwits Justice. God, no longer invoked into the court of words to speak in signs, was still the stable center of Justice and its ultimate monitor. Galbert could not live in a neutral world rearranged for each new occasion by noisy actors.

He is the serious man (in Lanham's sense) determined to connect the confused bravura gestures of his world with their common fixed center of meaning. At his most typical, he is unhappy about the outcome of an ordeal (every form of trial coexisted in twelfth-century Flanders) in which a certain Lambert of Aardenburg had cleared himself of complicity in the murder of Count Charles, although common opinion knew he was guilty. After that, Lambert had summoned "about three thousand vassals and friends and kinsmen"[90] and besieged a city in which his enemies lived: he was killed in the fighting. Galbert has mixed feelings: satisfied to see Lambert get his due, he is deeply discomforted at the thought that God was mistaken or missing at the first trial.

> It should be noted that in this battle Lambert, who had recently cleared himself by hot iron of the charge of having betrayed Count Charles, was now killed. For as long as he acted humbly towards God, God forgave him for having taken part in the murder of his lord. But, after being cleared by the ordeal, that Lambert and his men had arrogantly, without any sense of mercy, used a force of three thousand men to besiege a handful. . . . And so he deserved to be killed since he disregarded the mercy of God and the dispensation by which He had saved his life when he was about to be killed with the others, on condition, however, that he should carry out worthy acts of penitence, as he had promised God. . . . For when a servant acts humbly towards his lord because of an offense of which he is accused, the lord forgives him. . . . God supports the faith of the one acting justly, casting down the unjust man in his suit and confounding him in his obstinacy. So it happens that whilst in battle the guilty one is slain, in the judgement of water or iron the guilty one, if he is penitent, does not succumb.[91]

This is a very tortuous explanation, and most observers would surely not have been moved to attempt it. It records the night thoughts of a man who will not allow signs to lie, because their meaning has to depend on a God who is just, reasonable, and consistent. Galbert will not accept a dramatic reality tolerated by a God of rhetorical gestures; in lordless Flanders where calculated self-interest, fickle alliances, irreligion, and histrionic justice rapidly surfaced after the murder of the count, Galbert insists, at whatever cost of effort, that the surface reveal its inner meaning of right judgement and eternal truth.

He was not a rigid man; he lived comfortably in a town (Bruges is "our town," the burgers "our men") where shrewd free men were concerned with rents, tolls, trade, even self-governance, but he speaks of his volatile, urban-agrarian world, half bourgeois, half aristocratic, in the language of the *Song of Roland*, projecting onto life the traditional forms of lordship and vassalage, nobility and servility of birth and behavior, Christian honor and vile treason. And so he was deeply distressed when vengeance did not flow directly from the shock of that ultimate affront to order, the murder of a prince by his own vassals, but stalled unaccountably as various individuals, factions, and interests waited to see how events would turn.

> And so every man of peace and honor who had heard of the fame of this count now mourned him. But in our castle where our lord and most pious father was lying slain, no one dared openly to weep for his death.[92]

When finally the murderers and their accomplices have suffered a suitable public fate and parties have formed, dissolved, and reformed around the successive candidates for the countship until bribes, threats, and low calculation would seem to have exploded any lingering illusions of legitimacy and loyalty, Galbert is left to ponder the hidden significance of things in his agonized and deeply touching penultimate chapter:

> It may well be asked why, therefore, when God wished to restore the peace of the fatherland through the death of one of the two, He preferred that Count William should die, whose claim to rule the land was more just, and why on the contrary Count Thierry did not die who seemed unjustly put in his place; or by what justice God granted the countship to the one who forcibly seized the office. . . . And yet, because the countship pertained by hereditary right to Count Thierry, he holds it by right; and if he seems to have seized it unjustly, nevertheless, because before the election of that William, who is now dead, he had claimed that it belonged to him . . . he did right in seeing and conquering his heritage. . . . And so God rightfully preserved the life of Count Thierry in accordance with ancient justice. . . . Therefore God righted such a great wrong, which no human power could or would correct, in accordance with the line of strict examination . . . by contrition of heart and uprightness of mind they [men of Flanders] could have pleased God in this matter. But because they neglected this, they had to endure the one whom they had received as lord so rashly, as a tyrant and despoiler. . . .[93]

Galbert's "effort after meaning," considerably shortened here, strikes us as naive, but he was not a naive man. He knew, even before the murder, how men could talk and bluff their way into wealth and out of trouble; and he quickly acquired whatever he lacked in knowledge of hypocrisy, deception, oaths that do not bind, loyalties available to the highest bidder. But, perhaps with an urban impatience, he would not record the surface and leave the significance for a later generation. His voice throughout reminds us of an intelligible higher order, known to every Christian and not invented by him. His is the authentic voice of serious realism in medieval terms.

But, the historian yet demurs, does any of this artifice and apparatus of language exist outside the minds of word-intoxicated writers and critics? Here, in evidence, I submit two entries from the diary of Buonaccorso Pitti, patrician gambler and merchant from Florence. In 1377 he falls in love:

> While I was in these straits, I fell in love with Monna Gemma, the wife of Jacopo, Messer Rinieri Cavicciuli's son, and the daughter of Giovanni Tedaldini. She was staying at a convent outside the city at Pinta. As I happened to be passing by one day, some of her relatives invited me in for refreshments and I accepted. Although there were a number of people present, I managed to have a private word with her and told her very respectfully, "I am entirely yours and I beg you to take pity on me." "Does that mean," she asked me laughing, "that if I were to command you to do something you would obey?" "Try me." "Very well," she said, "go to Rome for love of me." [Rome and Florence were at war.] I went home and two days later, without a word to anyone, took horse and set out with one servant. [He contrived to get smuggled into Rome and found friends to help him get out and home safely—a rash and dangerous business.] When I got home I sent a woman to tell Monna Gemma how I had obeyed her. She sent back word that she had never supposed I would be so mad as to take such a risk on account of a challenge spoken in jest. That was in 1377.[94]

Unlike Paolo and Francesca who confused the rhetorical and the serious occasions of life, to their eternal sorrow, Buonaccorso Pitti and Monna Gemma were fully in control of their rhetorical play: the language of love and its choreography of offer and response are theirs to enact for mutual flattery and harmless delight. As soon as Pitti offers the first line, Monna Gemma takes her cue, and the couple transform themselves from idle young man and sensible Florentine matron to *cavaliere servante* and capricious Lady. In fact, the elegant game is played through quite far, although Monna Gemma, no Francesca, sooner returned to the ordinary business of life and had no intention of bestowing the last reward of love.

In 1391 Pitti marries:

> On reaching Florence I resolved to get married. Since Guido di Messer Tommaso di Neri del Palagio was the most respected and influential man in the city, I decided to put the matter in his hands and leave the choice of bride up to him, provided he picked her among his own relatives. For I calculated that if I were to become a connection of his and could win his good will, he would be obliged to help me obtain a truce with the Corbizi family. Accordingly, I sent the marriage-broker, Bartolo della Contessa, to tell Guido of my intentions. He sent Bartolo back with the message that he would be happy to have me as a kinsman and was giving the matter thought. A few days later he sent him a second time to say that if I liked I might have the daughter of Luca, son of Piero degli Albizzi, whose mother was first cousin of his own. I sent back word that I would be very happy and honored and so forth. I was betrothed to her at the end of July 1391 and married her on 12 November of the same year.[95]

Life's serious occasions are conducted in serious language. But quite ordinary people have perceptions, aspirations, selves, a "world of desires which is seen only by the mind," whose expression is too febrile or delicate, often too socially eccentric for more than intermittent appearance in the conventional course of life; this reality too, and its language, the constant preoccupation of the writer of fiction, are the historian's task, to see and honor, in past lives.

> The greatness, on the other hand, of true art, of the art which M. de Norpois would have called a dilettante's pastime, lay, I had come to see, elsewhere: we have to rediscover, to reapprehend, to make ourselves fully aware of that reality, remote from our daily preoccupations, from which we separate ourselves by an ever greater gulf as the conventional knowledge which we substitute for

it grows thicker and more impermeable, that reality which it is very easy for us to die without ever having known and which is, quite simply, our life. Real life, life at last laid bare and illuminated—the only life in consequence which can be said to be really lived—is literature, and life thus defined is in a sense all the time immanent in ordinary men no less than in the artist.[96]

NOTES

[1]John of Salisbury, *The Metalogicon*, trans. D. McGarry (Berkeley and Los Angeles, 1955), pp. 12, 131-45. (Hereafter cited as *Metalogicon*.)

[2]*Metalogicon*, p. 26.

[3]*Metalogicon*, pp. 66-70.

[4]Mary C. G. Dickey, "The Teaching of Rhetoric in the Eleventh and Twelfth Centuries," Thesis, St. Hilda's College, Oxford 1954 (on deposit in the Bodleian Library).

[5]Richard McKeon, "Rhetoric in the Middle Ages," *Speculum*, 17 (1942), 1-32.

[6]Richard Southern, "Medieval Humanism," in *Medieval Humanism and Other Studies* (Oxford, 1970), p. 32 and generally for his argument that medieval logic was a form of humanistic thought.

[7]Marcel Proust, *Remembrance of Things Past*, trans. C. K. Scott Moncrieff and Terence Kilmartin, 3 vols. (New York, 1981), 1:631.

[8]Augustine, *On Christian Doctrine*, trans. D. W. Robertson (Indianapolis, 1958), pp. 133-43 and generally.

[9]The efforts of James Murphy to bring the study of rhetoric back to life are widely and deservedly known, as are the works of Harry Caplan, George Kennedy, and Richard McKeon in this field; two especially excellent books are Stanley F. Bonner, *Education in Ancient Rome* (London, 1977) and T. P. Wiseman, *Clio's Cosmetics: Three Studies in Greco-Roman Literature* (Leicester, 1979); The essays by the other contributors to this volume speak for the ability of rhetoric to inspire scholarship of first quality.

[10]Cicero, *De oratore*, trans. H. Rackham, 2 vols. (London, 1942), 2:236-37.

[11]*De oratore*, 2:244-45, 249.

[12]Anon. [Cicero], *Ad Herennium*, trans. H. Caplan (Cambridge, MA and London, 1977), pp. 160-61.

[13]Nancy Struever, *The Language of History in the Renaissance: Rhetoric and Historical Consciousness in Florentine Humanism* (Princeton, NJ, 1970).

[14]*De oratore*, 2:236-37, 244-45.

[15]Erich Auerbach, "Fortunata," in *Mimesis: The Representation of Reality in Western Literature and Art*, trans. Willard Trask (New York, 1957), pp. 29-35.

[16]Tacitus, *A Dialogue on Oratory*, trans. W. Peterson and M. Winterbottom (London, 1970), pp. 290-91.

[17]Auerbach's perfect essay, "Sicharius and Chramnesindus," in *Mimesis*, pp. 67-83, remains the best, most sensitive response to Gregory of Tours and early medieval writing in general. His discussion of the change from classical literary Latin to Gregory's language in relation to the depiction of concrete reality is equally suggestive with respect to Bede's better Latin and organized history. See pp. 76-79.

[18]Orderic Vitalis, *The Ecclesiastical History of Orderic Vitalis*, ed. and trans. Marjorie Chibnall, 6 vols. (Oxford, 1973), 4:107.

[19]Quintilian, *Institutio Oratio*, trans. H. E. Butler, 4 vols. (London, 1921), 1:225.

[20]See Roger Ray, "Orderic Vitalis and His Readers," *Studia Monastica*, 14 (1972), 17-33.

[21]I am more and more convinced that medieval narrative was largely a casualty of the loss of the educational methods which underpinned rhetorical standards in antiquity.

[22]Quintilian discusses the construction of the *narratio* in *Inst.*, 2:49-121 (Bk. 4.2).

[23]*Ad Herennium*, pp. 28-29.

[24]Bonner, *Education in Ancient Rome*, ch. 18, "Progress into Rhetoric," pp. 250-76; ch. 19, "Declamations on Historical Themes," pp. 277-87.

[25]All medievalists who read the historians of the Middle Ages know how we read these authors for their "asides," implications, unknowing or indirect verification of other person's statements, and artless revelations—anything except a direct assent to the text, which we withhold as if by instinct. This reaction is an aesthetic emotion, not a rational judgement.

[26]It seems to me perfectly absurd to be quibbling in print with a book I read with such unreserved admiration and pleasure as Robert Alter's *The Art of Biblical Narrative* (New York, 1980). On parataxis, see pp. 5, 133-40.

[27]Alter quotes Eisenstein on montage in *The Art of Biblical Narrative*, p. 140. The analogy between narrative parataxis and cinematic montage flickered to mind in my chapter on literary form in *Serious Entertainments: The Writing of History in Twelfth-Century England* (Chicago, 1977), p. 205, in which I tried (fairly lamely, it now seems to me) to come to terms with parataxis. I have come to share more of Auerbach's views.

55

[28]Mordecai Richler, *The Apprenticeship of Duddy Kravitz* (Penguin Books, 1964), pp. 152-59: "Thank you very much, indeed," Mr. Friar said, "Unfortunately, the best parts were left on the cutting room floor." (This is a serious note.)

[29]John of Salisbury, *The Historia Pontificalis of John of Salisbury*, ed. and trans. Marjorie Chibnall (London, 1956), pp. 3, 1-4. (Hereafter cited as *HP*.)

[30]Erich Auerbach, "Figura," in *Scenes from the Drama of European Literature* (New York, 1959), pp. 49-56.

[31]Augustine, *On Christian Doctrine*, p. 10.

[32]Augustine, *On Christian Doctrine*, p. 64.

[33]See Calvin Kendall, "Bede's *Historia Ecclesiastica*: Rhetoric of Faith," in *Medieval Eloquence*, ed. J. Murphy (Berkeley, 1978).

[34]*HP*, pp. 11-12.

[35]*HP*, p. 51.

[36]Orderic Vitalis, *Ecclesiastical History*, 5:9.

[37]For excellent, succinct discussions of the relation between literal and allegorical truth in Dante's art, see Charles S. Singleton, *Dante Studies 1: Commedia: Elements of Structure* (Cambridge, MA, 1957), "Allegory," pp. 1-17, and "The Substance of Things Seen," pp. 61-83; *Dante Studies 2: Journey to Beatrice* (Cambridge, MA, 1958), "The Allegorical Journey," pp. 3-13, and "Justification in History," pp. 57-99.

[38]Proust, *Remembrance of Things Past*, 3:912.

[39]Thucydides, *History of the Peloponnesian War*, trans. Rex Warner (Baltimore, Penguin Books, 1954), p. 214.

[40]Thucydides, *Peloponnesian War*, p. 147.

[41]This is only the first step of an extended acknowledgement to the work of Richard A. Lanham, in this case his witty *Style: An Anti-Textbook* (New Haven and London, 1974), especially ch. 1, "The Prose Problem and 'The Books,' " pp. 1-20, on suspicion of style.

[42]Jane Austen, *Northanger Abbey*, first pub. 1818 (Oxford, 1971), p. 98.

[43]See Isaiah Berlin's excellent essay, "The Concept of Scientific History," in *Concepts and Categories* (New York, 1979), esp. pp. 103-08.

[44]Berlin, "Scientific History," pp. 122-24.

[45]Proust, *Remembrance of Things Past*, 1:972-74.

[46]This is an example of the "unfair generalization"; the exceptions know who they are.

[47]Hayden White, "Rhetoric and History," in *Theories of History* (Los Angeles, 1978); and "The Fictions of Factual Representation," in *The Literature of Fact*, ed. Angus Fletcher (New York, 1976), pp. 21-44.

[48]Geoffrey Barraclough, in *Main Trends in History* (New York, 1979),

pp. 1-45, gives a concise account of the failure of confidence in a "scientific" and consistent international historical enterprise. He himself insists on history-as-science and hopes that "the new generation, equipped with a more thorough groundwork of fundamental science, is far more willing than its predecessors to think in scientific categorie . . ." and will bring history to its "great leap forward . . . from the collection and description of data to generalization and the formulation of scientific propositions" (p. 207). Regardless of how one feels about this view of history, a glance at the new "scientific" generation's articles shows that they are not even hippity-hopping forward to "scientific propositions." The mosaic metaphor of the mythical common enterprise holds on with surprising tenacity. The always snobby question "Why in the world does he want to work on *that*?" often enough gets the answer, "Well, someone has to do it."

[49]Two special exceptions that must be lifted out of this "unfair generalization" are Peter Gay's *Style in History* (New York, 1974) which does take style seriously; and, of course, Hayden White's *Metahistory: The Historical Imagination in Nineteenth-Century Europe* (Baltimore and London, 1973).

[50]The collection of essays, *The Writing of History: Literary Form and Historical Understanding*, ed. Robert H. Canary and Henry Kozicki (Madison, WI, 1978) has had a fair amount of influence, although chiefly, as usual, among people already disposed to a "literary" point of view. The essay by Lionel Gossman, "History and Literature: Reproduction or Signification," pp. 3-39, is the "toughest" in its critical impatience with naive historians who think they can align word and world in mirror image; Hayden White's "The Historical Text as Literary Artifact," pp. 41-62, is also scathing on the "what really happened" school of history; the essays by Kieran Egan, Richard Reinitz, and Louis O. Mink on narrative are very interesting. Another good collection is *The Literature of Fact* [n. 47 above], which tends to take a kinder view of historians. An attempt to compile a bibliography of writing on language and history was made by *Style* in vol. 13 (1979).

[51]Augustine, *On Christian Doctrine*, pp. 8, 9.

[52]For those who do not "see" this similarity in detail, Hayden White's essays are very useful.

[53]Cynthia Ozick, Letter, *The New York Times Book Review*, 28 Feb. 1982; Epstein's review appeared 14 Feb.

[54]God can interfere with the narrative as He pleases; in this story, Abraham learns that to be human is to find, rendingly, that righteousness and well-doing, love of God and human love—both good and both demanded of us—do not give immunity from pain and confusion, but can come, with a horror of inevitability, into an opposition which only an angel can resolve. We are not as God; we are all Abraham.

[55]Assuming, against the odds, that there may be others as ignorant

as myself, I would offer a very few titles I have found especially helpful in this maze: Wallace Fowlie, *The French Critic 1549-1967* (Carbondale, IL, 1968), a compressed, cogent survey of French critical trends; Frederic Jameson, *The Prison-House of Language: A Critical Account of Structuralism and Russian Formalism* (Princeton, NJ, 1972) is a first-rate "hard" book which makes one understand the interior logic and terminology of structuralism; Jonathan Culler, *The Pursuit of Signs: Semiotics, Literature, Deconstruction* (Ithaca, NY, 1981); Thomas A. Sebeok, ed., *A Perfusion of Signs* (Bloomington, IN, 1977); and Michael Lane, ed., *Structuralism: A Reader* (London, 1970).

[56]Jameson, *Prison-House of Language*, pp. 30-33, 111-12.

[57]Proust, *Remembrance of Things Past*, 1:460, 3:188.

[58]Henry James, "The Art of Fiction," in *Henry James: Representative Selections*, ed. L. N. Richardson (Urbana and London, 1966), p. 82.

[59]James, "Art of Fiction," pp. 76-78.

[60]James, "Art of Fiction," p. 77.

[61]Gossman, "History and Literature," p. 39. There is a certain amount of malicious pleasure to be felt in much current sophisticated writing about history, as structuralist linguistics, semiotics, and non-realist fiction pull the rug out from under naive historical realism.

[62]A useful essay is Nancy Struever's "The Study of Language and the Study of History," *Journal of Interdisciplinary History*, 4 (1974), 401-15.

[63]E. H. Gombrich, *Art and Illusion: A Study in the Psychology of Pictorial Representation*, Bollingen Series 5, 2nd ed. (Princeton, NJ, 1969).

[64]Gombrich, *Art and Illusion*, p. 87; also pp. 90-110 on the process by which a preconceived "language" of forms is adapted to the requirements of representation.

[65]Gombrich, *Art and Illusion*, p. 173, and see ch. 4, "Reflections of the Greek Revolution."

[66]Erich Auerbach, *Literary Language and Its Public in Late Latin Antiquity and in the Middle Ages* (London, 1965), pp. 8, 14-19.

[67]Burke's very suggestive comments on the "Four Master Tropes" in Appendix D of *A Grammar of Motives* (Berkeley and Los Angeles, 1945), pp. 503-17.

[68]Lanham's *Style: An Anti-Textbook* has been already cited; his *The Motives of Eloquence: Literary Rhetoric in the Renaissance* (New Haven and London, 1976) is even bolder in its depiction of the creative powers of language. These are the rare kind of books in which the language itself does what it describes and makes the reader imitate and duplicate the process.

[69]This is first described in ch. 3, "The Opaque Style," of *Style*, pp. 44-68 and elaborated in *Motives of Eloquence* in chs. 1 and 2, pp. 1-64.

[70]Proust, *Remembrance of Things Past*, 3:924-25.

[71]Galbert of Bruges, *The Murder of Charles the Good, Count of Flanders*, trans. James Bruce Ross (New York, 1967), p. 84.

[72]Galbert, *The Murder of Charles the Good*, p. 84.

[73]*HP*, p. 15.

[74]*HP*, p. 26.

[75]*HP*, p. 26.

[76]Lanham, *Motives of Eloquence*, p. 4: "Rhetorical man is an actor; his reality public, dramatic. His sense of identity, his self, depends on the reassurance of daily histrionic re-enactment. . . . Rhetorical man is trained not to discover reality but to manipulate it."

[77]Gombrich, *Art and Illusion*, p. 173.

[78]Auerbach, *Literary Language*, pp. 257-58.

[79]Burke, *Grammar of Motives*, p. 508.

[80]Richard of Devizes, *The Chronicle of Richard of Devizes of the time of King Richard the First*, ed. John T. Appleby (London, 1963), p. 1.

[81]Richard of Devizes, *Chronicle*, p. 71.

[82]Richard of Devizes, *Chronicle*, pp. 65-67.

[83]See Richard of Devizes, *Chronicle*, p. 69; Partner, *Serious Entertainments*, pp. 175-78, for Richard's parody of Thomas of Monmouth's story of St. William of Norwich.

[84]Richard of Devizes, *Chronicle*, pp. 6-7.

[85]Richard of Devizes, *Chronicle*, p. 51.

[86]Lanham, *Motives of Eloquence*, p. 64. I have taken the opportunity of this essay to discuss Richard of Devizes again, having come close, but not close enough, to seeing him clearly in *Serious Entertainments*.

[87]Geoffrey of Monmouth has been very well analyzed by Robert Hanning in *The Vision of History in Early Britain from Gildas to Geoffrey of Monmouth* (New York, 1966).

[88]Orderic Vitalis, *Ecclesiastical History*, 6:201.

[89]Lanham, *Motives of Eloquence*, pp. 11-12.

[90]Galbert, *The Murder of Charles the Good*, p. 287.

[91]Galbert, *The Murder of Charles the Good*, pp. 288-89.

[92]Galbert, *The Murder of Charles the Good*, p. 124.

[93]Galbert, *The Murder of Charles the Good*, pp. 310-12.

[94]*Two Memoirs of Renaissance Florence*, ed. Gene Brucker, trans. Julia Martines (New York, 1967), pp. 27-28.

[95]*Two Memoirs*, pp. 45-46.

[96]Proust, *Remembrance of Things Past*, 3:910.

RHETORICAL SCEPTICISM AND VERI-SIMILAR NARRATIVE IN JOHN OF SALISBURY'S *HISTORIA PONTIFICALIS*

ROGER RAY

In the preface to his *Cronica*, written at the close of the twelfth century, Gervase, a monk of Christ Church Canterbury, distinguishes between "historici" and "cronici," historians and chroniclers. The difference lies mainly in varying techniques. The "modus tractandi" of the historian is said to be "full and elegant," that of the chronicler "brief and simple." Gervase made the distinction partly to put himself somewhat smugly among the chroniclers, partly to complain that certain unnamed authors violate their declared genre. Setting out to produce "cronica vel annales," they straightway exceed their professed limits and in fact write "more historici."[1]

John of Salisbury's *Historia pontificalis* was almost certainly a minor source of the *Cronica*.[2] It is therefore at least possible, though I think probable, that Gervase lodged his prefatory complaint mainly out of annoyance with John, for scarcely another medieval historian could have been more openly vulnerable to it. John presented the *HP* as a link in the great chain of Christian chronicles and himself as the latest of the "cronici scriptores." Specifically, he offered his book as a continuation of the *Chronicon* of Sigebert of Gembloux (d. 1112).[3] John's manuscript of this popular monastic chronicle included supplements down to 1148, which he took for Sigebert's.[4] The *HP* begins in that year, but otherwise has next to nothing in common with the Gembloux annals. The contrast, in Gervase's terms, is that between the "full and elegant" and the "brief and simple." John's "continuation"

61

is written "more historici," in the rhetorical manner that Gervase denied to chroniclers and annalists.

It has been suggested that John was perhaps pretending to be a continuator of Sigebert.[5] One of his later letters supports a different conclusion. In it John asks future "annalists" to score off Henry II of England for the tyrant he was in the Becket affair.[6] This was no appeal to the usual medieval annalists. I cannot imagine his thinking that a tyrant had anything to fear from the general run of them. For that matter I doubt that John ever credited very much at all to these laconic writers. He was not especially fond of the *Continuatio Gemblacensis*.[7] His epistolary plea to coming "annalists" shows that his view of historical writing owed nothing to the generic labels that interested Gervase. It reflects a belief that history by whatever name is always a field of rhetorical exposition. His own "annals" embody the assumption.

The narrative of the *HP*, as we have it,[8] covers but four years of papal history (1148-52), about half the reign of Eugenius III (1145-54). The pope himself is not the center of John's interest; he takes the *hystoria pontificalis*, the announced subject of the book,[9] in a wide theater that includes a number of great actors and stretches from Ireland to *Outremer*. During the narrated years, John was secretary and confidant to Archbishop Theobald of Canterbury, in which capacity he seems to have paid special attention to relations with Rome.[10] Theobald's business took him to the papal court at several times and places. About 40% of the *HP* originates in John's own recollections; all of it reflects long and close knowledge of the papal world's inner workings. The recent edition of the later letters makes it seem all the more probable that John wrote the *HP* entirely in 1164.[11] Early in that year John, now clerk and adviser to Theobald's successor Thomas Becket, preceded his lord into political exile on the continent, taking up residence at Rheims with a dear old friend Peter of Celle, the abbot of St. Remi. The *HP* is addressed to Peter.[12] It is empty of the brooding and even despairing attitude towards politics and society that notably marks the correspondence of 1165 and the remaining years of the exile.[13] The narrative is laced with humor and in general seems close to the spirit of the early letters, not to mention that of his more famous works the *Metalogicon* and the *Policraticus*, both completed in 1159. The *HP* seems to have been finished before the Becket matter began to erode John's morale. If he had written the work in the later years of the exile, it would surely have had a darker complexion.

The *HP* is well known for temperate and tentative judgements and for a remarkable density of convincing and amusing detail.[14] I hope to show that these characteristics owe much to rhetorical *inventio*, especially to the attitudes and methods sponsored by the theory of probability. To this end I take the *HP* within the context of John's other writings; I refer most often to the *Metalogicon* and the *Policraticus*, for they illuminate some of the inarticulate major premises of his work as a historian. The first section reviews his estimate of rhetorical sophistication, which is sometimes misunderstood. I then turn to the ciceronian scepticism with which John viewed contemporary human experience, whether of providence or politics. In the last part I discuss the previously mentioned prevailing characteristics of the *HP* in terms of their rhetorical grounds.

I

"It does not quite hang together," wrote Beryl Smalley of John's apparent attitude toward rhetoric and rhetorical study.[15] Others have observed that his defense of eloquence in the *Metalogicon* gives no formative place to rhetoric.[16] The principal interpreter of John's humanism, Hans Liebeschütz, concluded that rhetoric is in fact "entirely absent" from the *Metalogicon*, even though the work purports to be an apology for the verbal arts; at the other pole of opinion, Mary Bride wrote that the same book, for all its talk of logic, is "really a defense of rhetoric" in the great tradition of Aristotle, Cicero, and Quintilian.[17] At any rate Smalley's view is closest to the truth: John's attitude toward rhetoric is ambivalent.

A passage in the *Policraticus* touched off Smalley's remark. Directed against the Epicureans, it contains, among other things, ruminations about the prevalence of sin and misery.[18] In a few striking lines John suggests that in Paradise there was at first no speech. Then came language, and man praised the "magnalia Dei." At length, however, he became "verbiosor," more wordy, which led to disastrous talk with the tempter. Thus the first man fell and all mankind with him. The problem was not speech *per se* but the corrupt will that made hurtful use of it. All the same, this exegesis was written partly to stress the destructive power of language: it was at least a condition of the fall. "Sin accompanies loquacity," says Proverbs 10.19, as John notes in the *Metalogi-*

con.[19] In the same place he goes on to warn that the tongue unchecked can all but dismantle society.

By contrast the *Metalogicon* begins with the claim that eloquence gave rise to civilization. The belief that virtuous reason and cultivated speech set men apart from animals and drew together cities and nations was a commonplace of ancient rhetorical thought. It appears, for example, in Cicero's *De inventione* 1.1.1-4.5, his *De oratore* 1.8.30-34, as well as in Quintilian's *Institutio oratoria* 2.16.11-19. There is perhaps something of all these *loci* in John's own version of the myth of civilization.[20] To the received classical ideas John added Christian inflections. Grace perfects nature, making reason whole and competent; the philosophical wisdom that was for Cicero and Quintilian the source of responsible eloquence was for John "the relish, love, and observance" of divine truth. For the rest he closely follows his classical authorities. Like them he presents the myth to commend the formal studies that engender the civilizing eloquence; like them he directs his argument against those who maintain that this eloquence is not an art but a natural gift. In particular John aims at the so-called "Cornificians," an obscure contemporary group that appears to have held that the *trivium* adds nothing to the inborn language skills necessary to quick financial success.[21] He even catches the positive assessment of politics implied in his classical sources. There can be no happiness, he says, apart from a rightly ordered society, and whoever acts to diminish this "fraternitas" fights against the well-being of all. In *De inventione*, Cicero goes on to the same effect. For both Cicero and Quintilian, to deprive the state of properly educated orators is to invite its destruction. John declares that the Cornificians, by their rejection of the studies that produce eloquence, attack "not just one, or a few, but at the same time every city and all political life."[22]

The myth of civilization led John, however, to discuss grammar and logic, not the rhetorical doctrine that mainly occupied his Roman mentors. I might mention that Quintilian began his own discussion of eloquence with a long essay on the fundamental importance of grammar.[23] It is also worth bearing in mind that grammar and rhetoric were ever inseparable. Once Quintilian complained that grammar in his own time had become all but voracious, having nearly consumed the other departments of knowledge.[24] According to John, the grammarian teaches his student that fine literature images all the arts, including the "silvery eloquence" of oratory.[25] Actually the "logic" that the *Metalogi-*

con defends comprehends "all the instruction relative to words," thus subsuming grammar and rhetoric.[26] Rhetoric had its own sphere, however, and this comes out in John's discussion of "probable logic."[27] Unlike "demonstrative logic," probable logic concerns itself not with truth but with verisimilitude, things that people take to be true. Whoever uses it seeks to win over someone else, such as an opponent or a judge. It has two subdivisions, dialectic and rhetoric. John explains the difference between them in terms made popular in the Middle Ages mainly by Boethius.[28] The dialectician focuses upon an abstract "thesis" while the rhetorician trains interest exclusively on a "hypothesis," a question of particular human circumstances. The former proceeds by syllogisms and deduction, the latter by induction and oration. The rhetorician aggregates a case by finding material in the *circumstantiae*—who, what, where, by what means, how, why, and when. These belong, John notes, only to the rhetorician, which implies that he alone can treat historical questions. It is beside the point that all this has to do with but one part of rhetoric, *inventio*, the discovery of contents for effective discourse about human affairs. What matters is that John's defense of logic most certainly carries an apology for rhetoric, the study of which the Cornificians "despised" together with the rest of the *trivium*.[29] Rhetoric is not "entirely absent" from the *Metalogicon*.

As for John's own rhetorical education, he seems to have profited the most from the study of style and invention, and his instruction in the former perhaps came largely within the context of the grammatical *glossa auctorum*. His great preceptor in grammar was William of Conches, not Bernard of Chartres who was already dead when John travelled to France in 1136 to begin his twelve years of higher education.[30] Most of this long period was spent in Paris and at Mont St. Geneviève; whether John ever received instruction at Chartres remains controversial.[31] He makes it seem that his first intensive rhetorical study came from Thierry of Chartres and Richard the Bishop. He implies, however, that this work netted him less than he would have liked and suggests that later lessons from Peter Helias, one of Thierry's students, really took hold.[32] It is clear that John did not always agree with his teachers of rhetoric. Thierry and Peter, both vigorous commentators on Cicero's *De inventione*, took the ciceronian view that rhetoric is a part of "civil science," not logic or philosophy.[33] John preferred the position held by people like William of Conches, that rhetoric is a part of logic and thus of philosophy.[34] On a more important point he was completely at one with his teachers: all who talk about particular human affairs, the rhetorician's exclusive field, trade in verisimilitude, not truth.[35] This is a great methodological premise of the *HP*, as I shall argue below. Thierry and Peter were altogether serious students of the ciceronian rhetoric, serious even to the point of being critical of it.[36] They taught before the full discovery of Aristotle's *Organon* made it possible to separate clearly the dialectical and rhetorical methods, in a period when an overriding interest in probable argumentation still subsumed the study of rhetoric.[37] For this reason both stressed invention and perhaps favored Cicero's *De inventione* over the anonymous *Ad Herennium*, which includes a compressed discussion of invention but an account of all five parts of the rhetorical system. John himself was impressively attentive to Quintilian's *Institutio oratoria* and acquired for his own personal library a copy of Cicero's most mature ruminations about rhetoric, the *De oratore*. Both works he knew in incomplete texts.[38] He was well acquainted with the *Explanationes in Ciceronis Rhetoricam* of Marius Victorinus, a fourth-century commentary on the *De inventione*.[39]

One part of the rhetorical system—the art of memory—John says he never mastered, and he expresses regret that the discussion of it in the *Ad Herennium* is somehow lost on him.[40] Perfunctory performances in two hagiographical *vitae* (one of them on Becket) and his scorn of flatterers in the *Policraticus* make one wonder if he was sanguine about the laudatory side of demonstrative oratory.[41] In this connection it is perhaps significant that John wrote Letter 305, his most moving and elevated reflection on the death of Thomas Becket, by contemplating the *circumstantiae* of forensic rhetoric, almost as if he had made it a point to avoid both conventional hagiography and epideictic.[42] Yet the *Policraticus* attests that he could write vituperative prose almost as well as Jerome, though in better taste.

"Nothing is so incredible that artful speech cannot render probable; nothing is so dreadful and crude that oratory cannot polish it. . . ." These words from the proem of Cicero's *Paradoxa Stoicorum* John quotes in the *Metalogicon* to fortify an early crucial chapter titled "On the Commendation of Eloquence."[43] He seems perfectly comfortable with Cicero's equation of eloquence and oratory. John's praise of eloquence turns the argument from practicality and self-interest back on the Cornificians: If one wishes to win wealth, favor, and fame, then the rules of eloquence, quite apart from being superfluous, are made to order. He returns to the myth of civilization: If speech and reason set men above animals, the cultivation of these lifts some men above others. Eloquence is said to confer its benefits especially on the young. In good forensic style John reinforces the whole argument with questions: "Who are the most prosperous and wealthy among our fellow citizens? Who are the most powerful and successful in all their enterprises? Is it not the eloquent?" Then comes the quotation from the *Paradoxa Stoicorum*.

The lines from Cicero could have been used in a very different cause, to warn the reader that in the wrong hands artful language can delude; but John's purpose was the same as Cicero's, to laud eloquence. He could have quoted many other texts from Cicero to arm his audience against the "perverse and perverting" speech that he had rejected in the earlier-mentioned exegesis of Genesis 2. It is no doubt partly true that his attitude toward rhetoric was ambivalent because those of his classical authorities were ambivalent. "Eloquence without wisdom is futile," said Cicero in the *Orator*. This dictum helped John say that unprincipled verbal art is harmful.[44]

Bitter experience was surely another source of John's mixed view of rhetoric. His *bête noir* was Bishop Arnulf of Lisieux, who was for a long time a trusted counselor of Henry II. While Arnulf was still an archdeacon, John already disliked him. Even then, to hear John tell it in the *HP*, Arnulf was a master of verbal deception.[45] In 1156, after Arnulf had risen to the episcopacy, he persuaded the king that John had somehow been disloyal.[46] Probably he made his case from having heard John, at the papal court in the same year, support the high Gregorian views of Adrian IV. At any rate he managed to bring John into momentary disfavor with the king. Arnulf's great but hurtful asset, says John, was eloquence. In the episcopal courts he is said to have pursued seductive elegance at the expense of substantive pleading.[47] It was almost certainly John's animus for Arnulf that touched off his caustic praise of the "Luxovian tongue" in a letter of 1159 to a friend in Lisieux:

> My lords of Lisieux are not merely the fathers of eloquent men but might also be called the fathers of eloquence itself. In many respects they are the equals of the men of Orleans, who have vast knowledge and wide experience; and in one thing they easily surpass them,

> since at Lisieux they are born and grow to be so elo-
> quent that persons of every age and sex are steeped in
> the true practice of eloquence. What then shall I, a man
> of stumbling speech, say in answer to such a torrent of
> oratory?[48]

In the *HP* John even partly blames the eloquence of Arnulf for the failure of the Second Crusade.[49] Experience with men like Arnulf perhaps led John to remark cryptically that dialectic is a favored discipline because it cannot be "engulfed in waves of politics."[50] But John knew many men whose eloquence was not specious. William of the White Hands, an outstanding French churchman of the later twelfth century and one of John's prede-cessors as bishop of Chartres, was such a person. He had, John relates, great power with the French king and was a widely serv-iceable person because of his "prudence and eloquence."[51] If in the *Metalogicon* John claims that eloquence is a potent force in human affairs, and if in the *Policraticus* he recommends that kings study rhetoric,[52] it was not said for nothing. In fact John talked as if the verbal skill that partly results from rhetorical study was crucial to both church and state, and clearly he had in mind much more than the usefulness of prose and verse composition. For John rhetoric was a solid part of the humane curriculum that was the bulwark of civilization itself. In the writings of scholars like Thierry of Chartres, Peter Helias, and John, "the medieval under-standing of rhetoric came closest to the classical theory of elo-quence as the supreme social art."[53]

II

In one place John seems to say that historical writing is a sub-division of grammar.[54] But so does Seneca the Younger, and none would think he meant to exclude history from the orator's am-bit.[55] In the same place John also appears to have assigned the exposition of "court cases" to grammar, which is enough to prove that his mind was moving in the large interdisciplinary region of the *glossa auctorum*. In the Greek and Latin traditions it was never contradictory to think that history belonged to both gram-mar and rhetoric. At any rate it would not have escaped John's notice that his rhetorical authorities argue repeatedly that history is above all the orator's businsss. Thierry and Peter discussed historical *narratio* in the context of their lectures on rhetorical invention. They seem to have taken for granted that the historian's narrative method was the same as the orator's.[56] John's text of the *Institutio oratoria* included Quintilian's remark that the orator properly composes two things, "speeches and histories."[57] In Cicero's *De oratore* John no doubt read that rhetoric holds a monopoly in the entire field of cultivated prose exposition, of which history is a pre-eminent genre.[58] It may have been Victorinus who caused John's twelfth-century teachers to take up historical narrative as a topic of forensic rhetoric. The late Roman rhetor, commenting on Cicero's *De inventione*, taught more explicitly than his source that the rules for judicial *narratio* apply as well to history.[59] It would certainly have occurred to John that in fact the only available theoretical rules for reconstructing the past lay in the rhetorical manuals. In a fine book Peter Wiseman has recently contended that the uniqueness of this instruction is what made Greco-Roman historiography pervasively rhetorical.[60]

Another recent book implies that rhetoric was of little or no use to medieval historians because annalistic practices in one way or another held the entire field.[61] Erich Auerbach's studies in the medieval *sermo humilis* suggest that the received theology of history rendered the explanatory rhetorical style almost impious.[62] It has also been proposed that in the Middle Ages the vertical dimension of God's relationship with man made the horizontal plane of historical "facts" seem self-explanatory, in no need of the kind of elucidation that rhetoric might support.[63] Nancy Struever has claimed that Christian doctrine denied to the medieval period the basic assumption of truly rhetorical historiography, that man is the measure of all things. Thus among medieval historians the rhetorical tradition shrank down to mere verbal ornament, since theology had paralyzed the inventional method.[64]

To opinions of this sort John Ward has of late made a preliminary reply. He agrees with Struever that the Christian theology of history put classical rhetoric under medieval constraints but allows that further research in rhetorically trained historians may yield surprising results.[65] John of Salisbury's writings make it clear that classical rhetoric was not possessed in the same way by every historian who read it. They show that it was even possible to take a rhetorical approach to the Christian theology of history.

Johannes Spörl and Georg Miczka have drawn attention to John's apparent lack of interest in the various theological schemes of history that were prevalent in the Middle Ages.[66] He made no use, for example, of the doctrine of world ages that grew from the patristic exegesis of Genesis 1. Nor was he drawn to the notion of world empires, no doubt largely because of a pronounced dislike of the Germans. Even when in his later letters he likened an enemy to the antichrist, the term did not serve an explicitly eschatological view of historical movement.[67] There is a fair amount of figural and typological comment on contemporary persons and events in the often somber correspondence from 1165 onward; practically all of it was, it seems, epideictic, an attempt to praise or blame.[68] The *HP* contains no biblical figures and types.

For John it was enough to affirm generally God's just and benign providence, which he did in a remarkable section of the *Policraticus*, written to quash the popular astrology.[69] He confesses the paradox of man's free will and God's predestination; only heaven knows, he says, how these things fit together. The same mystery is said to shroud the movement of post-biblical history. The varying "times and moments of things" the Trinity "paints as if with certain *colores*" to give the appearance of events as men usually know them.[70] The rhetorical words "quasi quibusdam coloribus pingit" help John to say that God makes his deeds (history) look as if they were man's. All man can see is this appearance. John leaves no doubt that God is indeed the cause of all events.[71] But, he adds, since the divine will is an uncaused cause it is unintelligible to us; we can form no meaningful statements about it. Aside from the revealed manifestations of providence in the Scriptures, we have no power to comprehend the works of God in specific events of the past or present. Hence the astrologers should not pretend to know his plans for the future.

In the midst of this striking argument John takes a rhetorical attitude. He claims to be a ciceronian sceptic, an "Academic." Like Cicero and the New Academy, he will make only provisional statements about matters that do not permit certitude.[72] In this case he will not presume to say anything very definite about the hand of God in particular historical events. He had already avowed this rhetorical scepticism in the preface to Book 1: "In statements made from time to time in regard to providence, fate, freedom of the will, and the like, I am to be regarded as a disciple of the Academy rather than a dogmatic exponent of that which is still a matter of doubt."[73] In the early pages of Book 7 he renews the commitment, again mentioning providence.[74] Back in Book 1 he notes that Cicero, in old age, had taken refuge in the Academy, which is a clear reference to *De oratore* 3.36.145. John may have noticed that in *De inventione* 2.2.9-10, the youthful Cicero pledged to sustain a prudent and positive scepticism throughout his career, a promise he surely kept. This was written out of what George Kennedy calls "the rhetorical view of the world" that arose from the forensic doctrine of probability.[75] John too was ever the moderate Academic, not doubting all but remaining alert to the limits of reason. Actually he was sceptical about appeals to divine providence in specific current events because of a deep conviction that the works of God are far above mere human thought. From another angle he hoped to direct people away from futile speculation and toward the arena of their competence. "Truth itself," he says in his essay on providence, knows how things unfold; only "primitiva ratio" (divine wisdom) can "rightly and fully" penetrate the "iunctura rationum." Thus natural reason is better occupied with attempts to explain in contingent language the strictly human foreground of history than with hopeless efforts to understand the powerful but vague background of divine purposes.[76]

Signs and portents were generally thought to be evidence of this background. In the *Policraticus* John discounts both those who look everywhere for these things and those who claim to be expert in their interpretation.[77] The latter especially bother him. While some signs do give a hint of the divine will, the trouble with them all is that they are ambiguous. For that matter, many so-called signs are, says John, false. He comes down hard on the apparently fashionable art of dream interpretation. On the whole John warns the reader about speaking with any confidence in this entire murky area. "For to fall into error in many matters is a human weakness, while to possess nothing but the truth is an angelic and divine perfection."[78] This is part of a brief apology to those who may think him too full of doubt about alleged *mirabilia Dei*. For these persons there are several pages on the undoubted prodigies and portents of pagan and Christian antiquity. It is contemporary appeals to providence and the supernatural that prompt John's Academic reserve.

If John had revised the *Policraticus* in the 1170s, this ciceronian scepticism might have been curtailed. Several years after the canonization of Thomas Becket, John still found himself occasionally faced with critics of the post-mortem miracles attributed to the archbishop.[79] The defense of these wonders was for John the same as the defense of that *libertas ecclesiae* for which Thomas had died. In the previously-mentioned Letter 305, writ-

71

ten perhaps only days after the murder, John claims to have seen a number of miracles performed at his lord's grave. In words that surely respect his long-avowed scepticism, he explains that he would never have dared "for any reason" to write such things if his own eyes had not been witness.[80] As I observed earlier, John's involvement in the Becket ordeal seems to have altered his outlook. In 1165 he urged Thomas to trust now in prayer, not learned studies, for the latter "rarely or never inflame devotion."[81] Maybe this was momentary excess, but the preponderance of biblical over classical allusion and citation in the subsequent correspondence makes me wonder.[82] The advice to Becket is at least an extraordinary comment on the apparently earthbound atmosphere in which John had usually practiced the liberal arts.

The *HP* seems to breathe this atmosphere. The preface displays the expected Pauline words that the visible things of man reflect the invisible things of God.[83] Yet John wrote the narrative as if he himself stood little chance of catching the reflection. The *HP* does not document the Pauline view. It is entirely consistent with the discussion of providence and supernatural signs which John developed in the *Policraticus*. John was well aware that many historical works are, as he says, "filled with prodigies and portents."[84] It is therefore all the more significant that his own book of history contains but one. During a papal mass at Rheims in 1148, someone spilled a consecrated chalice.[85] The horrified pope ordered that the stained carpet be cut away and put among the sacred relics. The "opinio" was, writes John, that this unseemly happening augured ill for the whole church. "And certainly this opinion did not deceive," he goes on, for soon thereafter came news that the Second Crusade had failed, which was a disaster for the entire faith. John concludes the brief episode by citing the strictly human reasons for the collapse of the Latin expedition. There is no comment about the divine will.

Twice John calls the portent an *opinio*. This deliberate language was not meant to discredit the omen but to bring it within the terms of discourse about the sensible world. In the *Metalogicon* John remarks that some disciplines, like mathematics, consider intelligible reality, a subject matter that permits certain truth. But dialectic and rhetoric ponder sensible reality, about which it is so easy to be deceived. Hence they produce not truth itself but probable opinions. The "probable" John defines as that which always or usually happens or is thought to be true by many or at least by persons of good judgement.[86] When an *opinio* is widely acclaimed or accepted, it merits confident belief, "fides." And it is entirely permissible and desirable to say that a highly probable opinion is "true" as long as one does not confuse it with the very truth. Indeed human society could scarcely function if it were impossible to act on the probable truth; the courts are not the only institution that would be crippled. As for the portent of the spilled chalice, it was, of course, a particular event in the sensible world, something about which one runs the risk of being deceived. This event, however, "non fefellit," did not deceive. John speaks of it as an "indubitata opinio." The judgement of many persons, or at least that of the curia, had given it high marks for probability. The debacle of the crusade had conferred further verisimilitude. Presumably the *opinio* about the chalice had won *fides*. Nonetheless the omen was one of those things about which John did not want to be dogmatic. It only *seemed* true. Nor did it cause John to look away from the immanent causes that brought grief to the crusaders.

The doctrine of probable opinion is a major theme of the *Metalogicon*, the apparent crux of John's philosophy, and the substance of the ciceronian scepticism which he championed.[87] It was, moreover, the main burden of the inventional theory that was the focus of his rhetorical education and crucial as well to his dialectical studies. He notes that Cicero and Quintilian had praised Aristotle's *Topica* as the fountainhead of this theory.[88] Though his text of Quintilian did not provide a full discussion of invention, there was more than enough for John in Cicero and Victorinus. He quotes or alludes to them often, together with Aristotle, as he proceeds. Victorinus, an apparent favorite of Peter Helias, is notably prominent among the sources of the chapters on probability in the *Metalogicon*.[89] He was an especially rigorous exponent of rhetorical verisimilitude. On Neoplatonic assumptions he seems in fact to have radicalized the ciceronian doctrine of argumentation.[90] A philosophy of intelligible reality caused Victorinus to view the sensible world as an endlessly problematical object of thought. For him even apparently necessary truths about observable reality took their force from *opinio*. "If a woman gives birth, she has lain with a man," was one of Cicero's examples of a necessary argument about human affairs.[91] Victorinus points out that this line of thought may founder if one is addressing Christians, for in their *opinio* it is heretical to think that copulation always goes before childbirth. So it is, he claims, with all so-called necessary truths about this world: they turn out

73

to be somehow conditional. In Victorinus the doctrine of probable opinion comprehends the entire rhetorical method.

In *Metalogicon* 2.13 John, in the midst of his major essay on probable opinion, seems to have taken the rigorous position of Victorinus. In the course of arguing that "it is frequently dubious and presumptuous to assert that a thing is necessary" in the sensible world, he writes:

> Many ages took the following principle to be a necessary axiom: If a woman gives birth to a child, she must have had previous sexual intercourse. . . . But, finally, in the fulness of time, it has been shown that it is not such, by the fact that a most pure and incorrupt virgin has given birth to a child. Something that is absolutely necessary cannot be otherwise. But something that is conditionally necessary may be modified. Victorinus, in his work on rhetoric, explains this when he discusses necessity. He tells us that, while previous sexual intercourse may be inferred with probability, it cannot be deduced as absolutely necessary from the fact of childbirth.[92]

In what follows John makes it clear that the wise will not waste themselves in the futile pursuit of certain truths among changeable phenomena. They will realize that truth, "as our Academicians say," is as vaguely visible as if it "lay at the bottom of a well."[93] Hence he will equip himself with a knowledge of probabilities, which is "a master key whose use is universal."[94] Slightly later, John concludes that "one who understands probabilities will not be at a loss in any department of learning."[95] All this makes it seem that he learned well from Victorinus.

Certainly John absorbed the ciceronian view that there can be no unalterable claims about human affairs. He quotes with approval words from the *Disputationes Tusculanae* in which Cicero states it.[96] Much later in the *Metalogicon* he makes the same point in his own way. From recurrent experience, he says, one can have confidence, if not certitude, that the sun will rise tomorrow. "But since human affairs are transitory, only rarely can we be sure that our opinions about them are correct."[97] The apparent routine of nature permits statements of far higher probability than is possible in utterances about unrepeatable historical events. In a letter John wrote that historical experience is as fragile as a child's card house.[98] Elsewhere he treated the figures

74

of fortune and chance as fictions that cover the inability of the mind to keep track of constantly fluctuating life.[99] The human will struck him as especially mysterious. John counseled Becket to follow the Greek rule, to know himself; for only God can fully understand the motives of others.[100] In an earlier letter, to Peter of Celle, he reflects on the changeability of his own will. He tells his friend that his purposes, however often altered, seem more trustworthy when one sets them within the larger "rerum conditio." This general state John sums up in a stream of cliches ("the flight of time," "the mutability of things," etc.) which seem less commonplace in light of his articulate rhetorical scepticism.[101]

The Academic, John says, "will not presume to state definitely what is true in each and every case."[102] The reason is that the senses perceive highly frangible reality and so cannot produce totally safe generalizations. On these terms the assessment of most human activities will perforce be relative. If a heinous murder is wrong in any instance, the vast expanse of secular acts is harder to categorize. This is particularly true of *indifferentia*, morally neutral conduct like drinking wine. In the *Policraticus* John advises the reader to take this immense order of deeds case by case.[103] One can only appraise their "usefulness" and "honesty" (ciceronian criteria central to John's social thought)[104] "ex loco, tempore, modo, persona, et causa," that is, out of the relevant rhetorical *circumstantiae*. In this way one may find that even such typical wastes as hunting are occasionally worthwhile.

John's often discussed doctrine of tyrannicide illustrates peculiarly well his general respect for the ambiguity and relativity of human experience. Any talk of possibly killing a king was, of course, sensitive, but all the more so in a book (the *Policraticus*) addressed to the royal chancellor (Becket) and indirectly to a sitting sovereign (Henry II) with whom the author had recently been out of favor. Some have thought that John avoided further trouble only by falling hopelessly into contradiction, affirming tyrannicide on the one hand and Pauline quietism on the other. Further study has shown, however, that one can sort out the matter once one appreciates the function of John's ciceronian scepticism.[105] "Generally," John observes, tyrants deserve to die, for they fight against justice, the commonwealth, and thus God himself.[106] Not just law but logic and a great weight of historical precedents recommend this view. But John notes here and there many exceptions to it. Behavior toward a tyrant and even tyranny itself are topics that defy easy generalization. Ultimately John

75

assigns to God all responsibility for the punishment of tyrants. Here the complications really grow. For one thing, God has an enormous number of options for exacting retribution in time and eternity. Tyrannicide is only one of these options. Then too one can never be sure that a tyrant is not in fact a scourge of God visited upon a disobedient people. He may be, in other words, a tool of divine justice. In all cases his fate is a question of God's will in particular events. Since this kind of question tests the limits of reason, no answer to it can be certain enough to justify a specific plan of tyrannicidal action. Thus John in effect told Henry II to fear the justice of God, not the far less awful sentence of mere assassination. It is a message that the king could hardly have rejected, and John himself seems to have suffered nothing for having delivered it.

In Book 7 of the *Policraticus*, John totals up in one staggering sentence some of the topics that require the Academic approach.[107] Providence heads the long and rather odd list, which includes many of the more prosaic aspects of historical experience: time, place, speech (*oratio*), the source and function of virtues and vices, "the causes of events and their connection and opposition," and the duties and various issues that arise from social agreements, among others. The list leaves no doubt that John would have taken his scepticism to the reading of history. Twice in the *Policraticus* he remarks that historians often contradict each other. First he says that they are frequently at odds over military matters; then later, that the very complexity of events causes them to report conflicting things.[108] In the *Metalogicon* he writes that even the Gospels would seem out of joint if one knew nothing of their varying purposes.[109] Of course the Gospels do contain examples of apparent disagreement about times, places, and *orationes*. At any rate the Bible, "written by the hand of God,"[110] was for John a special case: in its pages the flux of events clearly points to the truth itself. All other books of history, the best of them created out of the eloquence which is "chiefly the work of man,"[111] state the probable opinion about human affairs, what is likely or at least thought to have taken place. On these terms the historian has no choice but to speak without prejudice to a better or even different view, in provisional words that respect the conditions of discourse in this sublunar world where, as John says in the larger *Entheticus*, verisimilitude reigns.[112]

III

In the preface to the *HP* John claims that his narrative contains nothing "nisi quod uisu et auditu uerum esse cognouero, uel quod probabilium uirorum scriptis fuerit et auctoritate subnixum."[113] I know of no other medieval historian who used the word *probabilis* to commend his sources of information. Perhaps the word is not here a forensic technical term; it may mean nothing more than "worthy" or "good." In light of John's estimate of rhetorical probabilities, the apparently idiosyncratic choice of the term is at least noteworthy. In any case I have no doubt that the theory of verisimilitude underlies John's claim to have written what is true, *uerum*. For John the Academic, neither the eyes and ears nor the testimony and writings of credible men could ever have given access to the actual truth of history. Only God knows that truth. "The Academy of the ancients makes to human beings the concession that whatever seems probable to each, that he has the right to defend," wrote John in his essay on providence.[114] On this premise the historian, however confusing his materials, may vouch for the probable truth about the past. It is this truth that John proposes to relate. The standard of rhetorical verisimilitude governs his narrative.

This means, to begin with, that in the *HP* the ambiguity of human experience gives John pause, just as it does in his other writings. Typically he proceeds with moderation and tentativity, as if one can have nothing more than provisional opinions about the forces that make history. At the same time the narrative embodies the rhetorical rule that verisimilar speech about human events must be explanatory. John's style was not the parataxis that in so many other medieval chronicles leaves the reader to supply the causal links. Actually I know of no case in which he seriously adopted the literary piety of the Christian *sermo humilis*. His standard was the hypotactical language of the slow ciceronian period, a syntax of subordinating relationships that is reasonable, natural, and thus verisimilar. Struever has argued that rhetorical sophistication causes one to draw from the reconstructed events themselves the things that explain them. In her view the apriority of Christian dogma robbed the Middle Ages of this method, but this generalization, valuable as it is, does not fit John of Salisbury.[115] His explanatory remarks owe little to theology. They come usually from direct reflection on the persons and events important to the narrative, from the materials themselves. And often they reflect the rhetorical scepticism that kept his attention trained on the horizontal plane of interacting human designs.

For example, midway in the extant text John relates briefly that Eugenius III, on the way home from the Council of Rheims, stopped in 1148 at Cremona to convene a synod of Italian bishops. At this meeting the pope dissolved the diocese of Modena to punish the fractious citizens of that city. John reports that a subsequent pope reversed the decision. Then he lingers for a moment to turn over possible reasons why not just this but other acts of Eugenius got the same disrespect.

> Indeed I do not know how it happened that many of Eugenius' judgements were so easily retracted, unless perchance [*nisi forte*] for two reasons: first, that he had perhaps [*forte*] merited it by so readily revoking the sentences of his predecessors, not to mention his fellow bishops, and secondly that he was too ready to rely on his personal opinion in imposing sentences.[116]

Pressing this latter point, John explains that Eugenius was slow to take advice because he was a "most suspicious" person. He tries to account for this foible, again with more than one reason. "I think" (*arbitror*, a verb that expresses a certain suspense of judgement) that the mistrust sprang, John says, from the pope's "weak nature" or from an awareness that his aids all suffered from "aegritudo," presumably a kind of occupational anxiety. Thus John begins this whole explanatory passage with a disclaimer ("Et nescio quo pacto") of any certain knowledge about the grounds for the reversed decisions; then gives not one but two likely reasons without favoring either of them and emphasizes his attitude with the rapidly repeated use of the word *forte*. About Eugenius' suspicion he is similarly cautious, as is clear in the choice of the verb *arbitror* and the impartial suggestion of more than one *causa*. The recurrence of the adverb *forte* gives substance to John's remark in the *Policraticus* that the Academic is likely to prefer "verba ambigua" like "si forte fortasse et forsitan" in places where other people might speak with less hesitation.[117] But the offering of multiple causes without preference for any is especially important recognition of the ambiguities of historical experience. This practice is typical of the *HP*. There are no fewer than ten cases of it.[118]

Some of these come in John's account of the proceedings against Gilbert of Poitiers that took place while the papal court was still at Rheims in 1148.[119] This part of the *HP* represents about one-third of the entire extant narrative and is one of the best known things John ever wrote. Its fame is due partly to the fact that John observed the trial, including the caucus in which Bernard of Clairvaux, the self-appointed prosecutor, tried heavy-handedly to determine the outcome in advance. The eye-witness quality of John's account has given it precedence over that of Otto of Freising, who was not present, and the moderation that suffuses the narrative has caused scholars to rate it higher than that of another eye-witness, Geoffrey of Auxerre, an apologist for the Bernardine party.[120] It is surely true that this moderation arose partly from John's relationship to Bernard and Gilbert: the abbot had recommended him for the appointment to Theobald's court, the post that John held at the time of the Council of Rheims,[121] and Bishop Gilbert was one of John's most revered teachers.[122] John was so close to both that he tried personally to intercede between them once they came into conflict.[123] Yet there is more to be said about the judicious temper of the narrative than that it reflects a counterpoise of respect for the two principal litigants.

John presents the two men by means of an extended comparison. First he makes it seem that they had one thing in common, a controversial reputation. The theological writings of Gilbert were treasured by some and assailed by others. Among the detractors John numbered Suger of St. Denis, Peter Lombard, and Robert of Melun. "I am uncertain," he then says,

> whether they acted out of zeal for the faith, or jealousy of his fame and merit, or a desire to propitiate the abbot, whose influence was then at its height and whose counsel was most weighty in the affairs of church and state alike.[124]

The sentence plants a disclaimer in its initial words ("Incertum habeo") and in the rest offers several reasons of apparently equal plausibility. Next John turns to the abbot, about whom also the *opinio* was said to have been various. People thought this or that depending on their attitude toward his warfare against intellectuals like Gilbert. At this point John offers his own estimate of both:

> But as for me I cannot be persuaded that a man of such holiness would have lacked zeal for God or that a bishop

79

of such gravity and learning would have committed to
writing anything whose meaning was not clear to him,
however obscure it might seem to others.[125]

Clearly John wrote this sentence without knowing what finally to
make of either man, as if their motives were a fair field for differing opinions. He was certainly concerned that the reader might
pause over his praise of Gilbert, for he goes quickly on to speak
further of his excellence in liberal studies and to say that he was
now reconciled anyway with Bernard "and the other saints" in
heaven (both men died about ten years before John finished the
HP). He adds that the apparent obscurity of Gilbert's works was
partly due to his mastery of patristic language that was not then
in general use. "This nevertheless is certain: that now several
terms are hackneyed in the schools which, when he introduced
them, seemed to be profane novelties."[126] The emphatic words
Hoc tamen certum est introduce a factual claim and lift the reader
out of the cloudiness of talk about human motives.

Then John turns to the events that preceded the trial. After
having failed to win over in advance a weighty group of men
against the cardinals, who as a body favored Gilbert, Bernard
secretly approached his old friend the pope, where he made some
headway. This momentary success John explains, first, with an
appeal to the reputed prowess of the abbot. "For he was a man
mighty in word and deed, before God, as is thought, and before
men, as is generally recognized."[127] The construction "coram
Deo, ut creditur, et ut publice notum est, coram hominibus" is
not a gentle barb directed at Bernard, as Chibnall's translation
makes it seem: "with God, as some believe, and with men, as we
all know." John chose the verbs *credo* and *nosco* because it was
one thing to speak of the abbot's secret power in prayer, but
another to talk of his observable sway with men. There is certainly no humor in the next remark: "Once given the chance of
speaking, he almost always made his will prevail." Then John
offers a second reason why Eugenius gave early consent to Bernard's views before changing his position later: "It was moreover
certain," says John, that some envious cardinals had slandered
Bernard, which spleen drove the pope to the side of his friend.
This is the one place in the entire work where John claims sure
knowledge of human motives—which only shows how little he
cared for the cardinals. But he expresses this untypical certainty

in the course of giving two possible reasons for Eugenius' temporary decision. The sceptical attitude prevails.

In the following pages John relates that Gilbert was able to acquit himself, Bernard's maneuvers notwithstanding, by clear arguments offered winningly in a spirit of moderation. He takes occasion to observe that Geoffrey of Auxerre's account of the proceedings lacked this rhetorical skill. The book "seems," John writes, to be a kind of invective and to embody "a formative bitterness." "However no human judge is competent to decide this," for only Geoffrey himself and God are privy to the true authorial motive.[128] "What is certain in any case" ("Hoc tamen certum est") is that Bernard, for his part, often attacked the bishop after the trial in spoken and written word. Again John has sharply juxtaposed the obscurity of human motives and the relative clarity of externally observable happenings. Having made these guardedly critical remarks about Bernard and his party, John goes on to a balancing statement, that some never stopped thinking that Gilbert triumphed by verbal dexterity. Then he returns to the comparison of the two chief actors, perhaps to suggest that they were in conflict because of unbridgeable strengths. Bernard's forte was biblical learning, pulpit eloquence, and practical affairs; Gilbert's was high patristic theology and, above all, secular letters. It is suggested that each lacked what the other possessed, and the point seems to be that they could find little common ground for discussion. The comparison comes to a climax with the assertion that these men set the standards in their respective fields: "Both these men had many would-be imitators, but I cannot call to mind one who could touch either of them."[129] Against this backdrop of evenly alloted praise, John turns aside in a long excursus to defend Gilbert by trying to clarify several of the matters on which some had thought the bishop culpably vague, or worse.

In the schools John had heard or read words to the following effect:

> It is a fault in making a comparison to think it necessary to disparage one thing when you praise the other. . . . Indeed it is not necessary, if you prefer one, to disparage the other; for you can manage, when you have given praise to one, to allot some portion of praise to the other, so that you may not be thought to have combated the truth under the influence of partiality.[130]

I give these lines from the anonymous *Ad Herennium* only partly because John's comparison of Bernard and Gilbert seems to have been cut precisely to the pattern. It is equally important to notice that they appear not in the section on style, where comparison comes up again among the figures of thought, but in the discussion of invention. Specifically they fall within a long review of faulty forensic proofs, arguments that stand little chance of seeming probable. The comparison of Bernard and Gilbert was a major part of John's attempt to aggregate a probable case for his former teacher. The moderation and tentativeness of the entire account were both a response to the ambiguity of the events themselves and an appeal to an audience among which opinion about the whole affair was still divided.

The only large topic of the *HP* on which John sometimes becomes intemperate is that of unprincipled clergy, especially papal legates, a theme that prompted some of the most scathing pages of the *Policraticus*.[131] Nonetheless he found it possible to give even his old foe Arnulf of Lisieux the benefit of a doubt. Though John makes it clear that the Norman bishop did much to ruin the Second Crusade, he allows that Arnulf had at least the capacity to have been a boon to the expedition.[132] There is only one consistently exemplary figure in the narrative, John's former lord Theobald of Canterbury. Not even an apparent belief that Bernard of Clairvaux was already a saint (the canonization finally came in 1174) kept John from viewing the abbot in some of his less holy aspects. Arnold of Brescia, says John, found Bernard to be full of vainglory and envy; it is not clear that John entirely disagreed. As for Arnold himself, John reviews the conflicting estimates of him and then takes a middle road.[133] A penchant for complex viewpoints and conditional comment is in evidence throughout the work. Whatever else this conscious bent may represent, it is certainly a function of John's rhetorical scepticism.

A wealth of persuasive and entertaining detail is the other often-noticed feature of the *HP*. John was, as I earlier remarked, an eye-witness to matters that fill something less than half of the surviving narrative; personal connections in high ecclesiastical places must have brought further grist for the mill. The work gives every appearance of having been written almost entirely from previously unrecorded materials. At the same time it seems to have been composed more than a decade after the events it recounts, which is at least arresting in light of John's repeated complaints that his memory was not the best. Two of these appear, respectively, in the prologues to books one and three of the *Metalogicon*.[134] They are given in respect of his schooling, things in which he would have been drilled. It is true that both remarks helped him to exhibit the expected exordial modesty. There is, however, no literary posturing when, elsewhere in the same work, he reveals that he never mastered the formal art of memory— though he now wished he had.[135] As of 1159, he seems to have felt that his powers of recollection were neither cultivated nor naturally strong. His ability to recall offhand literary quotations nonetheless lends support to Chibnall's belief that the *HP* owes much of its detail to a "trained and retentive" memory.[136] Poole liked to think that the narrative was written in stages, much of it while the facts were fairly fresh, with revisions intermittently up to 1163-64.[137] Finding no basis for this opinion, Chibnall preferred to cover the lapse of time by coupling praise for John's memory with the assertion that he "no doubt" worked from accumulated notes or a diary.[138] In the preface of the *HP* John does say that he had found "subnotationes" of memorable events in "church archives." He gives no particulars and even leaves one to wonder whether he actually used these "subscriptions" in his narrative.[139] He was just as vague about the "testimony and writings of credible men" to which he also made an exordial appeal. The truth is that we know nothing about his oral informants and scarcely more about his written authorities.[140] They may have been greatly detailed, but we cannot say.

What we do know is that the passing years, a fading memory, and incomplete secondhand information were not necessarily a hindrance to a historian trained in forensic rhetoric. The rhetors teach that the courtroom speech usually gives the facts of the case in a *narratio*. Quintilian observes that this narrative is in practice perhaps the most important part of judicial rhetoric, partly because the *narratio* is the one part of the orator's address to which the judge is likely to give full attention.[141] Hence, in his view it is critical that the orator know how to tell a good story, for it may be that a shrewd and charming narrative will all but win the case.

Training in the narrative art begins, according to Quintilian, early in the orator's education. The first lessons will come partly from the reading and analysis of historians, since *historia* is virtually the same thing as the forensic *narratio*.[142] All John's authorities teach that a narrative must be brief, clear, and probable, and all give due space to the first two of these traits while leaving no question that the third is the most important. There was general agreement about the conditions of *narratio probabilis*. It will reflect the familiar and the recurrent—what happens, as Cicero says, "in veritate," everyday life.[143] It will characterize persons so as to make it seem likely that they will have acted as they did. In other words, the narrator will do some type-casting, making politicians act like politicians, mothers like mothers, and so on. The plausible narrative will also give appropriate detail about the events in all their aspects. The narrator will recreate what John knew as the *circumstantiae*; he will somehow answer the questions who, what, where, and the rest. And he will be mindful of the "opinio" and the "mores" of the audience, lest he say something offensive. Victorinus was especially strong on the last point. If the narrative, however skillfully conceived otherwise, is at variance with the views and customs of the audience, it will be cast aside as implausible.[144]

All John's Roman mentors reveal the sharp pragmatism that underlies rhetorical narrative theory. The objective truth of the forensic *narratio* is in itself of little consequence; the power of the narrative to get the desired results is everything. Probability, not truth, is the final test; the audience, not the orator, is the final judge. The *Ad Herennium*, for example, advises that it is no use to tell the truth if for some reason the judge will not believe it. Thus even when the facts are true, the narrator must take thought to make them seem so.[145] If this seems to give implied authorization to conscious distortion and falsification, Quintilian left no doubt. He discusses at some length the *color*, the wholly fictitious narrative. In his view the orator may tell even the "big lie" if nothing will work better and if he can get away with it in a good cause.[146]

In general, rhetorical narrative theory gives broad berth to the imagination. The entirely falsified *color* aside, the rhetors take for granted that one's information will hardly ever be complete or fully clear, that one will usually have to augment the facts in one direction or another. This further material need not be true or evident, only likely and fitting and evocative. One "invents" (finds) data by asking what more will make the original *données* inherently probable to the audience. The great source of these supplementary "facts" is imagination, not research.

The classroom *controversiae* provided practice in the imaginary generation of narrative material. The teacher gave the pupil the bare bones of a story involving a possible criminal or civil issue, and then the challenge was to turn this incomplete information into a full and conclusive declamation. It is no accident, Wiseman has recently argued, that Roman historians trained in this practice were able to write far more than their apparent sources would seem to warrant. Attempting to illustrate how late republican authors like Aelius Tubero could have composed large works from a shard of information, Wiseman turns for an analogy to a twelfth-century historian, Geoffrey of Monmouth. Tubero and Geoffrey worked, Wiseman believes, in much the same way, by filling out their narratives from a cultivated use of the imagination.[147] The analogy is more interesting than Wiseman makes it seem. Geoffrey claimed to have produced the *Historia regum Britanniae* by translating from an ancient Celtic book. It is generally thought that this old *liber* never existed as such, which lends much fascination to Geoffrey's disclosure that the person who gave it to him, Archdeacon Walter of Oxford, was "a man learned in the art of rhetoric."[148] This may have been a teasing admission that the true source of the *Historia* was rhetorical inventiveness, Geoffrey's own and that of Walter.

I have no doubt that John was among the twelfth-century scholars who practiced the classroom *controversiae*.[149] In his view a good education combined theory and practice. "Theoretical principles must be consolidated by practice and exercise," he says in the *Metalogicon*.[150] There is no reason to suppose that John's teachers of rhetoric would have preferred, or even known, any alternative to the *controversiae* and *suasoriae*. He mentions with approval the "sophistical exercises" which are of great help to youths in the study of the verbal disciplines. These promote, he explains, "skillful oratorical expression" and dialectical facility—undoubtedly a reference to declamation on the one hand and disputation on the other.[151] These exercises represent the positive value of "sophistry," which John otherwise rejects for its radical scepticism and tolerance of lying. Despairing totally of the truth, the sophists prefer the appearance of probability, not probability itself. Deception is said to be the sophist's way of life. John sees nothing wrong, however, with playing sophistical games at school, since they engender eloquence.[152] We must take seriously his term "sophistical exercises." On his definition of sophistry, it seems to suggest activities in which truth and fact give place to convincing illusions. It would seem that John practiced rhetorical declamations with something of the same freedom of imagination that prevailed in the Roman *controversiae*.[153]

We must also take seriously John's attack on sophistry. He was averse to immoderate doubt and programmatic deception. At the same time he seems to have listened closely to Quintilian's advice about the benign strategic lie. In the prologue to Book 1 of the *Policraticus*, he confesses that the work contains certain "mendacia," all told to the public good. He gives no hint where these are; it has been suggested that his superior readers would have known.[154] Modern scholarship has spotted two. It is now widely accepted that John invented the so-called *Institutio Traiani* of Plutarch, which he claims to have ransacked for political ideas in books five and six of the *Policraticus*.[155] Janet Martin persuades me that he moved toward this large *mendacium* by first telling what, by comparison, is a small fib, that Plutarch wrote a political treatise titled *Archigramaton*.[156] Both works John seems to have imagined for a rhetorical reason, to give his own views more authority and effect. He would certainly have denied that his main purpose was to deceive; he was no cynical sophist. Yet these rhetorical creations, especially the *Institutio Traiani*, are remarkable examples of the verisimilar illusions that John learned how to use in "sophistical exercises."

I mention these apparent inventions not because the *HP* likely contains anything to rival them but because they are perhaps exaggerated yet entirely faithful evidence of the method that helped to give so much detail to the narrative. To the things he could recall or otherwise knew, John was trained to add further "facts," things that cohere with the original given, contribute to a likely picture, and give point and pleasing effect to the story. We cannot know how much information John started with, but it is clear that he was prepared to make the most of whatever there was. As a keen observer of the papal world, he had a strong sense of what was likely to happen within it. Thus by training and experience he was well equipped to conjecture verisimilar details for his papal history.

On solid textual grounds Martin has shown that John felt free to augment the written historical sources of the *Policraticus*. By a "reckless invention of spurious material" he expanded quotations from Suetonius; he took similar liberties with the Christian historian Orosius.[157] Martin discusses one case that says much about John's inventional practices.[158] In Book 4 he enlarges upon an anecdote from the *Satyricon* of Petronius. At table, Trimalchio relates that a certain craftsman once brought to Caesar some unbreakable glass he had made, expecting that the emperor would be pleased with it. Instead Caesar had the craftsman executed for fear that his remarkable handiwork would diminish the value of gold. To this little story John added, as Martin shows, more than elocutional touches. He contributed further material that brings out motives and expands the action. The result is a story considerably more detailed than what one reads in the *Satyricon*. And the added "information" clearly came from the amplifying imagination that John cultivated in rhetorical declamations. I give Martin's translation of a few lines that expand Petronius, complete with her emphasis on the original material from the *Satyricon*:

> So when he [the craftsman] had fashioned a vessel of this kind of the purest glass and worthy, as he thought, of Caesar alone, *he went to Caesar and was admitted*. The beauty of the gift was praised, the skill of the artisan commended, the devotion of the giver accepted. But the craftsman, in order to turn the onlookers' admiration to astonishment and to win more favor from the emperor, *took the vessel and threw it violently to the floor*.[159]

Though John notes that Trimalchio's tale may not be true (he is talking about his own augmented version of the story),[160] he leaves open the possibility that it was. In any case he treated Petronius with the same freedom with which he approached Suetonius. In rhetorical terms the further materials are "true" to the original facts. They fit with them; they enhance the inherent probability of the story. Clearly John thought it was his authorial prerogative to imagine this added detail, and there would have been no reason to think differently when it came to the sources of the *HP*.

The work was almost certainly written in the company of Peter of Celle, who took great delight in John's literary talents.[161] Probably Peter asked his guest to set down in a book some of the stories they had enjoyed together in the early months of their reunion. It has been proposed that the *HP* was all but intended for Peter's eyes only.[162] In one remarkable way the first ten chapters of the narrative have the look of a private communication. These represent all but four of the chapters devoted to the Council of Rheims and the trial of Gilbert of Poitiers. They include, as one would expect, many references to the presiding pope, but these are always made with words like *dominus papa* or *aposto-*

lus. John never mentions the name of the pope—not until the eleventh chapter, which begins about one-fourth of the way through the extant text. It is an entirely unconscious and thus revealing omission that shows how far John composed the work under the impress of a reader who already knew many of the major details.

Some of John's funniest letters are addressed to Peter.[163] It is therefore not surprising that a significant part of the *HP* was written for laughs. There is no doubt more humor in the narrative than we could ever catch. To any reader it should, however, be clear that John had a keen eye for the unseemly, the incongruous, the ridiculous, not to mention a flair for tongue-in-cheek and the witty verse. He has practically all his fun at the expense of bishops and the papal court. I can imagine Peter of Celle overcome with laughter at John's almost rollicking account of the legates *a latere* Jordan and Octavian on mission to the German crown in 1150.[164] He would perhaps have taken more bemused pleasure in John's picture of the sometimes weak and even silly Pope Eugenius III.[165] Eventually John praises "so great a pope,"[166] but not before much else had been said that hardly fits the belated compliment. He even found humor in the failure of the Second Crusade. Two of the chief participants, Arnulf bishop of Lisieux and Godfrey bishop of Langres, are made to seem the epitome of the raw ambition that in John's view often made ecclesiastical courtiers a laughing-stock.[167] They posed as papal legates partly to profit from sick and dying people willing to pay well for the "papal" blessing. But fraud and greed were all they had in common; for the rest they were always at odds, for no better reason than mutual dislike. They were on opposite sides of the question whether to return home after it became clear that the crusade was doomed. Godfrey wanted to stay, John says, at least long enough to do some "grandia," deeds worthy of God, king, country, and "the coming of such eminent men." Obviously John enjoyed writing that, as the princes were trying to decide finally what to do, the bishop of Langres was such a nuisance in council that he was sent with forty knights on a short reconnaissance mission just to get him momentarily out of the way.

Arnulf once quipped, says John, that Godfrey was rather like Cypriot wine, "sweet to the taste but lethal unless diluted with water." This barb John uses partly to prick Godfrey and partly to illustrate that Arnulf knew the great rhetorical power of humor. John had just observed that Arnulf was a man of parts, "eloquence" among them, "which he made beguiling under the *color* of

88

witticisms."[168] The words "quas sub facetiarum colore uenusta-
bat" were written to Arnulf's credit, for John did not want to
diminish the ridicule of Godfrey that follows them. They reflect,
at any rate, John's own regard for the allure of things spoken *sub
facetiarum colore*. The humorous coloration of the *HP* was John's
gift to Peter of Celle, but it was also part of his general concern
to find verisimilar detail for his narrative.[169] Cicero and Quintilian
emphasize alike the persuasive force of entertainment, a major
source of which is humor. According to Quintilian, Cicero was
always cracking jokes in the courtroom; indeed he thought his
great predecessor was both unduly given to the practice and the
unparalleled master of it.[170] The trouble with humor, says Quintilian, is that it usually consists of imaginary or at least distorted
material. To raise a laugh the orator will scarcely be constrained
by the facts. The utility of wit lies in what Quintilian calls its
"most imperious force." Things said with humor are almost impossible to resist.[171]

John's text of the *Institutio oratoria* did not contain Quintilian's discussion of wit. Yet it did include his long section on
narratio where the persuasive power of pleasure is an important
theme. The narrator must charm the judge, for "by pleasure he
is lured to belief."[172] On these terms a decorously witty narrative
will stand a fine chance of seeming true, whether it is or not.
There is a long passage on humor in Cicero's *De oratore*, one
which, I daresay, John relished.[173] Cicero praises the narrative
genre as the form *par excellence* of successful humor and recommends history as a rich source of witty matter. It comes out
boldly that the orator may sit lightly by the facts so long as he
raises mirth. It is in fact suggested that humor is a splendid mask
for outright lies.[174] The point is that wit is wonderfully persuasive:
people are inclined to believe what makes them smile or laugh.

We may be excused, I think, if we doubt that twelfth-century
ecclesiastical history was actually as funny as John makes it seem.
Nothing provokes more laughter, Cicero says, than the unexpected turn.[175] I believe that John concocted one of these for the
HP. He relates that Henry, the bishop of Beauvais and the brother
of Louis VII of France, fell into a tangle with certain great men
in the area.[176] The king not only sympathized with the bishop's
opponents but gathered an army to destroy Beauvais. Various
people interceded between the brothers, and the fratricidal war
never took place. Apparently demoralized by the experience,
Henry set off in 1151 for Italy, to ask the pope for full release

from his episcopal duties. Eugenius, at Ferentino, refused to grant the request. John offers three reasons for the papal decision without saying which, or even if any, was the truth. To this point in the narrative he had established that Henry suffered such personal and professional trouble that he was driven in depair to travel far in an embarrassing attempt to quit his job. In light of this highly-charged development, the reader readily imagines that the pope's negative reply would have burned itself into Henry's mind forever. Thus it takes one completely by surprise to find in one quick, matter-of-fact sentence a most unexpected turn: on returning home, Henry *forgot* what Eugenius had decided. One can only laugh at the thought of it, and that is exactly what John intended.

This detail was the worst of John's ridicule of Henry. He had just written that the bishop tried to resign either because of poor character, religious fervor, or a sense of being tainted. Most of these reasons tell against Henry, but not as much as his astonishing forgetfulness. John goes on to report soberly that Henry wrote to ask that the pope restate his position. Eugenius is then said to have replied in letters from his own hand. Poole, who called this episode a "strange story," points out that John referred to a papal letter dated 8 March 1151 and to another three days later. In the first the pope indeed wrote *propria manu*; in the second he became irritated with Henry.[177] Neither makes it seem that the continuing problem was Henry's short memory. Both suggest that the bishop, on further thought, found the pope's response somehow vague or perhaps contradictory, which may explain why Eugenius wrote without the knowledge of his notaries and then with a bit of pique. The letters are evidence that Henry's laughable lapse of memory was John's *color*. And the joke gets better when one takes into account that Henry became archbishop of Rheims in 1162. John, no doubt writing in that city about two years later, was apparently poking fun at the local diocesan, a twist that would perhaps have made the ridicule even more naughty to Peter of Celle.[178]

At any rate the beguiling lure of things said *sub facetiarum colore* was a charm that John understood very well, and its persuasive force would not have been misspent on readers besides Peter. The pursuit of humorous colors gave both scope to the imagination and insurance against disbelief. On the whole the witty bits of the narrative were part of the larger effort to fill the work with verisimilar materials.

In one kind of narrative detail John had little interest. The *HP* rarely includes calendar dates, and of the few John gives, all but one, says Chibnall, are wrong.[179] This lack of chronological detail is noticeable because John presents the *HP* as a continuation of the Gembloux annals, in which the basic organizing principle is the calendar. It is of interest here because a dearth of dates is typical of Latin rhetorical historiography from antiquity onward. Literary taste partly explains this fact; there is nothing elegant about calendrical information. Yet it must have mattered just as much that the theory of *narratio veri similis* makes almost nothing of dates. The narrator is supposed to put events in natural sequence and mind the difference between, say, summer and winter, or midnight and noon. But, as Cicero makes plain (*De inventione* 1.21.29), whether the time was sufficient ("si tempus idoneus") for the alleged action is far more important than what in fact the time was. In all, the evidence of calendar dates is not much of a weapon in the orator's arsenal. Obviously John wrote the *HP* as if it had little to do with the truth of his narrative.

There are not many speeches in the *HP*, and one wonders why. The work is well known for characterization, but not because John developed his views of people and issues in direct discourse. The longest and most interesting speech in the book is directed against Arnulf of Lisieux and the Normans.[180] Otherwise John restricts direct discourse to short spaces. It is widely recognized that medieval historians took much freedom in the creation of speeches. It is less well known that the relevant rhetorical assumption underlay, as well, the imaginative invention of things other than words. The *Ad Herennium* says that the orator may impute direct discourse so long as the speaker seems to stay in character.[181] In other words, it must be credible that such a person expressed such sentiments in such a connection. Not evidence or accuracy but inherent probability is what matters. It is the same standard that prevails in the rhetorical invention of other narrative materials. The imaginative discovery of direct discourse is not really a special case.

At the beginning of this essay I suggested that Gervase of Canterbury was perhaps thinking of the *HP* when he complained about the "full and elegant" rhetorical style of some would-be annalists. I wonder whether Gervase could have known the half of John's debt to classical rhetoric. Gervase was mainly worried about self-consciously artful prose and the sin of intellectual pride. By contrast, John was convinced that deliberately cultivated speech was the source of civilization. In any case, he knew that classical rhetoric was not only, or even mainly, a guide to Latin elocution, that it is primarily a theory of invention, a conspectus of tools for finding and shaping the contents of verisimilar discourse about human affairs. Gervase was perhaps innocent of this theory. It took from John's hands some of the usual equipment of Christian historiography, but he felt no sense of loss. There was manifold compensation. If rhetoric caused him to focus on human, not divine, choices and to puzzle over the unrepeatable and often deceptive course of events, it also armed him with attitudes and methods sufficient to the probable truth of history. It provided a moderately sceptical viewpoint and empowered the verisimilar amplification of an incompletely remembered ecclesiastical past. Rhetorical attitudes and methods, far more than the "full and elegant" style that seems to have bothered Gervase, set the *Historia pontificalis* apart from the average of medieval chronicles.

NOTES

[1]"Cronica Gervasii," in *The Historical Works of Gervase of Canterbury*, ed. William Stubbs, Rolls Series 73 (London, 1873), 1.87-88.

[2]*Ioannis Saresberiensis Historia pontificalis*, ed. and trans. Marjorie Chibnall (1956; rpt. London, 1962), pp. xlviii f. (Hereafter cited as *HP*.) The editor argues that Gervase's account of the Council of Rheims and the proceedings against Gilbert of Poitiers is in some ways too like John's to have been accidentally similar; she also gives evidence that Christ Church Canterbury owned a MS of the *Historia pontificalis* in the late twelfth century. William of Nangis is the only other medieval historian who is known to have made use of John's narrative.

[3]"Ut itaque . . . cronicis Sigeberti narratio nostra continuari possit, a concilio Remensi in quo ille suam finit, ordimur nostram. . . ." (*HP*, pp. 2-4, esp. 4).

[4]John's "Sigebert" is actually the anonymous *Continuatio Gemblacensis*, in which three different writers treat the years 1136-48. See *HP*, pp. xlvii, 95, where Chibnall gives details.

[5]Christopher Brooke, *The Twelfth Century Renaissance* (New York, 1969), p. 71.

[6]Ep. 275, *The Letters of John of Salisbury 2: The Later Letters*

(1163-1180), ed. and trans. C. N. L. Brooke and W. J. Millor (Oxford, 1979), p. 580. (Hereafter cited as *Later Letters*.)

[7]For his reservations, see *HP*, pp. 2-3. John says that Sigebert (the *Continuatio Gemblacensis*), for love of the Germans, "seems to have inserted" in his chronicle certain things at odds with the privileges of the church and the traditions of the Fathers. Chibnall points out (p. 3, n. 2) that the *Continuatio Gemblacensis* contains no such deviations. John's vague language—"inseruisse uisus est"—makes me wonder whether he himself had ever even seen the *Continuatio*.

[8]The *HP* survives in one MS (now Berne MS 367), written in the late thirteenth century at Fleury. For a description see *Ioannis Saresberiensis Historia pontificalis*, ed. R. L. Poole (Oxford, 1927), pp. lxxxii-lxxxix. The MS breaks off in the middle of a sentence.

[9]*HP*, pp. 3, 41. In both places the words *hystoria pontificalis* designate a theme, not a genre.

[10]See *The Letters of John of Salisbury 1: The Early Letters (1153-1161)*, ed. and trans. W. J. Millor and H. E. Butler, rev. C. N. L. Brooke (London, 1955), pp. xii-xxiv. (Hereafter cited as *Early Letters*.) Avrom Saltman, *Theobald, Archbishop of Canterbury* (London, 1956), pp. 169-75, and Giles Constable, "The Alleged Disgrace of John of Salisbury in 1159," *English Historical Review*, 69 (1954), 67-76, correct important details of John's early life. John O. Ward, "The Date of the Commentary on Cicero's 'De inventione' by Thierry of Chartres (ca. 1095-1160?) and the Cornifician Attack on the Liberal Arts," *Viator*, 3 (1972), 219-73, esp. 221-38, reconsiders the obscure chronology of John's twelve years of schooling on the continent. For his later life, see now *Later Letters* [n. 6 above], pp. xix-xlvii. On John's life and writings there is still much of value in C. C. J. Webb, *John of Salisbury* (1932; rpt. New York, 1971).

[11]Chibnall (*HP*, pp. xxiv-xxx) argues for this year, inclining to believe, against Poole, (p. lxxii), that the work was both started and finished within it. There is no evidence that the *HP* was produced, as Poole thought, over a period of years reaching from 1149 to 1164. While John was writing, Robert of Melun was bishop of Hereford (*HP*, p. 16) and Thomas Becket was still alive (p. 17); the former was consecrated in December 1163, and the latter died seven years later to the month. The canonization of Bernard of Clairvaux occurred in 1174, but in the *HP* (p. 24) John refers to the abbot as if he were already an acknowledged saint. There was an appeal for canonization in early 1163, while Pope Alexander III was at Paris. For various reasons, the petition was tabled. John's reference to *sanctus Bernardus* perhaps reflects the opinion, strong in northern France in 1163-64, that the abbot's sainthood needed nothing but official recognition. On the petition in 1163, see Adriaan H. Bredero, "The Canonization of Bernard of Clairvaux," in *Saint Bernard of Clairvaux: Studies Commemorating the Eighth Centenary of His Canonization*,

ed. M. Basil Pennington, Cistercian Studies, 28 (Kalamazoo, MI, 1977), pp. 63-100, esp. 83-86.

[12]*HP*, p. 4

[13]See the comments of Brooke in *Later Letters* [n. 6 above], pp. xxiii-xxiv. For an example of this sometimes bitter correspondence see esp. Letter 144 in *Later Letters*, pp. 32-34.

[14]For example, see *HP*, pp. xl-xlvi; and Beryl Smalley, *Historians in the Middle Ages* (London, 1974), pp. 111-13. The *HP* is often mentioned and praised, but rarely discussed at any length. The most illuminating general essay is Johannes Spörl, " 'Humanismus' und 'Naturalismus': Johannes von Salisbury," in his *Grundformen hochmittelalterlicher Geschichtsanschauung: Studien zum Weltbild der Geschichtsschreiber des 12. Jahrhunderts* (1935; rpt. Munich, 1968), pp. 73-113.

[15]Smalley, *The Becket Conflict and the Schools* (Oxford, 1973), p. 97.

[16]See Charles S. Baldwin, *Medieval Rhetoric and Poetic* (New York, 1928), p. 157; and Daniel D. McGarry, "Educational Theory in the *Metalogicon* of John of Salisbury," *Speculum*, 23 (1948), 659-75, esp. 671.

[17]Liebeschütz, *Mediaeval Humanism in the Life and Writings of John of Salisbury* (London, 1950), p. 85; and Bride, "John of Salisbury's Theory of Rhetoric," *Studies in Medieval Culture*, 2 (1966), 56-62, esp. 56. See Bride's article for further literature on John's view of rhetoric.

[18]*Policr.* 8.24 (2:414-15). The volume and page numbers, as given here and throughout this essay, are those of the C. C. J. Webb edition, *Ioannis Saresberiensis episcopi Carnotensis Policratici siue de nugis curialium et uestigiis philosophorum* (1909; rpt. Frankfurt am Main, 1965), 2 vols. For an English translation of the passage cited here, see John of Salisbury, *Frivolities of Courtiers and Footprints of Philosophers*, trans. J. B. Pike (Minneapolis, 1938), p. 402 (hereafter cited as Pike). It includes all of books 1-3, with selections from 7-8. The remainder has been translated by John Dickinson in *The Statesman's Book of John of Salisbury* (1927; rpt. New York, 1963). (Hereafter cited as Dickinson.)

[19]*Metal.* 2.8, p. 75. Page numbers given here and elsewhere in this study are those of the C. C. J. Webb edition, *Ioannis Saresberiensis episcopi Carnotensis Metalogicon* (Oxford, 1929). For an English translation of the passage here cited, see *The Metalogicon of John of Salisbury*, trans. Daniel D. McGarry (1955; rpt. Berkeley, 1962), p. 92. (Hereafter cited as McGarry.)

[20]*Metal.* 1.1, pp. 5-8; McGarry, pp. 9-12.

[21]On the Cornificians, see most recently Ward, "Thierry of Chartres," [n. 10 above].

[22]"Non ergo unam, non paucos, sed omnes simul urbes et politicam uitam totam aggreditur Cornificius noster, studiorum eloquentie imperitus et improbus impugnator" (*Metal.* 1.1, pp. 7 f.; McGarry, pp. 11 f. [His translation of the following has been slightly altered]).

[23]*Inst. or.* 1.3.1-1.9.6

[24]*Inst. or.* 2.1.4.

[25]*Metal.* 1.24, pp. 54 f.; McGarry, pp. 66-67.

[26]*Metal.* 1.10, p. 27; McGarry, p. 32.

[27]*Metal.* 2.3 and 12, pp. 64-65, 83-84; McGarry, pp. 79, 101-02.

[28]See Richard McKeon, "Rhetoric in the Middle Ages," *Speculum*, 17 (1942), 1-32, esp. 10-11; and Michael C. Leff, "Boethius' *De differentiis topicis*, Book IV," in *Medieval Eloquence*, ed. James J. Murphy (Berkeley, 1978), pp. 3-24, esp. 14.

[29]*Metal.* 1.3, p. 12; McGarry, p. 16.

[30]*Metal.* 1.5 and 24, pp. 16-17, 57; McGarry, pp. 21, 71. It is still sometimes said that John studied with Bernard; see James J. Murphy, "Rhetoric and Dialectic in 'The Owl and the Nightingale,' " in *Medieval Eloquence* [n. 28 above], pp. 198-230, esp. 203 . For John's account of his own education, see *Metal.* 2.10, pp. 77-83; McGarry, pp. 95-100; and Ward, "Thierry of Chartres" [n. 10 above], 221-38.

[31]R. W. Southern, *Medieval Humanism and Other Studies* (Oxford, 1970), pp. 61-85, has argued that there is no evidence that John ever studied in Chartres (see esp. pp. 72-73). Brooke, *Later Letters* [n. 6 above], pp. x-xi, accepts this view; but Ward, "Thierry of Chartres" [n. 10 above], 220, n. 1 contends that it is not conclusive.

[32]*Metal.* 2.10, p. 80; McGarry, pp. 97-98.

[33]On the rhetorical glosses of these two men, see Karin M. Fredborg, "The Commentary of Thierry of Chartres on Cicero's *De inventione*," *Cahiers de l'Institut du Moyen Âge Grec et Latin de Copenhague*, 7 (1971), 1-35; and her "Petrus Helias on Rhetoric," in a later number of the same Copenhagen series, *Cahiers*, 13 (1974), 31-41. Thierry commented on both the *De inventione* and the *Ad Herennium*; Peter glossed the former and perhaps the latter. Peter's commentary on the *De inventione* has not yet been published, except for the extracts in Fredborg's 1974 article. Thierry's work on the *Ad Herennium* still lies in MS. For parts of his glosses on the *De inventione*, see Nicholas M. Haring, "Thierry of Chartres and Dominicus Gundissalinus," *Mediaeval Studies*, 26 (1964), 271-86; Mary Dickey, "Some Commentaries on the *De inventione* and the *Ad Herennium* of the Eleventh and Twelfth Centuries," *Mediaeval and Renaissance Studies*, 6 (1968), 1-41; W. H. D. Suringar, *Historia critica scholasticorum latinorum* (Leyden, 1834), pp. 213-52, who prints an entire, though fragmentary, MS; and John O. Ward, "*Artificiosa eloquentia* in the Middle Ages," Diss. Univ. of Toronto 1972, 2:221-49. An indispensable study of medieval commentation on classical rhetoric is John O. Ward, "From Antiquity to the Renaissance: Glosses and Commentaries on Cicero's *Rhetorica*," in *Medieval Eloquence* [n. 28 above], pp. 25-67.

[34]See McKeon, "Rhetoric in the Middle Ages," in *Medieval Eloquence*, pp. 15-19.

[35]*Metal*. 2.3 and 12, pp. 65, 83-84; McGarry, pp. 79, 101-02.

[36]See Fredborg's articles [n. 33 above].

[37]On the impact of the "New Logic" on rhetorical study, see Ward, "*Artificiosa eloquentia* in the Middle Ages" [n. 33 above], 2:242-43.

[38]For John's knowledge of Quintilian, see Priscilla Boskoff, "Quintilian in the Middle Ages," *Speculum*, 27 (1952), 71-78; and Ward, "*Artificiosa eloquentia* in the Middle Ages" [n. 33 above], 1:420-21. The typical contents of the medieval *mutili* of the *Inst. or.* are summed up in James J. Murphy, *Rhetoric in the Middle Ages* (Berkeley, 1974), p. 125. Augustus S. Wilkins, in his edition of Cicero's *De or.* (Oxford, 1892), pp. 64-71, esp. 69, tabulates the parts of the work that were known in the Middle Ages before the fifteenth century. Among the books that John gave to the cathedral library at Chartres was the *De or.*; see Webb, *John of Salisbury* [n. 10 above], p. 168, for the evidence.

[39]Peter Helias seems to have made much of this work; see Fredborg, "Petrus Helias on Rhetoric" [n. 33 above]. I discuss below John's apparent affinity to the views of Victorinus.

[40]*Metal*. 1.20, p. 49; McGarry, p. 59.

[41]*Vita sancti Anselmi*, *PL* 199:1009-40; *Vita sancti Thomae*, in *Materials for the History of Thomas Becket*, ed. J. C. Robertson, Rolls Series 67 (London, 1875-85), 2:301-22. *Policr.* 3.4-15 (1:177-233; Pike, pp. 159-212) contains John's assault on sycophants.

[42]*Later Letters* [n. 6 above], pp. 724-38.

[43]*Metal*. 1.7, p. 23; McGarry, p. 27 (his trans.).

[44]*Metal*. 2.9, p. 76; McGarry, p. 93 (his trans.).

[45]*HP*, pp. 83-84.

[46]On this affair see Constable, "The Alleged Disgrace of John of Salisbury in 1159" [n. 10 above].

[47]Ep. 136, in *Early Letters* [n. 10 above], p. 10.

[48]Ep. 110, in *Early Letters* [n. 10 above], pp. 175-79.

[49]*HP*, pp. 54-56.

[50]*Metal*. 2.3, p. 65; McGarry, p. 79.

[51]Ep. 274, in *Later Letters* [n. 6 above], p. 578.

[52]*Policr.* 4.6 (1:255-57: Dickinson, pp. 29-31). See also Smalley, *The Becket Conflict and the Schools* [n. 15 above], pp. 96-97.

[53]Ward, "*Artificiosa eloquentia* in the Middle Ages" [n. 33 above], 1:534.

[54]*Metal*. 1.20, p. 49; McGarry, pp. 59 f.

[55]John quotes Seneca (Ep. 88) on grammar and history in *Metal*. 1.22, p. 52; McGarry, p. 63.

[56]This was, says Ward, the common assumption among eleventh-

and twelfth-century commentators on classical rhetoric; see "*Artificiosa eloquentia* in the Middle Ages" [n. 33 above], 1:399-406.

[57]*Inst. or.* 2.18.5.

[58]*De or.* 2.9.36.

[59]*Explanationes in Ciceronis Rhetoricam*, ed. Carolus Halm, in *Rhetores latini minores* (Leipzig, 1863), p. 203.

[60]Wiseman, *Clio's Cosmetics: Three Studies in Greco-Roman Literature* (Leicester, 1979), esp. pp. 3-53.

[61]Denys Hay, *Annalists and Historians: Western Historiography from the Eighth to the Eighteenth Century* (London, 1977), pp. 38-86. See my review of this book in *Speculum*, 54 (1979), 577-80.

[62]I have discussed Auerbach's now familiar views in "Medieval Historiography through the Twelfth Century: Problems and Progress of Research," *Viator*, 5 (1974), 33-59, esp. 48-50.

[63]Amos Funkenstein, *Heilsplan und natürliche Entwicklung* (Munich, 1965), pp. 70-77.

[64]Struever, *The Language of History in the Renaissance* (Princeton, 1970), pp. 34-36; for a helpful discussion of this important book see Ward, "*Artificiosa eloquentia* in the Middle Ages" [n. 33 above], 1:33-36.

[65]Ward, "Classical Rhetoric and the Writing of History in Medieval and Renaissance Culture," in *European History and Its Historians*, ed. Frank McGregor and Nicholas Wright (Adelaide, 1977), pp. 1-10.

[66]Spörl, " 'Humanismus' und 'Naturalismus': Johannes von Salisbury" [n. 14 above], pp. 92-95; Miczka, *Das Bild der Kirche bei Johannes von Salisbury* (Bonn, 1970), pp. 41 f.

[67]Miczka, *Das Bild der Kirche* [n. 66 above], pp. 41 f., n. 75, makes this point. For an example of John's practices see Ep. 152, in *Later Letters* [n. 6 above], pp. 54-56.

[68]See, for example, Ep. 175, in *Later Letters* [n. 6 above], pp. 152-64, which uses biblical *figurae* to pillory Gilbert Foliot.

[69]*Policr.* 2.19-26 (1:107-43; Pike, pp. 93-127).

[70]"Dispositioni ergo aptare tempora et rerum momenta uariare temporibus solus ille qui disposuit, potest; et cum multorum notitiam, secundum beneplaciti sui mensuram concesserit creaturae, hoc sibi Trinitas singulariter reseruauit. Quando itaque et quam diu quid futurum sit nouit, et etates temporum ille dispensat, per quem ipsa tempora facta sunt. Ipsa quoque tempora motu et uariatione rerum quasi quibusdam coloribus pingit, et uolubilem temporis rotam iugali quodam nexu rerum quo teneatur illaqueat, et ut rem incomprehensibilem ingerat intellectui, eandem mirabiliter rerum proprietatibus quasi suis informat" (*Policr.* 2.24 [1:134-35; Pike, p. 119]).

[71]*Policr.* 2.26 (1:139; Pike, pp. 123-24). Of God the first cause, John writes: "Adeo quidem prima est, ut si quaeratur de aliquo, cur ita sit,

rectissime dicatur, quoniam ille sic uoluit, qui omnia quaecumque uoluit, fecit. Si uero cur uoluerit inquiratur, inepta quaestio est, quia primae causae, uoluntatis scilicet, quaeritur causa, cuius nulla est omnino causa."

[72]*Policr*. 2.22 (1:122; Pike, p. 107).

[73]*Policr*. 1 Prol. (1:17; Pike, p. 10 [his trans.]). On John's ciceronian scepticism see Birger Munk-Olsen, "L'humanisme de Jean de Salisbury: Un ciceronien au 12ᵉsiècle," in *Entretiens sur la Renaissance du 12ᵉsiècle*, ed. Maurice de Gandillac and Edouard Jeauneau (Paris, 1968), pp. 53-69, esp. 64 ff. There are a few pages on the subject in Charles B. Schmitt, *Cicero Scepticus: A Study in the Influence of the 'Academica' in the Renaissance* (The Hague, 1972), pp. 36-38, but the author overlooks the evidence of the *Metalogicon*.

[74]*Policr*. 7 Prol.-2 (2:93-99; Pike, pp. 213-22).

[75]Kennedy, *The Art of Rhetoric in the Roman World* (Princeton, 1972), p. 228. For John's allusion to *De or*. 2.36.145 see *Policr*. 1 Prol. (1:17; Pike, p. 10).

[76]*Policr*. 2.22 (1:129; Pike, p. 114).

[77]*Policr*. 1.13-2.17 (1:54-101; Pike, pp. 44-88). In this connection see Barbara Helbling-Gloor, *Natur und Aberglaube im 'Policraticus' des Johannes von Salisbury* (Zurich, 1956); the author has little interest in the rhetorical basis of John's scepticism.

[78]*Policr*. 2.12 (1:86; Pike, p. 74 [his trans. slightly revised]).

[79]See Ep. 325, in *Later Letters* [n. 6 above], pp. 802-06.

[80]*Later Letters* [n. 6 above], pp. 724-38.

[81]Ep. 144, in *Later Letters* [n. 6 above], pp. 32-34.

[82]I make this judgement from the indices in *Later Letters* [n. 6 above], pp. 813-29.

[83]*HP*, p. 3.

[84]"Historicorum uolumina, quae de rebus memorabilibus scribuntur, prodigiis plena sunt et ostentis." (*Policr*. 2.13 [1:87; Pike, p. 74]).

[85]*HP*, pp. 11-12. For a comment on these pages that is keen indeed but different from what follows here, see Nancy F. Partner, *Serious Entertainments: The Writing of History in Twelfth-Century England* (Chicago, 1977), pp. 212-13.

[86]On probable opinion see *Metal*. 2.12-15 and 4.11-13, pp. 83-89, 177-79; McGarry, pp. 101-09, 220-23. See also *Policr*. 7.6 (2:117; Pike, p. 239).

[87]For John's theory of knowledge see Brian Hendley, "John of Salisbury's Defense of the Trivium," in *Arts libéraux et philosophie au moyen âge*, Actes du Quatrième Congrès International de Philosophie Médiévale, Montreal, 27 August-2 September 1967 (Montreal, 1969), pp. 753-62. Professor Hendley discussed John's philosophy further in "A Critique of the Critics of John of Salisbury," a paper read at Fordham University

on the occasion of the conference celebrating the eighth centenary of John's death, 25 October 1980. I thank him for sending a copy of this helpful study.

[88]*Metal*. 3.10, pp. 154-55; McGarry, pp. 190-91.

[89]Fredborg, "Petrus Helias on Rhetoric" [n. 33 above], esp. pp. 38-39.

[90]On Victorinus' rhetorical scepticism see Pierre Hadot, *Marius Victorinus* (Paris, 1971), pp. 47-58.

[91]*De inv*. 1.29.44. For Victorinus on necessity see *Explanationes* [n. 59 above], pp. 231-33.

[92]*Metal*. 2.13, pp. 85-86; McGarry, p. 104 (his trans.).

[93]McGarry's trans., p. 105.

[94]*Metal*. 2.14, p. 88; McGarry, p. 107 (his trans.).

[95]*Metal*. 2.15, p. 89; McGarry, p. 109 (his trans.).

[96]*Metal*. 2.14, p. 87; McGarry, p. 106. See also *Disp. Tusc*. 2.2.5. John quotes this text perhaps from memory in *Policr*. 7.7 (2:117; Pike, p. 239).

[97]*Metal*. 4.13; McGarry, p. 223 (his trans.).

[98]Ep. 273, in *Later Letters* [n. 6 above], p. 572.

[99]*Policr*. 3.8 (1:191-93; Pike, pp. 172-75).

[100]Ep. 301, in *Later Letters* [n. 6 above], pp. 708 f.

[101]Ep. 31, in *Early Letters* [n. 10 above], p. 49.

[102]*Metal*. 4.31, p. 199; McGarry, p. 251 (his trans.).

[103]*Policr*. 1.4 (1:31 f.; Pike, p. 23).

[104]See Liebeschütz, *Mediaeval Humanism* [n. 17 above], pp. 79-80.

[105]For what follows see Richard H. and Mary A. Rouse, "John of Salisbury and the Doctrine of Tyrannicide," *Speculum*, 42 (1967), 693-709. John's views on tyrannicide are scattered about the *Policraticus*.

[106]*Policr*. 8.17 (2:345; Dickinson, p. 336).

[107]*Policr*. 7.2 (2:98 f.; Pike, p. 221).

[108]*Policr*. 1 Prol., 7 Prol. (1:17, 2:92; Pike, pp. 10, 215).

[109]*Metal*. 1.19, p. 47; McGarry, pp. 56-57.

[110]*Policr*. 1.4 (1:27; Pike, p. 19).

[111]*Metal*. 1.9, p. 26; McGarry, p. 31.

[112]Ronald E. Pepin, "The 'Entheticus' of John of Salisbury: A Critical Text," *Traditio*, 31 (1975), 127-93, esp. 172, ll. 1129-36.

[113]*HP*, p. 3.

[114]*Policr*. 2.22 (1:129; Pike, p. 114 [his trans.]). See also *Metal*. 2.14, p. 87; McGarry, p. 106.

[115]Struever, *The Language of History in the Renaissance* [n. 64 above], pp. 24, 34-36.

[116]*HP*, p. 51. Here and on some other occasions I have altered Chibnall's fine translation to bring out the intended rhetorical significance of John's language.

[117]*Policr*. 7.2 (2:99; Pike, p. 222).

[118]*HP*, pp. 2-3, 12-13, 14, 16, 24-25, 53, 57, 70, 73, and 78. The Chibnall edition runs to eighty-nine pages.

[119]For this see *HP*, pp. 15-41.

[120]On the relative merits of these three accounts see Chibnall, in *HP*, pp. xl-xli; and Poole, *HP* [n. 8 above], pp. xxxvi-xlvi.

[121]See Brooke, in *Early Letters* [n. 10 above], pp. xvii f.

[122]*Metal*. 2.10, p. 82; McGarry, p. 99; *HP*, pp. 26-28.

[123]*HP*, p. 16.

[124]Ibid.

[125]*HP*, p. 17.

[126]*HP*, pp. 20 f.

[127]*HP*, p. 21.

[128]*HP*, p. 25.

[129]*HP*, p. 27.

[130]*Ad Her*. 2.28.45, trans. Harry Caplan (Cambridge, MA, 1964).

[131]*Policr*. 8.17 (2:348-58; Dickinson, pp. 339-49).

[132]*HP*, p. 55.

[133]*HP*, pp. 64-65.

[134]*Metal*. 1 Prol., 3 Prol., pp. 3, 119 f.; McGarry, pp. 5, 145.

[135]See n. 40 above.

[136]*HP*, p. xxviii.

[137]Poole, *HP* [n. 8 above], pp. lxxxii f.

[138]*HP*, p. xxxix.

[139]*HP*, p. 2.

[140]He quotes some brief theological propositions from Geoffrey of Auxerre's account of the Council of Rheims (*HP*, p. 24). There is no other clear evidence that John had a written source at hand as he was composing his narrative. At some time he had seen the register of Eugenius III and the records of the Council of Rheims (*HP*, p. 25).

[141]*Inst. or*. 2.1.10, 4.2.116-19. On forensic narrative theory see most recently Stanley F. Bonner, *Education in Ancient Rome* (London, 1977), pp. 261-63, 291-94.

[142]*Inst. or*. 2.4.2-3.

[143]*De inv*. 1.21.29.

[144]*Explanationes* [n. 59 above], pp. 206-07.

[145]*Ad Her*. 1.9.16.

[146]*Inst. or*. 4.2.88-100, 2.17.26-27.

[147]Wiseman, *Clio's Cosmetics* [n. 60 above], pp. 3-53, esp. 7-8, 21-26.

[148]My attention was drawn to these words by Valerie I. J. Flint, "The 'Historia regum Britanniae' of Geoffrey of Monmouth: Parody and Its Purposes," *Speculum*, 54 (1979), 447-68, esp. 459.

[149]For evidence of rhetorical declamation in the eleventh and twelfth centuries, see Ward, "*Artificiosa eloquentia* in the Middle Ages" [n. 33 above], 1:184-91.

[150]*Metal*. 4.28, p. 195; McGarry, p. 245 (his trans.).

[151]"Unde et ad frasim conciliandam et totius philosophie inuestigationes sophistice exercitatio plurimum prodest. . . ." (*Metal*. 4.22, p. 189; McGarry, p. 237).

[152]*Metal*. 2.5, p. 68; McGarry, pp. 83 f.

[153]On these generally see Kennedy, *The Art of Rhetoric in the Roman World* [n. 75 above], pp. 312-37, esp. 333: "At its best, declamation is an exercise of imagination. The student is confronted with a challenging case and asked to make the most of it, to imagine the possibilities in proof, exposition, and presentation."

[154]See Janet Martin, "Uses of Tradition: Gellius, Petronius, and John of Salisbury," *Viator*, 10 (1979), 57-76, esp. 67-68. See also *Policr*. 1 Prol. (1:16-17; Pike, pp. 9-10).

[155]The fundamental study is Hans Liebeschütz, "John of Salisbury and the Pseudo-Plutarch," *Journal of the Warburg and Courtauld Institutes*, 6 (1943), 33-39. For other literature see Martin, "Uses of Tradition" [n. 154 above], pp. 71-72.

[156]Martin, "Uses of Tradition" [n. 154 above], pp. 64-66.

[157]Janet Martin, "John of Salisbury and the Classics," Diss. Harvard Univ. 1968, pp. 116-41, esp. 136. I was fortunate to hear her unpublished paper "John of Salisbury and Orosius" at the previously mentioned Fordham conference [n. 87 above].

[158]For what follows see Martin, "Uses of Tradition" [n. 154 above], pp. 71-72.

[159]Ibid., p. 71.

[160]*Policr*. 4.5 (1:249; Dickinson, p. 21).

[161]On John's friendship with Peter see Brooke, in *Early Letters* [n. 10 above], pp. xlvii-lii.

[162]Chibnall, *HP*, p. xlvii.

[163]See, for example, Eps. 33 and 112, in *Early Letters* [n. 10 above], pp. 55-58, 183-84.

[164]*HP*, pp. 75-78.

[165]Weak, as in his unseemly and embarrassing grant of a divorce to Ralph of Vermandois; see *HP*, pp. 12-13 for this shady and very funny

affair. Silly, as in his attempt to rekindle passion between Louis VII of France and Queen Eleanor by requiring that they sleep together in a bedroom which he personally redecorated for the purpose (*HP*, pp. 61-62).

[166]*HP*, p. 82.

[167]*HP*, pp. 54-58.

[168]*HP*, pp. 55 f.

[169]On wit as a source of verisimilitude among rhetorical historians, see Wiseman, *Clio's Cosmetics* [n. 60 above], p. 35.

[170]*Inst. or.* 6.3.2-44 treats humor. On Cicero see 6.3.3-5.

[171]"Cum videatur autem res levis et quae ab scurris, mimis, insipientibus denique saepe moveatur, tamen habet vim nescio an imperiosissimam et cui repugnari minime potest" (*Inst. or.* 6.3.8)

[172]*Inst. or.* 4.2.119.

[173]*De or.* 2.54.216-2.71.290. Wilkins [n. 38 above] makes it seem that most or all of this pasage would have been in John's copy of the *De or.*

[174]*De or.* 2.59.240-41.

[175]*De or.* 2.69.284.

[176]See *HP*, pp. 69-70.

[177]Poole, *HP* [n. 8 above], pp. xx-xxi. For the two letters of Eugenius see nos. 433 and 435 in PL 180:1459-60.

[178]See Martin Preiss, *Die politische Tätigkeit und Stellung der Cisterzienser im Schisma von 1159-1177*, Historische Studien, 248 (Berlin, 1934), p. 48, for chronicle evidence of Henry's election at Rheims in 1162.

[179]*HP*, p. xlvi.

[180]*HP*, pp. 84-85.

[181]*Ad Her.* 4.43.55.

SOME PRINCIPLES OF RHETORICAL HISTORIOGRAPHY IN THE TWELFTH CENTURY

JOHN O. WARD

History-writing is a useful indicator of the level of humanism in any age. It is a form of writing close to speech, the human confrontation, the reality of personality. It is little concerned with abstractions, whether theological or scientific. An age characterized by a rich variety of historical writing will be an age in which a significant number of persons endowed with literacy find themselves in problematical or challenging social or political circumstances. The twelfth century was an unusual period in that persons of exceptional literary ability found the "web" of events (they use the word *tela*[1]) sufficiently challenging to devote more scarce time, ink, and parchment to it than at any previous time in western history. The same impulse that led to the compilation of learned histories also produced the first efflorescence of vernacular "histories"—the *chansons de geste*—and the first thorough application of the genre of *historia* to patently invented *materia*—Geoffrey of Monmouth's *Gesta Regum*.

My purpose here is not to comment on the circumstances that produced this remarkable efflorescence of historical writing but to examine the consistency with which the more learned historians practiced their art and to look at some of the principles that appear to have governed that art. Generations of subsequent historians and readers have puzzled over the apparent anomalies associated with the medieval attitude towards the writing of history, but despite a great deal of excellent recent work on the subject,[2] the anomalies remain. Part of the problem lies in the fact that history-writing flowed into the Middle Ages from Antiquity with something of an undertow: St. Augustine towards the end of his life concluded that it was an essentially invalid activity.[3] Despite an inevitable reversal of this conclusion, history-writing remained subject to a good deal of suspicion, partly because it concerned things of the flesh, of the *saeculum*, partly because it was an exercise in persuasion and, as such, open to inauthentic possibilities associated with the techniques and potential of pagan rhetoric, and partly because its antecedents were so patently pre-Christian. The undertow, of course, varied in strength: vernacular *chansons*, Easter Table annals, and rhetorical history that spilled over into polemic or defense of religious liberty[4] maintained momentum without noticeable inappropriateness, but full-scale learned history required an unimpeachable exordial apology. At the outset, therefore, the medieval historian was driven to harness history in ways that modern historians have been taught to find repugnant: history as set-piece rhetoric for a cause (imperial, national, ecclesiastical, moral, or the like) is anathema to modern ideals of objectivity.

A rehearsal of some of the anomalies more commonly associated with medieval history-writing will serve to introduce our subject. Why, to make a random start, is John of Salisbury's inappropriately full and curiously incomplete[5] *Historia pontificalis* found appended, anonymously, to a continuation of a continuation of a chronicler who died in 1112 A.D. and yet is said in the preface to John's "addition" to have followed ("secutus est eum Sigebertus") a writer who died in 1141 A.D.? What principles guided John in his selection of material? Why did he not take up the more patent and effective options that we know lay open to a twelfth century English would-be historian?[6] Why did Geoffrey of Monmouth put forward as *historia* what William of Malmesbury called "Britonum nugae . . . fallaces . . . fabulae,"[7] and William of Newburgh considered elaborate humbug?[8] Why did Otto of Freising distinguish between "plain diction appropriate to historical events" ("plana hystorica dictione") and "speech adapted to loftier philosophical pinnacles" ("ad altiora velut phylosophica acumina . . . oratio"[9]) and yet claim that the interspersing of one with the other is the proper method for his proposed *historia*? Why did Rahewin offer us a portrait of Theodoric II, king of the Visigoths, as a portrait of Frederick Barbarossa, or a description of Rome in the time of Catiline as one of Milan in the time of Barbarossa, or a picture of a Roman military camp drawn by Josephus as the disposition of a twelfth century A.D.

German military camp?[10] Why does it seem that both Rahewin and Otto omitted apparently important elements in their presentation of story or text?[11]

Why did the three chroniclers of Gilbert of Poitiers' trial at Rheims in 1148 disagree glaringly on crucial matters,[12] and why did all extant chroniclers of the Council of Rheims in that year see it in such curiously divergent ways? The continuator of Sigebert of Gembloux[13] saw it as a meeting that confirmed many things *super statu ecclesie*—for example the decrees of Innocent II (anathematizing those of Peter Leonis)—but chose to mention only the trial of Eudo de Stella (which John of Salisbury, in the very full account of the Council that forms the early portion of his *Historia pontificalis*, ignored). William of Newburgh likewise mentioned only the case of Eon.[14] Otto of Freising saw the Council as a synod for the condemnation of Eon but added that it ended with the promulgation of decrees confirming or re-fashioning old customs and received certain diplomatic embassies concerning German affairs (Waitz, p. 82). John of Salisbury saw the Council as a court for the hearing of ecclesiastical, jurisdictional disputes and a forum for the discussion and promulgation of *decreta*.[15]

Why do we find a crusading "chronicle" embedded in a manuscript containing material connected with the monastery of Ripoll in Catalonia and apparently intended "for the use of monks in the celebration of the Feast of the Liberation of Jerusalem"?[16] Why did historians in the Middle Ages so consistently and conscientiously promise truth and then offer something else?[17] Why was so much historical effort wasted on material already chronicled? Indeed, much of the better historical writing of the twelfth century is a re-working of some adequately extant earlier work.

Modern historians offer explanations of varying plausibility for these and similar difficulties: conspiracy, confusion, ignorance, a frivolous love of ornate language, poor notes or sources, the lack of a clear contemporary didactic method for the historical discipline, and the like. The combination of such explanations has earned medieval historiography a poor name: one must approach it with caution, be prepared to endure gross partiality and omission, winnow loads of chaff for a few grains, or, at best, approach it on its own terms, or label it "rhetorical" and make various resultant allowances, one of which is to admit and attempt to measure a perceived distance between "rhetoric" and "reality."[18]

Modern writers readily advance formative influences on medieval historiography: the Bible,[19] the *Ad Herennium* or the *De Oratore*,[20] Augustine's *De doctrina christiana IV*,[21] basic notions of *series temporum*,[22] but there is little close analysis of the way these notions or texts structured twelfth century learned narrative. Perhaps more seriously, modern writing on subjects for which twelfth century historians are a major source is vitiated by the assumption that what such historians say is likely to be factual unless there are clear grounds for suspicion arising out of the facts themselves (as they are inferred from a variety of evidence) or from some alternative source for these facts that is preferred by the modern inquirer. In truth, any assessment of the factual basis of a learned twelfth century narrative can only proceed from a firm grasp of the rhetorical purpose and techniques of the medieval historian in question, and, thus, much modern scholarship on important aspects of the first crusade, for example, is built upon sand, as I hope to demonstrate later.

The obvious starting point for an analysis of what twelfth century historians thought they were doing is recognized to be the *exordium* prefaced to most histories. Recent research suggests that these *exordia* were meant as quite precise guides to contemporary historical ideas.[23] Certainly, where they are absent, we are often confronted with "an apparently mindless jumble" of "mixed genres."[24] This suggests the range of historical writing referred to by Cicero and Gervase of Canterbury:[25] on the one hand, "histories" in which the structuring factor is an entity or entities quite external to the order of historical events (e.g., liturgy, monastic recitation, notions of monastic *libertas*,[26] the resonance of *imperium*,[27] and the like); on the other hand, "chronicles" in which the structuring factor is essentially the product of the order of events in time, however carefully selected, fused, dispersed, woven into language.

This range of attitude towards history mystifies and maddens the modern historian: the annal is factual but "stupid" and "random"; the history is fluent and sometimes critical but "misguided," "rhetorical," "unfactual." This confusion on the part of moderns results from a failure to face the first principle of rhetorical historiography, that history is a "language-construction" rather than a critically ordered and communicated sequence of more or less verified facts. Let us note how plainly this is announced in some *exordia* and how plainly it is acted upon.

John of Salisbury

John of Salisbury has a famous and relatively lengthy preface to his *Historia pontificalis*. In it he uses the term *historia* to refer to the facts as existing in time, independent of the act of chronicling.[28] The words used to describe both the work and the person of the historian are interesting. The richest range concern the act of constructing the narrative: "describens," "texit," "enarrat," "producit/produxit," "depingit," "preconatur," "seriem temporum digessit," "succincta narratione complexus est," "scripturi sunt," "studuit immorari," "retulit/digna relatu/referre," "pervenere noticiam," "perstringere," "prepositis exemplis," "dicturus sum," "scribam." The activity of being a historian is referred to simply as "studium." The written product of the historian's labors is described in words which suggest (adjectively) the notion of time-sequence and (substantively) speech or writing acts ("sermo," "descriptio") or the act of writing ("telam") or, once, simply "book" ("cronicis descriptionibus," "telam narrationis," "cronicum librum," "suis cronicis," "sermonis").[29] The raw materials of the historian, the "facts," are personal observations, brief records, the previous writings and authority of credible men ("subnotationes rerum memorabilium," "visu et auditu cognovero," "probabilium virorum scriptis et auctoritate"). The historian is a "time-conscious writer" ("cronici scriptores").

Notable here is John's failure to describe his own work as history, himself as a historian, anyone else as a historian, or the activity as history. Everywhere his terminology consciously stresses the creating and conscious writer who "describes," "weaves," "narrates," "produces," "paints," "praises," "arranges," "embraces in clear narrative," "writes," "zealously dallies," "lightly touches upon," "relates (carries back)," "places examples," "speaks." There is no sense, as there is in the modern historical preface, of the miniscule historian wrestling with the vast, intractible, and "real" past through a variety of approved approaches and methods. The balance is easily lost in translation: when Marjorie Chibnall translates John's return from his lengthy digression into the views of Gilbert of Poiters,[30] she puts more weight on the facts ("These matters . . . nature of the subject") than on the author's action ("have dwelt . . . longer"), whereas John actually packs the former into a single unspecific three letter word ("hec") and uses his words on the action of the author: "diffusius . . . quam ratio propositi exigebat [the reason behind the author's selection of words] prosecutus sum," and stresses that the central occasion for the digression was a personal request by a proposed auditor. John then specifically reuses the word *hystoria* to refer to the unchronicled events which the author surveys for action ("superest ut ad pontificalem redeamus hystoriam"): the central essence of history is the author and his action of writing; next to that is the personal occasion or request that produces the action of writing; and behind all lies the sleeping and amorphous mass of past events.

John's preface is not necessarily typical of twelfth century historians. Nevertheless, it cautions against too ready an assumption of equivalence between the modern genre "history" and what we take to be its medieval forebear. It cautions the modern historian in other ways also. It is a deceptive guide to what John really wants to do, in that, despite the impression it creates that the work is a chronicle, in a chronicle tradition, the reality is otherwise. It will be instructive to demonstrate this.

I have mentioned "the sleeping and amorphous mass of past events." John is not, in fact, so undiscriminating. With the words "omissis aliis"[31] he indicates clearly that the facts are already pre-arranged into categories; papal as distinct from other matters, for example. As Roger Ray says, "*res* expresses not the literal occurrence but the edifying shape of the actual happening."[32] Three tiers of historical reality might, thus, be proposed for the twelfth century historian: (1) raw, unformed historical facts or events, which cannot be written about; (2) partially shaped, selected, formed facts, which can be written about (papal, imperial, royal, monastic history, etc.); and (3) the finished narrative presentation of the historian. What warrant did John of Salisbury have for the pre-selection of *materia* (at level 2, above) for his chronicle? There was no precedent, for example, in his alleged model, Sigebert of Gembloux. A brief content analysis of the *continuatio Gemblacensis* of Sigebert's chronicle for the years 1140-48 (which John must have had in mind, because he cites it in his preface) is, in fact, instructive. A full fifty-five of the 173 lines in the *Monumenta Germaniae Historica, Scriptores* edition concern climatic conditions and related prodigies. The second largest emphasis is upon crusading matters (thirty-two lines); after that, disputes involving Lotharingian and Eastern French dukes and bishops (twenty-nine lines). Next come matters affecting the German *regnum* (twenty lines). The papacy occupies nine lines, on a par with a variety of lesser subjects (the English crown, the

French crown, heresy, and miscellaneous religious matters). John is not, therefore, following the pattern of the chronicle to which his own writing has been added. Nor can he have derived his notion of *materia* from the other historical models he cites in his preface, unless, that is, we return to the very beginning of the preface and pick up the emphasis upon Scripture and the *infantia* and *processus ecclesie*. Here, carefully disguised under the appearance of a continuous line of universal chronicling, from *Paralipomenon* to Hugh of St. Victor, lies the key to John's "weaving," and the result is a document that stands out from contemporary historical writings in that it is not a history of the Church (John is antipathetic to the institutional Roman Church[33]), not a papal biography, not a universal chronicle, not a specialized history. An analysis of what is in the *Historia pontificalis* in terms of the clue just mentioned above from the preface will help unravel John's thinking.

The subject-matter of the *Historia pontificalis* falls approximately into four categories: the pope as adjudicator and administrator of the Church Universal and the Roman Church (21%); the pope and affairs of the Church Universal—reform, crusade, trial of Gilbert of Poitiers (38%); relations between pope and secular princes (29%); and the pope as regulator of the affairs of secular princes (8%). The whole work can thus be brought within the rubric "The Pope in Society."[34] The theme of John's work is the pope in society, not the papacy, not the pope as a man. In this respect, the *Historia pontificalis* takes its place alongside Gratian's *Decretum*[35] and Bernard of Clairvaux's *De consideratione*[36] as a document inspired by the ideals of the Innocentian schismatics during the 1130s: the world should be governed by a pope of outstanding personal holiness, moderation, and diplomacy, not by a financial bureaucracy, not by the whims of kings or emperors. The *Historia* conforms to the sacerdotal view of government expressed in the *Policraticus*.[37] An illustration will clarify John's emphasis.

In the *Historia* John is at pains to demonstrate the personal touch that Eugenius brings to his task.[38] An outstanding example of this is chapter 41, which concerns Count Hugh of Apulia, who had long been striving to secure a separation from his wife. John describes the impressive steps taken by Hugh to assure his case: pomp, bureaucracy, episcopacy, and corruption were all applied to the suit. Eugenius meets this barrage with simplicity of emotion and purity of vision. At the crucial moment he bursts into tears, prostrates himself before the Count, and his mitre rolls into the dust: "suffusus ergo lacrimis, de sede corruens, in conspectu omnium, quantus erat, prostravit se ad pedes comitis, ita eciam quod mitra delapsa capiti pulverulenta, postquam eum episcopi et cardinales erexerant, inter pedes stupefacti hominis inventa est." Four short, plain phrases arranged in simple *isocola* ("con-par," *Ad Herennium* 4.20.27) paralleling the sequence of emotions among observers (John says "hiis presens interfui . . .") are fol-lowed by four slightly longer phrases, arranged again in *isocola*. There is no subordination; word order is plain; the only tension between English and Latin order is the suspension of the verb for *mitra* until the end—and here the point is undoubtedly to under-line the extraordinary nature of the event—and John stresses his presence to parry the charge of fiction.[39] John concludes this striking example of *sermo humilis* with a reiteration of the point of his *Historia*: he has recounted ("curavi enarrare") these things "ad gloriam Dei et honorem tanti pontificis." Thus, the *Historia pontificalis* illustrates a first principle of rhetorical historiography: the conscious statement of literary intent, choice and selection of subject-matter in accordance with stated intent and persuasive aim. John is keen not to provide a general chronicle at all, but to shape his appreciation of the past (tier 1, above) by singling out the *materia papatiae* (tier 2) and presenting a narrative (tier 3) that will serve as a type for the envisaged pattern of future polit-ical society regulated by divine equity and actualized in the per-son of a man of pre-eminent tact and holiness. Even the smokescreen John throws up by referring to the chronicle of Sig-ebert of Gembloux is a clue to the novelty of his purpose: he must insinuate his view of the desired future into the minds of his readers as innocently as possible. What better way than to disguise his writing as a chronicle continuation? The disguise may seem to us rather transparent: the papal theme is ascribed to Peter of Celle, and such a narrowing of theme surely exposes John to exactly the criticism he levelled at Sigebert: partiality of emphasis. It may also have been no part of John's intention to attach his work physically to manuscripts of the Sigebert chron-icle and its continuation: that may have been a piece of tidiness on the part of the scribe of MS. Bern 367 or its archetype, for John does say: "cronicis Sigeberti narratio nostra continuari pos-sit, a concilio Remensi, in quo ille suam finit, ordimur nostram, subtexentes ea que ab illo constat fuisse preterita" (*HP*, p. 4). Nevertheless, when the subject-matter is as unusual as John's and the preface strains as hard as it does for the atmosphere of the general chronicle, we may be pardoned for sensing a smokescreen.

I have stated that John's preface is not typical. His approach to history, however, is characteristic of twelfth century learned historians in that he makes no pretense at chronicling facts at level 1 of the tiers listed previously and deploys the resources of Latin rhetoric to give effect to the narrative at the level of tier 3. If we transfer our attention to John's great contemporary historian, Otto of Freising, we may find a more ambitious theme (at the level of tier 2) developed with equal artistry. Otto's great historical theme arises out of his consideration of power relationships in contemporary society: *reges, imperatores, pontificatum*.

Otto of Freising

In his *Deeds of Frederick Barbarossa*, Otto of Freising initiates the development of his theme heavily in the first sentence, complete with subjunctive temporal / causal clause and contained relative clause, a loaded ablative absolute, and classical word order, driving home the crucial point: the *rei novitatem*, the papal decreee of anathema against the king *a suis destitutum*. A taut string of subordinated clauses stresses the theme of the history, a world-engulfing power struggle between two larger-than-life entities: the emperor, announced first but in the oblique case, and the pope, announced second but in the nominative or subject case. In a single sentence we receive, as simultaneously as Latin syntax can provide, the scene: "imperium scissum"; "parte . . . maxima obtimatum principi suo rebellante"; "tota . . . regni latitudo. . . . ferro, flamma fedaretur"; "imperatore"; "Gregorius qui . . . Romae pontificatum tenebat"; and "anathematis gladio." This opening is entirely of Otto's choice. His announced and commissioned theme (Waitz, pp. 1-5, esp. p. 5, ll. 9-10) is the deeds of Frederick Barbarossa, and it is only his sense of historical theme that takes him back to the investiture controversy.[40]

Setting out from this compact beginning, Otto proceeds with such rapid economy that the modern reader is tempted to dismiss his history as aimless chronicling. The German resistance to the papal anathema is concisely put in strong language ("novitatem," "vehementius," "indignatione," "inflammati," "pseudomonachus vel nicromanticus"), climaxed by an eruption into direct speech arranged around the *color contentio*.[41] Carefully constructed sentences present the simultaneous parallelism of theme

111

and provide set pieces in the complicated drama: a single *queri-monia* unites both *laici*, inflamed by consideration of secular honor, and *episcopi*, pressed by the clergy on the issue of clerical marriage, to the will of the prince. The rhetorical ploy of the emperor's manipulation of his supporters is emphasized by the parallelism between the enclosing words "querimonia" and "voluntati," between which the sentence bifurcates into *laici* and *episcopi* and back again. The pope's refuge in Sicily, described in the next basically narrative paragraph (2) makes necessary an explanation of the situation in Sicily (3). This is not a digression but another part of the background tableau, necessary for later events, since Sicily was the great bone of contention between Pope and Emperor. It is necessary for Otto, however, to advance his major theme, the dynasty of the Staufen, rich with nobility, far-seeing in their advice, vigorous at arms, loyal servants at court, ready in a time of peril to succor the imperial office (8). To get to this point, the Saxon wars require mention. This is no digression either, as these have already been alluded to (Waitz 13.2-3) and the phrase "principi suo rebellan(te)" is carried over (Waitz 13.2, 15.4) to emphasize the point.

This rapid scene setting is then fractured, as we would see it, by 6½ pages of "philosophizing" into which Otto tumbles solidly by advancing from his mention of the Saxon Wars to his location of their origin in the unwise imperial challenge to Saxon military heroism and valor (Waitz 15.24-26) and then to a consequent admonition to all princes of the world to temper their temporal transience by consideration of their creator: "discant ergo principes orbis." This leads finally to a peak, an opportunity to probe the *rerum causas*—appropriately, a line from Vergil (*Georgics*, 2.490).[42] This little piece of philosophizing, a kind of showpiece of Otto's theological and intellectual credentials, buttresses a basically dual interpretative axiom about which a statement has become relevant in view of Otto's mention of the Saxon Wars: the ineffable permanence of God—the single uncompounded creator—and the inevitable impermanence of man—the compounded creation—ever rising, levelling off, and declining. The German king's remark in Saxony is, thus, emblematic of the rationale, inherent in the structure of events, that governs the existence of emperors and popes and the historical course of their relationship. Despite appearances, Otto has a notion of the *seriem narrationis* (Waitz 58.1) and is aware of his departures from it ("iam ad propositum redeamus" [Waitz 22.19], "ad narrationis seriem redeamus" [Waitz 54.4, 58.1]). It would be a mistake to apply modern criteria of relevance here and accuse Otto of digressing. *Digressio* did not carry the diversionary implications that the notion of digressing has today; in fact, it had good rhetorical curriculum status: for example, in Marius Victorinus' commentary on the *De inventione* as a *genus narrationis* designed for accusation, delight, or amplification; in Martianus Capella's *De nuptiis Mercurii et Philologiae* for inciting the jury or defusing the case; in Isidore of Seville's *Etymologies* (unusually under the term *epanalepsis*) implying additional commitment to one's theme, the motive for digression being *calor dicendi et dignitas rerum*.[43] The way in which the digressions in Otto's *Gesta* Book 1 expand the interpretative axiom and provide an interlace narrative pattern rather than a pattern of theme and (in the modern sense) secondary digression (or departure from the theme) can best be appreciated by analysis of them. This will enable us to consider the preface to Otto's *Gesta*, where the key to his notion of theme and digression lies.

These are the announced digressions in Otto's Book 1.

(1) First is the philosophical digression already discussed.

(2) A second digression is announced as an explanation of the political confusion within the Empire prior to the *hystoriam* proper of the second crusade which transforms the turbulence of the Empire into peace (Waitz, 48.3-54.3 and Mierow, pp. 64-69). Chapter 34 is an announced digression from the theme of confusion within the Empire yet is thought pertinent because it preceded the full-scale march on the East which we call the second crusade, with its well-known anti-Greek feeling (Waitz 53, 54.3 ff.).

(3) Next comes the announcement of a further digression, within (2), explained by the need to give proper perspective to Hungary as an important, adjacent, subordinate realm and by Otto's sense of the rich tapestry of history (Waitz 49.11-51.19: "sed de predictae gentis ritu haec dicta sufficiant"). Cf. the famous digression on Lombardy (Book 2, 13-15).

(4) The *seriem narrationis* is then interrupted by the text of a letter which demonstrates the crucial importance of

the crusade as a focus of papal authority (Waitz 55.1-58.1).
Such reasoning justified description of the crusades in every
important chronicler of the day, whatever the announced
theme.

(5) Otto calls the next digression (concluding Waitz 80.32
and Mierow p. 94: "sed haec hactenus. Nunc ad hystoriae
seriem revertamur") a prefatory *divisio* (Waitz 77.15). It is
philosophical in content and occurs within the famous Gilbert of Poitiers digression, which is not announced but is
framed between digression related phrases: "sed de his
hactenus" (Waitz 67.27) and "hactenus ista" (Waitz 88.14).[44]
Otto's account of the crusades is, in fact, split around the
Gilbert of Poitiers episode, as the time sequence requires
(Waitz 88.15). The link between the two is the role of St.
Bernard and the pope. The two episodes provide evidence
of the unity of Christendom and a dual illustration of transience: crusade failure (broached Waitz 67.18, immediately
prior to the Gilbert of Poitiers episode, preceded as it is
by the adjacent topic of Peter Abelard) and heresy or doctrinal instability.

Otto's ordering of events here is unusual, and to separate the
main thread of the narrative from the digressions it may help to
set out the sequence of topics in order, using Waitz's chapter
numbers.

(30) Part of the base narrative of the book, confusion within
the Empire terminated by a sudden transformation—the
unity of crusade peace.

(31) A digression which elaborates on confusion within the
Empire.

(32) A digression concerning Hungary.

(33) A resumption of (31).

(34) An isolated chapter regarding Roger of Sicily's aggression against Greece, suggested by contemporaneity ("circa
idem tempus," 53.12) and proximity of subject to (35).

(35-47) A description of the crusades Part A, including a letter as an internal digression (36). Part A concludes, as if it were a digression, "sed de his hactenus" (p. 67, l. 28), although at the end of (34) it is classed as a return to the main theme.

(48-61) A digression concerning Gilbert of Poitiers and Abelard with contained digression at (55).

(62-64) A description of the crusades Part B (completed).

(65-66) *Perorationes* to the crusades description, effecting a transition back to the narrative of imperial affairs. (65) is parallel with Otto's first philosophical digression in that it reiterates the dualities permanence / instability and prosperity / reverse which Otto sees evidenced in the ups and downs of imperial affairs.

The first thing to note about this sequence is the symmetry of the contained digressions (32), (36), and (55). Second is the symmetry of the Gilbert of Poitiers / Abelard digression, in effect a digression contained within the crusades description. In content, however, the relevance of the Gilbert / Abelard digression is not as clear as is that of the just-mentioned contained digressions. Yet, both the Abelard / Gilbert affairs and the crusades are projects of St. Bernard and illustrate the reverses suffered by sanctity (cf. Waitz 87.26 ff. and 93.32 ff.). Furthermore, Sigebert's entry (or, more accurately, his continuator's) for 1148 also covers both crusade reverse and Council of Rheims / heresy. Otto, erroneously, believes the trial of Gilbert to be part of the Council (Waitz 87.4), though perhaps this is a slip (Waitz 82.11 ff.). Whereas Sigebert adopts a sequential (paratactic?) order, Otto adopts a concentric one (hypotactic?).[45] The third point to note about Otto's order is that in (30) he advances both confusion and its termination in peace. He then has to return to confusion to elaborate it and return to the peace and elaborate it. A more "modern" order would have been to announce and deal first with confusion and then peace. Otto's method, however, indicates more tightly the thematic dualism of confusion and peace which is part of the theme he comments upon philosophically in chapters 5 and 65. Finally, we may adduce some reasons why the crusade narrative is given the appearance of being the main thread: the fact that it involves the German ruler Conrad; that it is an integral part of the history of Germany, terminating the confusion which is presented almost as a footnote (chs. 31-34); and the fact that it illustrates Otto's principal theme (chs. 5, 65). It is, nevertheless, noteworthy that Otto has introduced an element of balance and interlace by interweaving his themes and minimizing the distance between theme and digression.

To modern eyes, the whole of *Gesta* Book 1 must seem an elaborate prefatory digression from the announced theme, the deeds of Frederick Barbarossa. Yet Otto's purpose is to heighten and enhance his principal subject. Book 1 concludes with an appropriate summation which sets the scene for Frederick's entry and includes these elements: peace in France and Germany (Waitz 98.8); the predecessors of Frederick Barbarossa approach but do not achieve the imperial crown (thus imparting to Frederick the position of climaxing a development which would have been unclear had the narrative begun in 1152 [Waitz 98.9]); tension vis-à-vis Sicily (Waitz 98.10); King Conrad's death in *curia*; his designation of Barbarossa "ob multa virtutum suarum clara facinora"; his burial in accordance with the convenience and honor of Church and Empire. Thus, "by a certain thread of narrative" (Waitz 12.7) the picture of Frederick I is already heightened ("clariora," 12.8) by anticipation and the setting of the stage.

Otto, however, was unable to make proper use of the massive book-long introduction to the *Deeds of Frederick Barbarossa*; he produced only one further book, of slightly smaller dimension than Book 1. Had the *Deeds* been completed, it undoubtedly would have been the largest and most sophisticated of all medieval historical writings. Just how sophisticated is suggested by a glance at the opening of the *Gesta Friderici I imperatoris in Lombardia*.[46] The slenderest of historical justifications ("ad utilitatem posterorum scribere temptabo") is followed by an annalistic style (I follow the Latin word order exactly):

> in the year of the Lord's incarnation 1154, in the month of October, entered King Frederick, a man industrious, most wise, most strong, Lombardy with a great army. And then the Milanese with the Pavians were at war, which was begun in the month of July previously. He came therefore, having taken counsel, that the Lombards in wondrous wise he might subjugate.

116

Note the paratactic elements: absence of subordination, the simple, clumsy connectives, and the almost vernacular word order.

Today, Otto's philosophical digressions must seem the most anomalous; yet, these are most carefully envisaged in the preface to his work. Unlike John of Salisbury, Otto openly uses the word "hystoria" to describe his finished narrative account and refers to the act of writing as "narratio" (Waitz 9.33, 12.2, 12.27, and cf. 150.11 ff.). He prepares the reader for digressions (12.9) of a routine sort and also of a philosophic sort, drawing the aforementioned distinction between "plana historica dictio" and "oratio" elevated "ad altiora velut phylosophica acumina," the latter being indulged in when an opportunity is reached "ad evagandum" ("evagor" is a word Quintilian often uses for digressions in speaking). Otto gives Lucan, Virgil, and other Roman writers as his authority for "philosophic" history, just as his authority for digressions at the level of *plana dictio* is the fact that the *narratio* of all kingdoms and peoples leads back to the situation of the Roman republic as if to a source (Waitz 12.9 ff.). What does Otto mean here? How can the *status Romanae rei publicae* legitimate digressions? At one level (and Otto probably uses the terms "imperii" [Waitz 12.16-17] and "rei publicae" loosely) he simply means that since the Roman Empire is a universal phenomenon, the history of all nations is relevant to it. At another level, the late Republican and early imperial writers are seen as the source of all history-writing (*narratio*, 12.13). The distinction between *philosophica* and *historica* is evident also in the *Chronica*, where reflections on the state of the times[47] are obviously not history, for it is necessary to conclude them with "sed iam ad hystoriam revertamur" (321.6). Fulcher of Chartres similarly envisages history as the *narratio* rather than the digressions. He concludes his account of the dissension between Urban II and the anti-pope Wibert of Ravenna, presented as a homily on the theme of the ills of Europe and the cure of crusade, with "nunc igitur ad historiam stylus est vertendus."[48] Yet Otto clearly considers his whole book (his *Deeds*) to be history, both narrative and digression (Waitz 12.2). This is the confidence of the rhetorical historian, contrasted with the temerity of the annalist or the caution of the exegete, who like to keep the historical sense to the simple linear narrative, the first meaning of a piece of writing, and reserve interpretation to other senses and levels.[49] The exegete's distinction between the historical or literal level (text / event) and the allegorical level or interpretation (things / spiritual meaning) forms an analogy for the distinction Otto draws between narrative (facts) and digression (interpretation). Yet Otto is confident enough of the interpretative or selective process evident in both narrative and digression to aggregate the whole as history, and here he means, clearly, not simply the "letter" or the first, literal level of meaning for a text or event but the complete assemblage of text / event and all implicit things, meanings, interpretations. The term *historia* is thus promoted, in the arena of writing about past facts, to incorporate the exegete's first or literal meaning and derived, secondary meanings.

Although difficult for moderns to perceive, Otto's Book 1, as a whole, has a guiding theme and structure which is neither annalistic nor paratactic and which operates at least at two levels: the factual (announced in Waitz 12.4 ff.) and the allegorical or moral, the level at which the book must be seen as a mirror for princes: "discant ergo principes orbis . . ." (Waitz 15.31). The use of digressions serves to amplify and diversify the narrative by breaking up long sections, creating the impression of warp and weft, an impression not far from the minds of twelfth century historians who drew continual analogies between writing and weaving.

William of Malmesbury

Enough has been said to clarify the element of conscious artifice in twelfth century rhetorical historiography. The metaphor of weaving, as mentioned, is significant. Otto wove his *Chronica* as a tragedy (Hofmeister 3.2, 317.7)—in his head, presumably, as his *capellanus* Ragewinus (Rahewin) took it down from his mouth (3.20)! The *Chronica* is clearly described as *historia* (2.31, 3.20, 317.7, etc.) with an appropriate thematic structure—the tension between "mutabilitas" (307.17, 308.3, 22) and "eternitas" (6.17-18). The element of conscious structure is made plain by a programmatic adoption of the opening sentence of one of the most popular of all classical Latin textbooks, Cicero's *De inventione*, which begins with a reflection on the mutability of rhetoric: "sepe et multum hoc mecum cogitavi. . . ." Otto began his reflection on mutability with "sepe multumque volvendo mecum."[50] Even so patent an admirer of the *plano et suavi sermone* of Bede (who does not, incidentally, "weave narratives" but "gives out" ["edideram"][51] "facts" that require authority) as William of Malmesbury speaks of the difficulty of finding "those who have given

attention to the weaving of histories of England in Latin speech"
(Stubbs 1, Prologue, p. 1).

Whereas Bede devoted the bulk of his preface to matters of
authentication, William of Malmesbury expresses less concern
with authentication (though he makes up some ground in Book
2, Preface) and a little more concern with avoiding the chronicler's manner or vernacular idiom; he places Eadmer, who writes
"sobria sermonis festivitate" (cf. *Ad Herennium* 1.8.13 "sermonis
festivitatem") and whose "diffusa et necessaria historia" (Stubbs
1:2) indulges in digression ("licentius evagatus") ahead of Ethel-
werd, whose level is that of the chronicler (*chronica*). William of
Malmesbury's role, delineated in his preface, is partly to fill a gap
(here he anticipates the prefatory jargon of the modern historian)
and partly to season ("condire" rather than "condere" which is
regularly used of "fashioning" a history) the "temporum seriem
. . . romano sale," the latter a word which classical writers commonly used with *lepos, suavitas*, etc. to imply tasteful literary
polish. At different points William stresses the link between history and rhetoric,[52] perhaps most clearly in his eulogy of Bede
historicus (Stubbs 1:58 ff.) whose "sermonum sobrietatem . . .
incuriosae sed dulcis . . . eloquentie" (1:63) surpasses conventional *eloquium* and bids fair to being the most noteworthy thing
about him.

An examination of William of Malmesbury's notion of *materia* and digression will serve as a transition to the major digression included in most learned histories of the time, the account
of the first crusade. We have seen how critically the notion of
crusade underlies the interpretative axiom in the work of John of
Salisbury and Otto of Freising. We shall find that the first crusade
functions as the keystone of the arch of historical interpretation
for many of the most learned twelfth century historians: it is not,
as we might today be tempted to see it, a digression from their
theme, but a kind of *summa* or manifest sign of it. For other
historians, as we shall see, the first crusade formed, by stated
intent, an organizing theme in its own right for historical creativity.

William abridges Bede's work to less than a fifth of its original
length. This is partly because his purpose is stricter ("de gestis
regum Anglorum" versus Bede's "historiam gentis Anglorum ec-
clesiasticam"[53]), yet it was not too strict: a long digression on
Glastonbury fills almost as many pages as precede it, and it concludes with: "nostra oratio prosequatur historiam." We gather
from the subjunctive that William acknowledges this departure

from history, though it is not clear whether this includes the whole Glastonbury digression or simply the remarks on Aldhelm (see: "nisi quia alias avocamur," 1:31). William's narrative continues, oscillating between strict *gesta regum* (cf. "ut in proemio dixi," 1:96 and see 1:102) and a history of Glastonbury. He readily admits his digressions, which are concluded with phrases like "nunc quod in manibus erat repetam" (1:67, on Bede); "sed ut ad inchoatum revertar" (1:72, on the lineage of the Frankish kings); or "quae verba, ad cautelam legentium posita, hunc in ista historia locum habeant" (1:74, on Alcuin). As with Otto, a document is considered to interrupt the *historiae ordinem* (1:82) and requires a conclusion such as "ut historiam repetam" (1:84). The conflict between thematic order and chronological order elicits the occasional remark from William: at one point (Stubbs 1:86) he wishes to insert documentary material and, while realizing that to do so would take the reader out of chronological order, he decides to risk it on the grounds that it is more difficult to "weave together" bits and pieces of a theme broken up to suit chronology than it is to accommodate occasional violence to the chronology in order to follow through a theme already advanced: "regalis igitur epistolae partem, simul et pontificalis, apponere dignum reor, quamvis anticipare temporum seriem videar; sed ideo hoc faciam, quia difficilius contexo interrupta, quam absolvo instituta." The problem for the historian (the "weaver") is alluded to again a little later: after the death of King Kenelm, the Mercian kingdom sank to a level fit only for a chronicler; there was nothing the historian, as man of letters, might "weave"; "nihil quod littera[54] dignetur comminisci habuit" (Stubbs 1:95). Yet, William is quite willing to list names "ne quis nos arguat semimutilatam historiam interrumpere."

Book 2 provides more information on the Franks than Book 1, occasioned by natural links with England and by the justification offered at p. 69. As he proceeds, in fact, William finds it harder to control his narrative. The Gerbert episode is a good example of his loss of control: "et quia diverticulum feci" (p. 203) ". . . praeterea non indecens aestimo si multicolori stilo varietur oratio." The same apology is repeated at the end of Book 3: "nulli varietatem relationum displicituram opinor" (p. 355). Although William clearly gives up here any pretense of a thematic thread to his history, he is still working within rhetorical curriculum requirements. The author of the *Ad Herennium* writes: "sed figuram in dicendo commutare oportet, ut gravem mediocris, mediocrem excipiat adtenuata, deinde identidem commutentur, ut facile satietas varietate vitetur" (4.11.16). The *genus narrationis* based on persons, says the same author (1.8.13), "debet habere sermonis festivitatem," and he mentions pairs of extremes including *rerum varietates*. Cicero, in the *De oratore*, implies that the historian should distinguish and polish his narrative "varietate colorum" and "verborum conlocatione et tractu orationis leni et aequabili" (2.13.54).[55]

William's most shameless digression, recognized in the preface to Book 4 as such, is his account of the first crusade, which Stubbs calls "a work of art rather than a proper chronicle" (2:cxviii). Curiously, William would have agreed, but with a reverse emphasis: the re-writing of Fulcher ("not," laments Stubbs, "the result of a comparison of authorities, but a simple paraphrase of one particular account of the crusade") was an exercise in *historia litteris* (i.e., "art") and by no means a contemptible chronicle. William's gain was Stubbs' loss. William's rewriting of the first crusade, together with the rewrites of some other early twelfth century historians, will detain us for the remainder of this chapter, because they expose most clearly the purposes and techniques of the rhetorical historians of the time. They also illustrate the danger for modern historians of treating medieval historians as quarries for facts without grasping the principles of factuality that prevailed among the rhetors. The first crusade is, in fact, a crucial point of intersection for modern and medieval historical ideas: both modern and medieval writers betray a compulsive fascination for the subject, yet along opposing fronts. For the medieval historian the first crusade was a marvellous and authoritative point at which to construct history, to weed out anything that obscured the revelatory insight and to amplify the key points of that insight (Urban's Clermont speech, the role of Adhemar, the "coronation" of Godfrey at Jerusalem, and others). In the unconscious search to reverse the effects of this process, the modern historian cuts up and puts on cards the bits and pieces of the twelfth century crusade historians, as if they were, or might be, raw facts (at the level of tier 1). The result is a good deal of modern perplexity: what did Urban really say at Clermont? Was Adhemar really deputed in any sense to be the leader of the crusade? Did Godfrey really become a king at Jerusalem or rule a kingdom? The list of perplexities could easily be extended. I shall confine myself here to those upon which the reader may expect some comment.

Rewrites of the First Crusade

The notion of rewriting earlier versions of a legend, story, history, is not in itself curious. Periodical revisions of a text to accommodate changed literary sensitivities or expectations is a stock-in-trade for the medieval writer, whether in reworking a *Chanson de Roland*[56], a Saint's life,[57] a previous historian's version of an historical event or person,[58] or a prayer.[59] Nevertheless, the explosion of literary interest in the first crusade that followed the capture of Jerusalem in 1099 is a phenomenon of the first significance for the student of medieval historiography. Too often, however, historians have simply wallowed in this rich mud, looking for salvageable facts rather than observing the phenomenon for what it is. What follows is an attempt to redress this balance.

William of Malmesbury states quite clearly that for part of his account, at least, he will follow the narrative of Fulcher of Chartres (Stubbs 2:434). Such an exercise requires writing *accuratius* by transforming Fulcher's almost rustic style ("stilo non quidem agresti") into one with pointed polish and combative strength ("nitore ac palaestra"). The latter phrase is taken from Cicero's *De legibus* 1.2 and seems to imply the well-oiled sheen of the wrestler's body combined with overtones of the combative virtuosity of the rhetor's schoolroom, often termed *palaestra* (Quintilian, *Institutes of Oratory*, 10.1.79). I have suggested elsewhere[60] how William executes his task, and the result conforms exactly to the picture I have constructed here of the twelfth century rhetorical historian. The present discussion, however, will focus on the jewel of the first crusade accounts, the Council of Clermont, and to a lesser extent on related episodes such as the death of Adhemar of Le Puy and the election of Godfrey of Bouillon to the *regnum* of Jerusalem. If the crusade rewrites are the gem of twelfth century historiography, these episodes lie at the heart of the gem.

It is first necessary to indicate just how uncertain our evidence is for the time-hallowed crusading element in the Council of Clermont.[61] This will require an excursus. Some time in the middle of the year 1094, Pope Urban II, having regained some control in Rome from the Anti-pope Clement III, set out on tour to hold councils and consult with important clerical individuals and bodies, with a view to re-establishing his claim to be the legitimate pope by advancing the goal of clerical reform. This culminated in two great councils, Piacenza (March 1095) and

Clermont, in southern France (November 1095). The question of a military expedition to the East came up at both councils, but we are unsure of the details. Our only source, despite some claims, is Bernold of St. Blasien (d. 1100 A.D.), a cleric who may well have accompanied his bishop to the Council of Piacenza and who wrote a chronicle of the last years of the eleventh century. Bernold writes that the Piacenza Council received a delegation from Byzantium:

> Likewise an embassy from the Emperor of Constantinople came to this synod and implored, in the manner of a suppliant, the lord Pope and all the faithful of Christ, to send him help against the pagans, for the defence of the Holy Church, which the pagans had now almost destroyed in those parts of the world. He added that the pagans had seized that part of the world right up to the walls of Constantinople. The Lord Pope therefore urged many to provide this help, asking that they take an oath to go to those parts, at the nod of the Lord, to bring aid to the same Emperor against the pagans, as far as they were able. . . . According to the reports, this synod was attended by almost four thousand of the clergy, and more than thirty thousand of the laity.[62]

It should be noted that Bernold's short account of the later Council, Clermont, makes no mention of crusade or of a military expedition to the East. Clermont, according to Bernold, simply confirmed the statutes promulgated at Piacenza, especially the excommunication of King Philip of France.[63]

The information Bernold provides about Piacenza is strangely at variance with that provided by our main Byzantine source, Anna Comnena, daughter of Emperor Alexius (1081-1118), who states that Alexius always thought deeply about a project and then worked with tremendous energy to complete it; that he was completely surprised by the approach of the crusaders, reported to him by "rumour"; that he had no love for Franks (Kelts), believing them to be erratic, irresolute, greedy, treacherous; and, finally, that he prepared for war with them.[64]

This is hardly the picture of the man who asked for aid at the Council of Piacenza. Anna makes no mention of Piacenza or Clermont and claims that the crusades were due to Peter the Hermit, a Kelt who had made a pilgrimage to the East, received some rough handling, and, having returned home, decided to obtain retribution by preaching a crusade. Nevertheless, according to Anna herself, Alexius had received military aid from Count Robert of Flanders earlier; did employ western mercenaries in his army; and had a high opinion of Norman fighting prowess. Anna, it must also be remembered, was writing as late as the 1140s and displayed characteristic Byzantine contempt for westerners. The canons of the Council of Piacenza, however, make no reference to the crusade:[65] they deal, in the main, with simony and related matters of church reform. The synod also, as we have seen, dealt primarily with the matter of King Philip of France's adultery with Bertrada of Montfort, wife of his vassal, the Count of Anjou.

Such general evidence as we have suggests that these matters were also uppermost in Urban's mind when later in the year he travelled north over the Alps into France[66] to hold three major church councils and have sessions with leading clerics and ecclesiastical communities. The first and most important council was that at Clermont, November 18-28, 1095. The *acta* of this Council survive in some fourteen versions, none authoritative, none full, and none contemporary. Strange as it may seem, there was no set, formal procedure for recording the debates and decisions of large church councils at this time, though records of a sort must have been kept. They were presumably informal notes, headings, and summaries taken by those attending for use in their own dioceses; the papacy, no doubt, kept a register of main issues and decisions. Delegates to the Council probably kept notes only of items which concerned them individually. The early copies and originals of these notes have not survived, so that, in many cases, we have only later copies, some not even medieval. In all the versions and groups of versions of the *acta* of Clermont now extant, sixty-one separate canons are mentioned *in toto*. Only two have anything whatsoever to do with the crusade: items 3 and 60 in Somerville's list.[67] Item 3 (Crusade indulgence) exists in four of the fourteen extant versions, item 60 (Goods of crusaders remain under the Peace of God) in one.[68] Let us examine these more closely.

Item 3 reads: "whoever, for devout reasons only and not for the purposes of acquiring fiefs or money, sets out to free the Church of God at Jerusalem shall be entitled to consider the journey as the equivalent of all penance." This canon occurs in three versions of a single connected group of versions called "the

124

Northern French group" and in another early twelfth-century manuscript also connected with this group, where, however, the wording is different and suggests that the canon had nothing to do with crusade but concerned only provisions for those making the pilgrimage to Jerusalem: "it was advised that in connection with people making a journey to Jerusalem to execute penance, they and their goods shall be protected by the Truce of God."[69]

Item 60 in Somerville's list forms canon nine in a version stemming probably from official papal sources:[70]

> Then also an expedition of horsemen and foot soldiers was made to cast out from Jerusalem and the other churches of Asia the power of the Saracens. And the provisions of the peace were extended to cover the goods of those who took part, right up to their return.

This canon does not say that the crusade was official business at the Council, but it does make clear that extension of truce provisions to crusaders (or pilgrims?) was part of the official business, if an incidental part. The authoritative Anglo-Norman tradition of the Council, preserved in William of Malmesbury and Ordericus Vitalis, contains no mention of crusading canons.[71]

Two possibilities face us. Clermont may have, in a routine sort of way, extended the provisions of the truce of God to cover pilgrims to Jerusalem and their goods. No other reference to the crusade appears to have been made at the Council, although afterwards Urban may have furthered his private negotiations with certain lay princes in regard to an expedition of relief to the Eastern churches. Alternatively, Clermont, in one of its [lost?] canons, may have proclaimed the crusade and legislated with regard to penance and protection of crusader goods. This latter alternative, however, poses difficulties. If we accept it, we should expect to find the novel notion of crusade looming large in the business of the Council, and we would expect it to have survived in all or most versions of the *acta concilii*, perhaps forming a block of canons. In fact, as indicated above, only two clauses within the entire corpus of sixty-one surviving canons cannot be explained away as referring to routine penitential pilgrimages: "To free the church of God at Jerusalem" (Somerville item 3), implying armed pilgrimage, and canon nine (Somerville item 60), mentioning an expedition. The first phrase occurs only in one version of the canons of the Council, and item 60 merely mentions that an expedition was undertaken, not that it was the particular business of the Council.

Aside from the *acta* and the chroniclers, we have Urban's own letters on the subject of crusade. These letters are curious. The first, to the Flemish (December 1095?), is strangely precise: it says that the pope visited Gaul in 1095 largely to urge the princes of the area to free the churches of the East as a preparation for the remission of all their sins. The rest of the letter has overtones of Gregorian reform: Adhemar is papal deputy, with power to bind and loose, and all on the expedition should obey his commands as if they were the pope's own. Urban adds the important phrase that people should obey Adhemar's bindings and loosings "as far as shall seem to belong to such an office." This is important evidence that Gregorian motives lay behind our extant versions of the pope's Clermont speech: here is the pope himself directing lay princes in secular affairs, and the Gelasian qualification is added, referring to the traditional limitations on the exercise by one power of both swords. The letter states that Urban enjoined the obligation of crusade upon the princes of Gaul at the Council of Clermont and makes mention of Jerusalem only to illustrate the extent of Turkish depradations. The expedition or journey to the East is not seen as a Jerusalem pilgrimage. There is also mention of a vow.[72]

If this letter were genuine, it would settle most points, as it is, for the most part, in agreement, for example, with the Clermont account of Fulcher of Chartres, except that it refers to dealings between Urban and the lay princes at Clermont, which Fulcher does not seem to know. It suggests, however, that a large part of Urban's purpose in visiting Gaul was to organize the crusade, and this does not follow from Fulcher or from the emphasis at Clermont and in the sources on reform, lay investiture, and the like. Nevertheless, the letter provides no warrant for the notion of Clermont as a Council dominated by a long and powerful pulpit plea to the assembled masses, followed by hysteria. For this we have to await the pleasure of the rhetorical rewriters. The second papal letter, to Bologna, merely indicates that by that later date (September 19, 1096) Urban was aware that the urge to visit Jerusalem was getting out of hand, under the banner of an *expeditio* to the East, and that controls were necessary. With this background, we may turn to the principal chroniclers of the first crusade. They may be grouped as "primitives," "rhetors," and "later rewriters."

JOHN O. WARD

Chroniclers of Clermont

First are four "primitive" accounts by historians who claim to avoid oratorical style and to adhere to "naked truth," or else, who so act without proclamation.

> (1) The so-called *Gesta* (*Francorum et aliorum Hierosolimitanorum*),[73] written perhaps in c. 1100-01 A.D. by a secular follower of Bohemond.

> (2) The account of Fulcher of Chartres, a cleric in the company of Stephen of Blois, then chaplain to Baldwin of Boulogne ("regis Balduini notarius" [*HC* 3:309]) and probably present at Clermont. The relevant portion of Fulcher's account seems to have been written c. 1101.[74]

> (3) The *Historia Francorum Qui Ceperunt Iherusalem* of Raymond d'Aguilers, chaplain to Raymond of Toulouse, written c. 1102-05.[75]

> (4) The *Historia de Hierosolymitano Itinere* of Peter Tudebode, priest of Civray. This account is mostly the same as the *Gesta* but makes no mention of Clermont or of papal inspiration for the crusading movement and was written before 1111 A.D.[76]

To these one should add Albert of Aix, writing over a quarter of a century after the Council and, hence, without the same authority as the others. Albert's *Historia Hierosolymitana* is, nevertheless, on the author's admission, a primitive account: Albert refers to his own "puerili et incauto stilo" (*HC* 4:271).

The difference between Fulcher's account of Clermont and that of the other primitives is striking. At the beginning of his account, Fulcher has Urban concerned for the turbulent state of Europe. Hearing that Romania had been devastated by the Turks, he crosses into Gaul and summons to Clermont a council of 310 members, bishops, and abbots, to whom he delivers a sermon on the evils of the time, "die ad haec praenominato." This sermon ("allocutione dulciflua") is announced as the *causam conventus*, and it occupies chapter 2 of Fulcher's history (*HC* 3:322-23). It does not refer to the crusade, the Turks, or Constantinople and ends with the renewal of the Truce of God in Europe. When those

127

present, "tam clerus quam populus," gave assent to Urban's ad-
monitions, the pope straight away ("illico") announced, in a further speech, the need for an expedition to carry aid to the
Christians in the East against the Turks. The appeal is tied in a
complementary manner to the imposition of peace at home. This
crusade speech purports to be what Urban said ("inquiens" [*HC*
3:323E], "his dictis" [324F]), and may be broken into four blocks.
(1) Following on from the refurbishment of truce in Europe is a
test for new-found will—"confratribus vestris in Orientali plaga
conversantibus" (the provision of aid to Christians in the East);
(2) The Turks have ravaged *Romaniae fines*; (3) God orders people
of all ranks and conditions to relieve the situation, and remission
of sins is the reward; and (4) Only shame can follow refusal: let .
those who previously befouled Europe with war attain eternal
reward by carrying war to the East. Many among the audience
vowed to go to the East on hearing this, among them Adhemar
of Le Puy "who afterward, acting as vicar apostolic prudently
and wisely governed the entire army of God and vigorously inspired it to carry out the undertaking." The Council then broke
up. Subsequently, peace was refurbished *passim per provincias*,
and crusade crosses were sewn on garments.

Such is Fulcher's account, and, as presented, it is patently
untenable. Fulcher has no sense of the business of the Council
and presents it as if it took place on a single day. The crusading
speech is an equal part of the business with reform, Adhemar's
"appointment" and the sewing on of crosses take place *after* the
Council (the rhetors will seek to include them *in* the Council). It
is noteworthy that a contemporary primitive reworking of Fulcher,
commonly ascribed to a Bartulf of Nangis,[77] telescopes Fulcher's
narrative of Clermont neatly to accentuate the crusading speech;
he omits the first speech on the ills of Europe and the refurbishing
of the *Treuga Dei* (*HC* 3:491-92). Obviously, the crusade legend-
builders soon learned to dispense with what may well have been
the real (and only?) business of the Council of Clermont.

Fulcher's account is markedly different from that found in
the *Gesta*, which Fulcher later uses to supplement his narrative.[78]
The author of the *Gesta* speaks of a wave of religious agitation
spreading through Gaul, urging people to follow their Christ by
enacting Matt. 16:24: "If any man will come after me, let him
deny himself, and take up his cross and follow me." Urban then
joined in this agitation and, coming to Gaul with his archbishops,
bishops, abbots, and priests, subtly began to preach sermons urg-

ing people to save their souls by following in Christ's footsteps.
Consequently, many sewed crosses onto their clothes and followed their Saviour who had redeemed them from Hell. In this
account we find no Clermont and no legend of papal initiative in
the crusade: the pope adds his voice to a movement already in
progress. There is no specific call to military service—Rosalind
Hill translates "fecerunt denique Galli tres partes" as "the Franks
ordered themselves in three armies"—and the movement has all
the marks of a millenarian pilgrimage movement.

How can the discrepancy between Fulcher and the *Gesta* be
explained? It is worth noting that the *Gesta* was probably written
by a layman and that Raymond d'Aguilers' chronicle, which, despite Raymond's southern French background, makes no reference to Jerusalem, Urban, or Clermont at all in the beginning
(and, as far as Urban and Clermont are concerned, anywhere
else) was written jointly by a cleric and a knight (Pons of Balazun,
knight from the diocese of Viviers). A preliminary suggestion,
therefore, might be that the *Gesta* and Raymond represent the
popular idea of the crusade, only vaguely aware of Urban and
Clermont, while Fulcher represents the better informed (or better
"woven") clerical understanding of events. More radically, Fulcher
may have reshaped the facts to fit more easily his basically Gregorian viewpoint, which required papal initiative and leadership.
The "lay primitive" view lasted a long time: it was picked up by
Albert of Aix and, as a consequence, by William of Tyre, who
used him. Albert has Urban responding belatedly to existing pressure for a crusade and ascribes the initiative to Peter the Hermit.
He has only the vaguest notion of Clermont: "deinde ad Clarum
Montem in Alvernis proficiscitur, ubi, audita legatione divina et
ammonitione apostolica, episcopi. . ." (vowed an expedition to
the sepulchre of the Lord).[79]

Typical of the pretensions of the primitives is an avowal of
the value of "truth" versus "style." For example, according to
Raymond d'Aguilers, Fulcher "veraci stylo digessit" (*HC* 3:309),
and, according to Fulcher's own admission, "Francorum
gesta. . . . stilo rusticano, tamen veraci. . . . digessi" (*HC* 3:319;
Hagenmeyer, p. 116). Later, Fulcher refers to himself as "scientia
rudis, ingenio debilis, temeritatis naevo notari quam haec opera
non propalari, prout oculis vidi vel a relatoribus veridicis per-
scrutans diligenter didici" (2:34; Hagenmeyer, pp. 504-05). He
then prays his readers to indulge charitably his ignorance (of
style?) and to correct if they wish his *dictamen* which is "nondum

129

a quolibet correctum oratore locatim / iocatim," but not so as to change the "seriem historiae" on account of "pulchritudinem partium pompaticam" (the latter a late Latin word, found, for example, in Julius Victor's *Ars rhetorica*, Halm *Rhetores Latini Minores* 411.24, and fashionable in the twelfth century), "nor to confound mendaciously the truth of the things done." The primitives thus group themselves as chroniclers rather than as historians, in the terminology of Gervase of Canterbury.[80] Geoffrey of Monmouth parodies the distinction as one between "big-bellied diction," that is, words, and *historia*.[81]

Passing over for a moment the second group of crusade historians, the rhetors, who must detain us extensively, we should complete our picture by briefly mentioning the third group, the later rewriters. These have left full accounts of the crusade and the Council of Clermont, but sewn into larger chronicles with other purposes. They are less interesting for our purpose, but they deserve some discussion in this context. I adduce three: William of Malmesbury, whose *Gesta Regum*, as already noted, includes an account of the crusade, written c. 1120-30; Ordericus Vitalis, monk in the Norman monastery of St. Evroul, whose *Ecclesiastical History of England and Normandy* Book 9 contains an account of the first crusade, written c. 1135; and William, Archbishop of Tyre, whose *Historia rerum in partibus transmarinis gestarum* was written in the third quarter of the twelfth century.[82]

William of Tyre bases his account of Clermont on Fulcher, making far less drastic changes to Fulcher's language and content than William of Malmesbury, but, with the *Gesta* and other primitives, has agitation for the crusade precede Urban's involvement and assigns priority to Peter the Hermit (following Albert of Aix). William reverses Fulcher's order when dealing with Clermont, the schism between Henry IV and Gregory VII, and its aftermath for Urban II (William, Book 1, ch. 13, *HC* 1:36; Fulcher Book 1, ch. 5, *HC* 3:325). William telescopes Fulcher's account of the reforming decrees of Clermont and has Peter the Hermit present with suggestions. He also adds the presence of several of the secular "chiefs of those parts" (*HC* 1:39) and concentrates on the crusading speech, which is a *sermo*, studded with scriptural citations, on the theme of the sacredness of the Holy Land and the horror of its impious desecration. The theme of an expedition with remission or indulgence of sins or penance is advanced, and reference made to the presence of Peter the Hermit. In the end,

Urban extends protection to pilgrims, rather in the manner of the canons of the council discussed above. It is, indeed, curious how late this probably factual element of the Council is worked into the legendary accounts. Like Baudry—a rhetor to whom I will return shortly—William has Urban exhorting the clergy to preach both crusade and "treuga" (p. 42). Like Fulcher (*HC* 3:324), William has Adhemar take the cross after the dissolution of the council (*HC* 1:44): William uses Fulcher's words to describe Adhemar's assumption of delegated papal leadership, implying that it followed the Council.[83] William was not writing a specialized Jerusalem-saga like Baudry or—another rhetor—Robert the monk; his purposes were broader. He is, thus, less bound than the rhetors to the rhetorical picture of the papal initiation of crusade at Clermont and is closer to one of the primitives (Albert) than to the rhetors in certain crucial respects. He nevertheless altered the primitive account in order to stress the crusading element at Clermont.

William of Malmesbury's account begins deceptively like Fulcher's (Stubbs 2:390; *HC* 3:321), with a long date. There the similarity ends: William focuses immediately on Urban alone, while Fulcher gives the rulers of Germany and France, together with a keynote statement about the vacillating faith in Europe. William reinforces the centrality of Urban's position with the epic word "culmen" (cf. Vergil, Lucan; Fulcher simply says "urbi Romae"). William omits the chronicler's tag, *vir egregius vita et moribus*, etc., and creates an impression of deadly haste with the ablative absolute phrase "evasis Alpibus," the verb neatly framed between this unit and the matching directional indication *in Gallias*. William's readers might have sniffed Vergilian echoes in the choice of words: the line "evado ad summi fastigia culminis" is found in the *Aeneid* (2.458). William passes rapidly, via a reference to the circumstances of Urban's expulsion from Rome by the Anti-pope Wibert, to Urban's *repositius propositum* (the former a rather rare Vergilian word), whereas Fulcher dallies excessively with Urban's pious concern with the quarreling and confusion present in Christendom (a cause for Urban's advent, ignored at this stage by William) and does not move him across the Alps until this had been followed by a reference to the devastation of Romania by the Turks. William corrects Fulcher's account of the Council by noting that the delegates debated for several days the state of Christendom. He then appends a version of the actual decrees of the Council, which were not given by

Fulcher. William concludes the decrees with a curiously anonymous "posteris diebus processit sermo ad populum sane luculen-
tus et efficax qualem decet sacerdotis esse, de Christianorum
expeditione in Turchos." William purports to give this speech
from the viewpoint of persons who heard it. He cannot, he says,
recreate the *vigor facundiae*, so gives only the *integer sensus verborum*. What follows, if it does capture the gist of what Urban
said, makes a liar of Fulcher, and if it does not, makes a liar of
William. William expands Fulcher as far as Fulcher goes, but
from the beginning of his chronicle of places attacked by the Turks
(Stubbs 2:394, l. 26) begins to freewheel elaborately, making precise the reference to Jerusalem (omitted in Fulcher). He then
alights briefly again upon the text of Fulcher,[84] only to go beyond
it with another fixture in the legend of Clermont: the sewing of
crosses (*specimen crucis*) on garments. A return to Fulcher[85] is
concluded with a reference to the *famosa Francorum virtus* and
a long peroration on martyrdom for which there is no warrant in
Fulcher's text. This feat of virtuosity is followed by some wry
candor on William's part: "I have written down the tenor of this
speech, fetching out a few things in [the original] unedited discourse [*incastigato sermone*], but setting rather more of it free of
the original words" (Stubbs 2:398). What did William expect his
readers to make of Fulcher's text—the "original" for his reworking? Something to be set aside in view of the testimony of William's unnamed informers? What would a reader suppose who
came across both William's account and that by Ordericus Vitalis,
Ecclesiastical History 9.2, which, though basically similar (keeping the same order as William and presenting a very similar version of the canons of the Council), puts forward a very short
"crusade" speech entirely devoted to the ravages and rapacity of
the Turks and having little to do with William's version? What did
William expect his readers to make of the numerous other rewrites that competed in the market of crusader readership? Ordericus might not have had much circulation, but other rewrites
did. Can these questions be answered without first assuming a
radical discrepancy between the twelfth century notion of the
relationship between historical reality and language and the modern notion?

It is time to return to the rhetors, our middle group of re-
writers. Three rhetors in particular will come under scrutiny here.
Guibert, abbot of Nogent-sur-Coucy, wrote his *Gesta Dei per
Francos* around 1109 A.D. Baudry or Baldric, abbot of Bourgueil-

en-Vallée, then archbishop of Dol, wrote his *Historia Jerosolim-itana* perhaps between 1108-10. Robert, monk at Rheims, wrote his *Historia Iherosolimitana* around the same time or a little later.[86] These literary historians, who rewrote the *Gesta* in the early twelfth century, completely rewrought their subject to suit new emphases and preoccupations, following the principles of classical Latin prose composition. Before looking at their own statements and the nature of their rewriting, it will be useful to elaborate upon Latin prose style in the twelfth century: it was neither so unclassical nor so completely obscured by paratactic style as is sometimes imagined.[87]

The use of literary Latin in the Middle Ages has been subtly classified by Marc Bloch as an act of "translation" and, as such, "deformation." The original was always at least slightly deformed:

> to most of the men who made use of it, [Latin] presented the grave inconvenience of being radically divorced from the inner word—the term that stood naturally, in their minds, for the concept—so that they were forced to resort to perpetual approximations in the expression of their thoughts.[88]

In explaining the absence of "mental precision" in the feudal period we must adduce "this incessant movement to and from between the two planes of language." Erich Auerbach, however, put the matter more positively, and, as far as the learned rhetors were concerned, more usefully:

> Latin was not necessarily an obstacle; it offered great freedom in word order, rhetorical models for the use of this freedom, a rich vocabulary permitting of surprising effects, and an abundance of phonetic figures. In addition, Latin had the advantage of offering stylistic models from antiquity and late antiquity and, above all, the text of the Bible with its inexhaustible opportunities for typological and allegorical interpretation. Erudition was required for the mastery of all these instruments; expression was possible only where learning and spontaneous drive went hand in hand.[89]

These observations progressively apply to the vernacular in the twelfth century, as well as Latin:[90]

133

> when a vernacular has become sufficiently stabilized
> and widespread to produce literature, questions of style
> begin to arise: what is the best mode of expression?
> How can expression be modified to suit a particular sub-
> ject or to appeal to a particular audience? What means
> can be discovered for attracting and holding attention or
> for securing applause?[91]

By the end of the twelfth century the vernacular had adopted, in the Romance, much of the choice range available to Latin, except that it had no models to incorporate as a meta-language, and it restricted itself to the less rhetorical "middle" style. Nor was it so readily controlled by the Church, which tended to assert a monopoly and uphold the special, almost liturgical status of Latin. As Peter of Blois said, "things can be passed over lightly in the vulgar tongue, whereas the dignity of Latin demands longer treatment."[92]

The elements of choice and the special effects consequent upon these elements were not lost on the crusade rewriters who needed to give their subject-matter the longer treatment Peter of Blois mentions. In certain basic aspects of sentence structure (*compositio*), the difference between the rhetors and the primitives is clear enough. Quintilian (*Institutes of Oratory* 9.4.26), for example, recommends the classical requirement regarding ending a sentence with the verb: "in verbis enim sermonis vis est." The primitives did not trouble to adhere to this rule (which conflicted with their native speech habits) as systematically as the rhetors, whom one sometimes suspects of considerable artistry. Baudry, for example, in a random narrative passage (*HC* 4:20-22, sect. 12-14) ends fourteen sentences regularly with a finite verb, one with another part of a verb, and five with a non-verb. Of the latter, at least three secure especial effect thereby, in accordance with Quintilian's rule at *Inst. Or.* 9.4.29 ("hospitium," *HC* 4:21G, "insidiae," 22A). In a more powerful passage, a description of famine (*HC* 4:70, sect. 11), eight of seventeen sentences end with a finite verb (the less dramatic sentences), and an equal number with a non-verb (colorful words like *macies, maculentos, deliciis, anxietates et penurias*). One sentence where the word order has been distinctly ruptured begins with a finite verb ("coacti sunt") and ends with the infinite verbs, which carry the impact of the sentence.

As explained by Scaglione, the complex Latin periodic sentence can be viewed as, in some respects, a restructuring of the factually chronological order into a rhetorical / linguistic relationship selected for emphasis. In Scaglione's example, the chronological priority (i.e., the historical veracity) of the different elements of the action is deliberately subordinated to the thematic crux of the sentence: "homines interfecerunt."[93] As John of Salisbury says, "the splendour of *oratio* derives from appropriateness ["proprietate"], as when adjective or verb is joined elegantly to noun, or from transference [metaphor, "translatione"], as when *sermo* is led across from an expected meaning ["causa probabili"] to an unfamiliar meaning ["alienam significationem,"[94]] that is, it does not depend on any sequence derived from "history." In fact, alluding to the standard textbook description of *narratio*,[95] John talks of the addition of "tanta disciplinarum copia [the seven liberal arts] et tanta compositionis et condimenti gratia" to the "rudem materiam historie aut argumenti aut fabule aliamve quamlibet."[96] The grammarian should, as part of his *prelectio*, show "metaplasmum scematismumque et oratorios tropos, multiplicitatem dictionum, cum affuerint, et diversas sic vel sic dicendi rationes." Bernard of Chartres, when recommending his students "imitari vestigia" of the poets and orators of the past, would point out the "iuncturas dictionum et elegantes sermonum clausulas" (Quintilian *Inst. Or.* 9.4.32 *et seq.* 9.4.29 and Augustine, *De doctrina Christiana* 4.20.41). Whether John is accurately describing Bernard of Chartres' methods or simply extrapolating from Quintilian, his chapter indicates what currency study of classical sentence structure had among men of learning at the time, and it is precisely from such circles that our historians are drawn.

In his letter to Lysiard, bishop of Soissons, Guibert of Nogent says that the "dictandi. . . . immo quod gravius est, translatandi. . . . intentio" was struggling within him. No one should wonder, he says, that he used in his crusade history *stilum* different from that found in his *Expositiones Geneseos*, "decet enim licetque prorsus operosa historiam verborum elegantia coornari" (carefully wrought elegance of words), while in regard to the *mysteria* of sacred eloquence, simplicity should replace poetic concentration upon words (*HC* 4:118). The preface to Guibert's *Gesta Dei* (*HC* 4:119) elaborates his notions of style and truth: "for the execution of the present little work, no confidence in *scientia litteralis* (of which I have but *forma pertenuis*) spurred me on, but *historiae spiritualis auctoritas*." God, who guided the crusaders through such tribulations as they experienced on the first crusade, would doubtless "endow me with the truth of what happened in ways best suited to him, and would not deny to the arrangement of appropriate matters the ornaments of composition" (*ornamenta dictorum*). A history was indeed extant ("erat siquidem eadem historia"), but woven ("contexta") in words more than commonly plain, exceeding the bounds of grammar in many places, and calculated to deflate the reader with the insipidity of its often vapid discourse. This *historia* seems adequate enough to those of little learning, or those who care nothing for the *qualitas locutionis*, simply because of their appetite for novel happenings, nor do they think it should have been put any other way than they perceive, by the author. For those, however, to whom probity ("honestas") is valued as the nourishment of eloquence ("pabulum eloquentiae"), while they consider these things less aptly said where an unaffected intimacy of narrative ("comitas narrationis") is recognized to be expedient, and composed ("prolata") succinctly where the dense variety of soothing eloquence ("facundiae paregorizantis") was fitting, when they see the arrangement ("seriem") of the material undertaken to march with bare feet,[97] they sleep or laugh, as the poet says (Horace, *Ars Poetica*, 105); in fact, they look askance at the badly drafted speech ("orationi") which they think should have been sung in a very different manner. The *sermo* of those speaking ("orantium") should be suited clearly to the status of events[98]: acrimonious words should convey warlike deeds; things related to divinity should be presented in a more moderate vein ("gradu temperatione"). This Guibert promises to do, within the limits of his powers, as the recent popularity of grammatical studies makes him reluctant to leave *historia* "in the scabbiness of unstructured speech" ("inconditi scabredine sermonis"). When he has occasion later to comment on Fulcher's history (*HC* 4:250), Guibert uses the same phrase: "scabro . . . sermone," but perversely implies that he will shake "pure history" out from the clutter of Fulcher's *colores*, "for while Fulcher scatters big-bellied and yard-long words[99] and smoothes out the wrinkles in his inane apparatus of lurid *colores*, I preferred to lay hold of the naked bones of fact ("nuda verum . . . . gestarum . . . membra" [*HC* 4:250H]) and not to weave over ("contegere") the sham weft (*praetexta*)." The context of the *Ars Poetica* and Guibert's earlier remarks suggest that Fulcher's sin, in Guibert's eyes, lay in matching style to matter inappropriately, that is, without the sense of appropriateness that John of Salisbury said provides *oratio* with *splendor*. We may not have here the distinction between the trite and meaningless application of *colores* which forms the common modern assumption about medieval rhetoric and what Nancy Struever refers to as an informed sense of "good periodic style,"[100] but it would be unwise to accuse Guibert of indulging in meaningless stylistic polemics.

Some of Guibert's friends suggested that he adopt verse as his medium, some prose, but for this "gem," his crusading *historia*, Guibert, in his maturity, rejects the rattling of verses ("versuum crepitibus") and words that might win applause ("verbis plausilibus"), feeling that so unprecedented a series of events "should be arranged with greater maturity than all the histories of the Jewish Wars [Josephus, a model for Rahewin also], if there was anyone to whom God would vouchsafe such *copiam*." Guibert admits (p. 120) that it was the capture of Jerusalem that stimulated his historical imagination ("nec diffiteor me post Iherosolimae captionem . . ."):

> about to attack the exemplar of the history itself [to which he referred above] with a view to its correction, or even demolition, I proposed to deal first with the causes and necessities which resulted in the expedition, as I had heard them, and, having done this, I resolved to weave [*attexere*] the pattern of things done on to this base.

Guibert says he supplemented or compared his sources with eye-witness testimony and intelligent insight on his own part ("aut per me ipsum agnoverim").

True to his assertion, Guibert deals first with causes, and the Turkish attack on "Palaestinam, tum Iherusolimam ac Sepulchrum Domini" occurs in the second line of his history, after an extremely protracted *exordium* (absent, of course, from other chroniclers) on doctrinal heresy stretching out from the eastern Mediterranean and climaxing in the invasion of Palestine.[101] Guibert's account moves carefully along this path: the Turks press Constantinople; Alexius writes to Robert of Flanders for help; and Guibert includes parts of the letter "verbis tamen vestita meis." Urban does not appear until Book 2, when a dual theme is established: the need to rescue Jerusalem from the heretical East, and the superiority of the Franks (p. 136) over all other nations that might theoretically lend succour. In Guibert's account, the Council of Clermont becomes a crusade rally, held in

137

France because the Franks are the chosen race. Besides the four hundred bishops and abbots present, "illic . . . totius Franciae et appendicium comitatuum litteratura confluxit" to hear and see Urban (*HC* 4:137A). All other business apart from the excommunication of the king of France falls away as Urban attempts to persuade the Franks to rescue the East, and Guibert, true to form, gives not the words of Urban but the *intentiones* he used! What Guibert offers is an elaborate thematic sermon on Jerusalem and the need to rescue it. It begins with an elaborate syllogism which can best be set forth in two parts:

A i. Particular reverence ought be accorded churches distinguished for apostolic links or royal connections;
A ii. Jerusalem is such a church;
A iii. therefore, Jerusalem ought be accorded particular reverence.

B i. Most reverence ought be accorded the church most distinguished thus;
B ii. Jerusalem is the most distinguished such church since it is linked with Jesus Christ;
B iii. therefore, Jerusalem ought be accorded most reverence.

The next segment expands (Bii) and is followed by the *argumentum*: since Jerusalem is polluted, the *milites Christiani* (an argument *ex comparatione* [Cicero, *Topica* 4.23] is here drawn from the Maccabees) should earn martyrdom by carrying war there. This portion of the speech reaches a rhetorical climax which is again couched in the form of an argument *a minore*: if pilgrimages are valid, how much more zealously should one be prepared to rescue the cross itself, the blood of Christ, the land of his birth? The use of "exclamatio" (*Ad Herennium* 4.15.22), "denominatio" (*metonymy*, 4.32.43), "interrogatio" (4.15.22), and "repetitio" (*epanaphora*, 4.13.19) heighten the climax. It is at this point that Guibert makes reference to the notion of truce of God (*HC* 4:138E, cf. Fulcher *HC* 3:324D), but only in a suppressed fashion and tied to the "rescue Jerusalem" theme. It is, however, brought in, as with Fulcher, after the main appeal. The taking of the vow and the sewing on of the crosses follow Urban's speech, after which Guibert writes "terminatio itaque concilio quod Claromonti habitum" (*HC* 4:140H).

The whole business of Clermont becomes the expedition to save Jerusalem, an event which fits Guibert's eschatological view of history. Much the same transformation takes place in the almost contemporary *Historia de peregrinatione Jerosolimitana* by Baudry of Bourgeuil, subtitled "How the Christians from remote parts of the world made such great efforts to seek out Jerusalem, attack it, and keep it." The crusades become an episode in the messianic history of Jerusalem. The first word of Baudry's history is Jerusalem:

> Jerusalem, totius Judaeae metropolim, non ignobilem nec ignotam civitatem, regalibus honorificentiis in immensum multotiens decoratam, multotiens a tyrannis hostibus obsessam, et ad solum usque dirutam, et a propriis filiis in captivitatem abductis orbatam, variasque temporum tumultuationes ante Salvatoris adventum perpessam, noverunt vel qui historiographorum libros saltem tenuiter legerunt, vel qui computantium relationi aures audiendi avidas accommodaverunt (*HC* 4:11):

> (Jerusalem, capital of all Judaea, noble and famous city, Jerusalem, resplendent with royal honours, so often oppressed by tyrannical enemies, razed to the ground, widowed and childless with its sons in captivity, crushed by the tribulations of the time before the advent of the Saviour, Jerusalem they know who read the writings of the historians, however occasionally, Jerusalem they know who have bent avid ears to the tales of historical annals.)

This is Baudry's first, rhetorical sentence. The word "Jerusalem" is expanded in a triad of phrases (one word, three words, five words, respectively) all terminating in accusatives.[102] This device of *similiter cadens* (homoeoptoton, *Ad Herennium* 4.20.28) used as in *conversio* (antistrophe, 4.13.19) at the end of a phrase is employed to give unity in the next five adjectival phrases, all of which end with the first declension feminine accusative ending (*-am*). The crucial verb, "noverunt," begins its clause ("adiunctio" [*Ad Herennium* 4.27.38]), is structurally in the middle of the sentence and is tied to the last word in the sentence, which has the same ending (*similiter cadens*). The emphasis upon stylistic effect displayed here is explained clearly enough in Baudry's prologue (*HC* 4:9). There we find a self-effacing apology for the author's lack of polish and his exiguous talent:

but since in our days great was the abundance of Sallusts
and Ciceros, who yet wished to busy themselves with
this not ignoble pastime [Vergil in *Georgics* 4.564 hints
that verse-writing is an "ignoble pastime"[103]] there was
a threat of sterile shortage: I have undertaken this work
as a reproach to our greater writers who were either
asleep or lost in sloth, and lest a *historia* worthy of
relation should fall into the oblivion of envy, I have applied my almost sixty-year old hand to writing. [If the
facundiores do get round to the task, they may correct
me, but let not envy cause them to detract from my
work.] I did not deserve to take part in this blessed
soldiery, nor have I narrated what I have myself seen.
Rather, some anonymous compiler put out a rather rustic little book on this subject, yet one into which the
truth was woven [*texuerat*], but the noble subject-matter
was befouled by the crudeness of the codex [*inurbani-
tatem codicis*] and an uncouth and untidy text for recitation [*lectio*[104]] was rapidly turning the simple off. . . .
Succinctly, therefore I will recapitulate what I have carefully weighed up in the above-mentioned codex and relying partly upon the narrative relation of those who
were there, I will sew in what I have heard.

Peter, abbot of Mailly-le-Château, to whom Baudry sent the book,
professed himself satisfied and described it as a volume "ubi con-
catenatio multiplicium sententiarum consonat, partium quoque
junctura regulari censura liberoque gressu discurrit; nihilque lec-
tor diligens absonum inibi repperiat" (*HC* 4:8).

After his first sentence, quoted above, Baudry goes on to tell
of the sufferings of Jerusalem and the Antiochene Church under
the barbarians. Then:

The Roman Pope, Urban by name, came into Gaul to
preach publicly, and, in so far as he was an eloquent
man with a ready flow of words, sowed the word of God
everywhere. Having celebrated a general council at Piacenza the Pope, a little afterwards, came into Auvergne
and there held another general synod with many bishops
and abbots of Gaul. There, having despatched in advance things pertaining to the faith, he delivered a sermon concerning the already mentioned tribulations of
the Christians of Antioch and Jerusalem. There came
to the Council from many parts great men and numerous
dignitaries, mighty in the array of the lay militia.

Baudry then goes on to set down what purports to be a speech from the pulpit to the assembled throng. This is all the detail he provides about the Council of Clermont, which has become a purely crusade assembly. The laity have crept in in large numbers, and Baudry gives the impression that Urban delivered the bulk of his speech to the laity and then turned to the bishops and urged them, much as in Fulcher, to publish the crusade announcement and to preach the journey to Jerusalem (*HC* 4:15).

Urban's speech, in Baudry, is an artistic evocation of the theme of the pollution of Jerusalem sacred in its associations ("descriptio," *Ad Herennium* 4.39.51), the formation of a holy militia, the attraction of martyrdom after the model of Christ, the need to turn aggression from among Christians in Europe to the East. The speech is greeted with the by now familiar enthusiasm (tears, panic, discussion), and crosses are sewn onto garments. An unexpected element is the sudden and fortuitous appearance of the envoys of Count Raymond of St. Gilles, who announce his intention to take up the cross with numerous followers, having, presumably, pre-arranged it all with the pope (if there is any truth in the episode). At this point the Council was dissolved and "each of us hurried back home" (*HC* 4:16). Baudry thus claims to have been present.

Baudry's is a carefully orchestrated account. Along with Guibert (*HC* 4:140G), he has Urban unequivocally give command of the expedition to Adhemar, the first to come forward after the pope's speech: "insuper et ab apostolico mandatum promeruit, ut omnes ei obedirent; et ipse pro officio suo in omnibus exercitui patrocinaretur" (p. 15H). There follows the advent of the envoys of Raymond of Toulouse who declare "ecce sacerdotium et regnum, clericalis ordo et laicalis ad exercitium Dei conducendum concordant. Episcopus et comes, Moysen et Aaron nobis reimaginantur." We hardly need to be told that there is nothing of this symmetry in Fulcher or William of Malmesbury who re-words him. Fulcher gives no real priority to Adhemar but mentions him alone among those who responded to Urban's call, because he later acted as the pope's lieutenant, "qui postea vice fungens apostolica" (*HC* 3:324). The significance of Baudry's symmetrical church and state scenario at Clermont will become apparent later when we consider his remarks on the election of Godfrey of Bouillon to the crown of Jerusalem.

Robert, the monk of Rheims, is blunter than the other rhetors (*HC* 3:721). After the customary apology for inurbanity, he mentions that a certain Abbot Bernard showed him an acephalous and uncultivated *historia* and instructed him to add the proper beginning, that is, the Clermont episode: "praecepit igitur mihi ut, qui Clari Montis concilio interfui, acephalae materiei caput praeponerem et lecturis eam accuratiori stilo componerem." Recall William of Malmesbury's use of the word *accuratius* when claiming to rewrite Fulcher (Stubbs 2:434). Thus, the failings of the primitive account of the crusade were easily remedied. Robert concludes his *apologeticus sermo* by using familiar stylistic language: he will avoid the decorated style ("phalerata compositio") because he has no notary to do the writing and, hence, cannot afford the luxury of too many words. His decision to "walk with pedestrian speech" ("pedestri sermone incedentes") signifies his desire to elucidate the obscure rustically rather than obscure the clear philosophically. The phrases "sermo exactus" and "plebeio incessu" complete his choice of stylistic mode. His prologue isolates these elements from history for focus: the crucifixion, the *iter* to Jerusalem (the second most marvellous event after the creation of the world, excepting only the mystery of the crucifixion), and the pre-election of the Franks to carry out the *iter*.

As instructed, Robert begins his history proper with Clermont (*HC* 3:727), which he describes as an assembly "episcoporum quam et principum." After ecclesiastical matters had been dealt with, "the Lord Pope went out into a certain spacious courtyard, because the enclosed Church could not accommodate all those present," and delivered his speech. The speech begins with a reference to the "Gens Francorum . . . a Deo electa et dilecta"—absent in other versions—and then proceeds to the *descriptio* of the pollution of the Holy Land, especially Jerusalem. The Franks are urged to bestir themselves by contemplation of the "gesta . . . Karoli Magni regis et Ludovici filii" and other kings who attacked pagan kingdoms and enriched the church.[105] Robert ends the main part of the speech with a short description of *Iherusalem umbilicus terrarum*. As in Baudry's account, the rest of the speech is delivered as a separate portion (in Baudry, addressed to the bishops). Robert has the populace cry *Deus vult* between portions. The second portion contains instructions to different classes of persons regarding the crusade and is not elaborated elsewhere;[106] the pope then issues personal instructions regarding the sewing of crosses on garments. Use of the line "qui non bajulat crucem suam et venit post me non est me dignus"[107] is common to both Baudry and Robert. Robert then breaks off to tell of the action of a certain cardinal Gregory, who led the masses in confession and to stress that from the evidence of the whole world it was known "quod Iherosolimitanum iter in concilio sic stabilitum fuisset . . . a Deo, non ab homine." He then contradicts Baudry by saying that the laity went home but that Urban retained the bishops for a conference on the following day, when he took advice on what to propose to the multitude of eager pilgrims, "since no one of the nominated princes was among them." The bishops then *elected* Adhemar, who was unwilling but undertook "ducatum ac regimen dominici populi cum benedictione Domini Papae ac totius concilii . . . quasi alter Moyses."[108] Thus Robert reflects, complicates, and renders false Baudry's ornamental rewrite of the Clermont events. With Baudry, however, he shares a central focus on Jerusalem: neither chronicler takes his labors beyond the conquest of Jerusalem in 1099 and its immediate aftermath, the establishment of the first crusader kingdom.

Adhemar's election at Clermont is a potentially powerful element in the case for papal control of the new regime at Jerusalem. Had not the election of Godfrey and the succession of Baldwin been so decisive, we might have heard more of the clerical case for rule in the Holy City. By the time the rhetors wrote, however, it was a wraith that could not be resurrected, although its emphasis at Clermont suitably enriched the "head" provided for the acephalous *Gesta*-type chronicle. In miniature, the accounts of Adhemar's death and Godfrey's election at Jerusalem match the account of Clermont: there is the same opportunity to demonstrate a clerical thesis, the same confusion, the same dissimilarity of account. In particular, the latter two episodes demonstrate the inevitable abandonment of the rhetorically powerful clerical narrative principle: the "facts" prove too overwhelming; the clerical thesis is undermined by the sub-theme of Frankish, knightly virtue, which makes it quite acceptable, thematically, to have secular *militia* ruling in the end. Only Baudry, as we shall see, grasps the rhetorical possibility of developing a consistent theme. Clermont could demonstrate clerical primacy, but the election of Godfrey dispels the illusion. The only solution is a balance of *sacerdotium* and *regnum*: hence the advent of Raymond's envoys at Clermont and the speech accompanying the election of Godfrey, which we shall examine in a moment.

Robert the monk's account of the death of Adhemar (p. 839) is harmless and says nothing about crusade leadership or the problem of leadership succession. It follows Tudebode and the *Gesta* (as do Guibert and, to some extent, Baudry)[109] and depicts Adhemar as counselor and shepherd. Fulcher, however, in the first recension of his history,[110] inserts an extraordinary letter which touches directly upon the papal initiative thesis: Urban began the crusade and should end it (Fulcher 1.24.14). There is no other reference to the question of leadership or succession (apart from the sentence "ille Podiensis episcopus, quem tuum vicarium nobis commiseras," 1.24.12). Hagenmeyer thinks Fulcher omitted the letter from the second recension of his history because it seemed repetitious and, in any case, had no useful outcome.[111] It is found, apparently, in six first recension manuscripts and three manuscripts independently. It is curious because it appears in no later rewrite, nor is there any other reference to it, despite the fact that many rewriters probably had access to the first recension of Fulcher's chronicle rather than the second.[112] The letter offers powerful possibilities for building on the Clermont thesis of papal design and leadership of the crusade. One can only presume that the circumstances of Godfrey's election made any reworking towards the notion of direct papal rule patently vain, with the result that the letter was not made into an instrument for furthering their rhetorical design by the rewriters. Whether it was ever sent or even approved by the leaders its *intitulatio* mentions may be doubted.

William of Malmesbury (Stubbs 2:421) calls Adhemar "Christianorum vexillifer, illius boni auctor praecipuus" but does not hesitate after the capture of Jerusalem (2:428) to write "Godefridus in regem eligitur . . . dilato interim de patriarcha consilio." I have suggested elsewhere how his account of Baldwin's seizure of the succession at Jerusalem suggests a proper combination of timely and calculated opportunism untroubled by reflections on papal initiatives, approval, or rule. William's account of Godfrey's election is a curious departure from Fulcher, who states that there had been no coronation of Godfrey, nor had he been entitled *rex* (though his function was *regere* and the land he exercised it over was a *regnum*[113]). Robert the monk is happy enough to describe Godfrey's election as the outcome of a debate "de ordinando rege"; he notes that it was a matter of "regiam dignitatem . . . in tantum etenim regiae dignitati praefuit et profuit" (*HC* 3:870). Tudebode makes no mention of a royal election or coronation,[114] but the *Gesta* has Godfrey elected "principem civitatis, qui debellaret paganos et custodiret Christianos."[115]

144

Raymond d'Aguilers says Adhemar was spiritual leader at the fall of Jerusalem and has him instructing the leaders in dreams; however, it was a kingship that was offered to Raymond and finally accepted by Godfrey.[116] Raymond uses the phrase "in regem" and has one of the clergy admonish the princes to select a spiritual leader "sicut sunt aeterna priora temporalibus" before a king to preside over secular affairs.[117] The clerical position, however, was weak, due to the death of Adhemar ("ablato Domno Ademaro") and the princes, annoyed, refused.

Raymond's account suggests the kind of tensions that probably surrounded the question of control once the city of Jerusalem had been captured and the crusaders found themselves in possession of the promised land. Baudry of Bourgeuil rose artistically to the occasion. He was fully aware of the crucial *sacerdotium / regnum* balance and had so arranged his account of Clermont to suggest his thesis: joint (Gelasian!) command: Raymond and Adhemar, *Moysen et Aaron* (*HC* 4:16 and cf. 3:301B). Thus, the election of Godfrey had to be, for Baudry, a matching piece, reconciling the historiographically necessary triumph of his principle with the uglier eventuality of facts. The result is the last great set speech of a history more than usually studded with speeches.

Baudry leaves no doubt that it was a question of kingship (despite Fulcher), because tradition knew only kings and priests. "One after another the leaders [*majores*] made use of [*habuerunt*] speech [*sermonem*] of this kind." The speech follows this theme: God has brought the journey of his servants to a harbor of rest, but before anyone returns home, provision should be made for the rule of the city and the governance of the *plebs*. We can prove that this royal city has known a long line of kings. It has also been presided over by bishops, or, using the terminology of *modernior Christianitas*, patriarchs. Let us therefore look for a man preeminent for royal virtue who shows himself a servant to God as he feels himself a king to men, for the *monarchia* needs a *militia* to defend itself against the Saracens. A patriarch too is necessary: the kingdom needs the priesthood and vice-versa. Without further ado, let us elect duke Godfrey "quem huic civitati subrogatum praeficiamus." An exhortation to the king to fight the Lord's battles follows "et manibus injectis, eum apprehenderunt dicentes '*et ecce te regem post Deum signamus*' " (*HC* 4:105). Arnulf is then elected patriarch "erit enim et populo Dei et ipsi regi necessarius."

145

This speech is half as long as the Clermont speech, which it matches in tone as closely as reality will allow. It illustrates how important ideological and thematic symmetry was for the rhetorical chroniclers, but it also tells us about the twelfth century use of dialogue ("sermocinatio," *Ad Herennium* 4.43.55, or "ethopoeia," "notatio," 4.50.63 ff.[118]) or speeches, a tried device of ancient, medieval, and Renaissance historiography. Speeches, for the rhetorical historian, were a vital creative tool, whether ideological set-pieces such as Frederick Barbarossa's outburst against the Roman citizens or his opening address at the Diet of Roncaglia, Bishop Ulger's declamation in John of Salisbury's *Historia pontificalis* (with its opening use of *repetitio* "mirum est . . ."), Queen Ethelburga's decisive speech to her husband in William of Malmesbury, elaborate pre-battle addresses such as the speech of Walter Espec in Ailred of Rievaulx's *Relatio de Standardo*, or architectural fictions such as Urban's speech at Clermont.[119] The primitives, in their account of the *iter* to Jerusalem, did not make much use of set rhetorical speeches. As far as Fulcher was concerned, Urban at Clermont, God and the dead at Book 1.20, and the Moslems at 1.22 are exceptions. The *Gesta* author frequently enlivened his narrative with dialogue or short direct speeches. His nearest approach to set rhetorical speech was the extended dialogue / speech of Karbuqa's mother with her son, chosen as a vehicle for an extremely important ideological statement.[120] Small and quite effective set speeches (*sermones*) were also used here and there by other primitives: Raymond d'Aguilers sometimes puts a short speech into someone's mouth, for example, Adhemar's, or crusade leaders meeting in assembly to discuss the election of a Christian ruler at Jerusalem, or matters relating to the siege of the Holy City itself.[121] Significantly, none of the primitives except Fulcher included a Clermont speech, and Fulcher's was tame compared with those of the rhetoricians. The primitives' use of dialogue is similar to that found in the *chansons de geste* and the vernacular French histories. It differs somewhat from that found in the rhetors.[122]

The use of speeches in the rhetorical rewriters seldom worked to probe and set forth the continued duality of ambivalences, conflicts, and tensions in a historical situation. In this they were unlike the great ancient and Renaissance rhetorical historians. Even primitives, such as the French vernacular chroniclers, as mentioned, sometimes used their simpler dialogue to air both sides of a conflict.[123] But the rhetors, though they used long and highly wrought speeches, did not often set up an antinomy or antilogy.[124] Letters—a form of speech—were sometimes so used, and Otto of Freising could match speeches in a Thucydidean way;[125] Odo of Deuil could put debate on crucial issues in the form of short set speeches, or else put advice he wished to castigate into the form of a speech "magis verisimili quam veraci," making use of *similitudo* (*Ad Herennium* 4.45.59), *exemplum* (4.49.62), *sententia* (4.17.24), and *contentio* (4.45.56).[126] However, Otto of Freising can pass up a magnificent chance for a Thucydidean Melian debate: instead of pairing set speeches exploring the arguments on both sides, he advances his counter-arguments within the speech of the townsmen of Tortona, presenting thus only one speech.[127] Baudry's speech on the election of Godfrey, like the Clermont speech, is also not a rhetorical exposition of antinomy: he did not seek via paired speeches to play up the tensions hinted at in Raymond d'Aguilers' account of the election of Godfrey. His single speech was, instead, resolvent, it assembled and resolved the elements of conflict (the secular and spiritual cases) and then laid out a formula which, even if not factual in the strict sense, was factual in that it mirrored the eternal verities which prevailed at the level of spiritual reality.[128]

If we ask why this speech should function in a resolvent rather than an antinomic way, we reach the heart of medieval rhetorical historiography: the *sacerdotium / regnum* tension was not resolvable at the level of fact (our reality). It was only resolvable by either positing an eschatological framework for historical development and an (eighth) post-historical book—as Otto did in his *Chronica*—or adopting a linguistic solution that would reflect this eschatological reality. For a rhetorical historian to abdicate this linguistic office and use rhetorical powers to expose, lay bare, point up the irreconcilability of *sacerdotium* and *regnum*, would have been to feed the medieval order to a savage and devouring flame: the stakes were too high, the balance too fragile, the identity of the historian too marked, to permit the luxury of Greek sophistic or Renaissance humanist modes. In the Renaissance, history functioned, in part, to establish and enrich the world view of relatively new men in novel social and ideological situations. Humanist historians did not, for the most part, come from the ancient civic magnate families who stood above the constitution. For Leonardo Bruni,[129] rhetoric opens, keeps a dialogue open, and prevents factional tyranny; and rhetorical history erects this into a principle of interpretation. In the twelfth century, however, rhetorical history functioned, like liturgy, to close out doubt and encourage and create certainty: it was practiced by the technical leaders of society, many of whom were linked with the best families: the bishops, the abbots, the upper clergy. The thesis history is to demonstrate is known, it does not lie in antinomy or antilogy eloquently expressed in paired speeches that form the "soul of history."

Consequently, we need to view the speech of Urban II at Clermont and many related aspects of the history of the first crusade as modern writers have reconstructed it, not as fact but as persuasive fiction within the rhetorical framework of the twelfth century historian. Urban may have delivered one, or many, crusading speeches at Clermont, but the modern historian can neither assert this as a fact (tier 1) nor venture any remarks regarding the contents of such speech(es) as delivered. Here, as in other contexts, the modern scholar must treat sources as texts, not as potential facts, and if the medieval historian is allowed to teach something about the art of writing history, the modern scholar can avoid the tedious impasse in which much modern history-writing is trapped.[130]

Conclusion

I have stressed in this essay a twelfth century commonplace, the opposition between two groups of historians: the chronicler who is "impeditus sermone sed non scientia," who writes "tenui orationis figura," who offers "veritatem humili sermone" but speaks "balbutiendo,"[131] and the rhetorical historian to whom the chronicler offers "veritatem litterali eloquentia venustandam."[132] I have outlined some of the ways the latter group operated and elaborated their notion of truth. The lesson for today's students of these writings is simply that our modern notion of historical factuality was, for the rhetorical historian, but a *pro tem* thing, a temporary resort for the inarticulate or the preoccupied. It was at best a half-truth,[133] and one can imagine the angry astonishment in the first years of the twelfth century as the learned men of Europe's abbeys and churches discovered that the third most important development in the whole history of humankind was written up in the form of a child's babble. The worth, the "reality" of the story, lay in the *re*-telling, and the re-telling was a creative literary challenge in which the man of letters brought his skills at Latin, with all its resonances from the best models of antiquity, all its rich resources of well-taught *colores* and devices of *compositio*, to the *nuda verba* of the annalist and thereby "created" *historia*.

NOTES

I owe particular thanks to David McRuvie and Deidre Stone, current and former graduate students at the University of Sydney, for reading and commenting on this chapter. My colleague Dr. John Pryor and the anonymous reader for the Press have also been of much assistance to me. If I have not adopted all their suggested improvements, time alone is to blame. Ms. Lana Johnstone very kindly typed the notes for me.

[1]John of Salisbury, *Historia pontificalis*, ed. and trans. M. Chibnall (London, 1956), p. 2. (Henceforth cited as *HP*.) On the metaphor of "weaving" as applied to ancient poetry, see William Berg, *Early Virgil* (London, 1974), pp. 111-12.

[2]Well surveyed in R. D. Ray, "Medieval Historiography Through the Twelfth Century: Problems and Progress of Research," *Viator*, 5 (1974), 33-59. See also *Speculum*, 54 (1979) for reviews of Galbert de Bruges, *Le Meurte de Charles le Bon* (568) and Denys Hays, *Annalists and Historians: Western Historiography from the Eighth to the Eighteenth Centuries* (577-80).

[3]R. Hanning, *The Vision of History in Early Britain* (New York, 1966), pp. 32-37; J. O. Ward, "Classical Rhetoric and the Writing of History in Medieval and Renaissance Culture," in *European History and its Historians*, ed. F. McGregor and N. Wright (Adelaide, 1977), p. 3; and R. A. Markus, *Saeculum: History and Society in the Theology of St. Augustine* (Cambridge, 1970), pp. 157 ff. and passim.

[4]For example, the *Historia Vizeliacensis monasterii*, ed. R. B. C. Huygens, in *Monumenta Vizeliacensis*, vol. 42 of Corpus Christianorum Continuatio Mediaevalis (1976) or *Patrologia Latina* 194: cols. 1561 ff. (Henceforth cited as *PL*.)

[5]See *Historia pontificalis*, ed. R. L. Poole (Oxford, 1927), pp. lxxxii-iii.

[6]Nancy Partner, *Serious Entertainments: The Writing of History in Twelfth Century England* (Chicago, 1977), indicates some of these options. Yet Sigebert's chronicle was not obscure. Over sixty manuscripts once existed, of which forty-four survive. Over fifty subsequent writers took material from it, and there were thirty continuators; see D. Hay, *Annalists and Historians* (London, 1977), pp. 46 ff., and Peter Classen, "*Res Gestae*, Universal History, Apocalypse," in *Renaissance and Renewal in the Twelfth Century*, ed. R. L. Benson and G. Constable (Cambridge, MA, 1982), p. 399. For Orderic Vitalis and Sigebert see A. Gransden,

Historical Writing in England c. 550 to c. 1307 (London, 1974), p. 162. John's *continuatio*, however, was little known or used.

[7]William of Malmesbury, *De gestis regum Anglorum*, ed. W. Stubbs, 2 vols., Rolls Series 90 (London, 1887), 1:11. (Henceforth cited as Stubbs, 1 and 2.) See also Suzanne Fleischman, "On the Representation of History and Fiction in the Middles Ages," *History and Theory*, 22 (1983), 278-310.

[8]Partner, *Serious Entertainments*, pp. 63-67. William of Newburgh's language expresses clearly an opposition between "history" and "fiction": "ridicula . . . figmenta contexens . . . fabulas de Arturo. . . per superductum Latini sermonis colorem honesto historiae nomine palliavit. . . ." (*Historia Rerum Anglicarum*, proemium to Bk. I, *Chronicles of the Reigns of Stephen, Henry II and Richard I*, ed. Richard Howlett, Rolls Series 82 (London, 1884), 1.11-12).

[9]*Ottonis et Rahewini Gesta Friderici I Imperatoris*, ed. G. Waitz, vol. 46 of *Scriptores Rerum Germanicarum in usum scholarum* (Hannover and Leipzig, 1912; rpt. 1978), p. 12. (Henceforth cited as Waitz.)

[10]*The Deeds of Frederick Barbarossa, by Otto of Freising and his Continuator, Rahewin*, trans. C. C. Mierow, vol. 49 of *Records of Civilization, Sources and Studies*, ed. Austin P. Evans (New York, 1953, 1966), pp. 207, 233, 331. (Henceforth cited as Mierow.)

[11]See the Munz-Gillingham controversy regarding Otto and Rahewin in J. B. Gillingham, "Frederick Barbarossa, a Secret Revolutionary?," *English Historical Review*, 86 (1971), 73 ff.; and his "Why did Rahewin Stop Writing the *Gesta Frederici*?," *English Historical Review*, 83 (1968), 249 ff. See also Partner, *Serious Entertainments*, p. 44, for a parallel point in regard to Henry of Huntingdon.

[12]See N. Haring, "The Writings Against Gilbert of Poitiers by Geoffrey of Auxerre," *Analecta Cisterciensia*, 22 (1968), 3-83, and "Notes on the Council and the Consistory of Rheims (1148), *Mediaeval Studies*, 28 (1966), 39-59, esp. p. 49, n. 3; and R. L. Poole, *Illustrations of the History of Medieval Thought and Learning* (London, 1920), ch. 6. See n. 39 below and R. L. Poole, *Historia pontificalis*, pp. xxxvi ff.

[13]*Monumenta Germaniae Historica, Scriptores* 6 (Hannover, 1844, 1963), p. 390. (This series hereafter cited as *MGH*.)

[14]Partner, *Serious Entertainments*, pp. 76, 130-31. (The business of the Council did not, incidentally, include the trial of Gilbert of Poitiers, and the latter can by no means be described as, in Partner's phrase, a "more respectable heretic.") *Guilielmi Neubrigensis, Historia Sive Chronica Rerum Anglicarum*, ed. T. Hearne (Oxford, 1719), pp. 63 ff. (I.19).

[15]*HP*, sects. 1-3.

[16]John France, "An Unknown Account of the Capture of Jerusalem," *English Historical Review*, 87 (1972), 771-83.

[17]For example, William of Malmesbury, *Gesta pontificum Anglorum*, ed. N. E. S. Hamilton, Rolls Series 52 (London, 1870), p. 4: "ut et integra non vacillet veritas." See Ray, "Medieval Historiography Through the Twelfth Century," p. 43; R. W. Southern, "Aspects of the European Tradition of Historical Writing: The Rhetorical Tradition from Einhard to Geoffrey of Monmouth," *Transactions of the Royal Historical Society*, s.5, v. 20 (1970), 178; and W. J. Sayers, "The Beginnings and Early Development of Old French Historiography," Diss. Univ. of California, Berkeley 1966, pp. 279, 293 ff. M. L. Levy, "As thyn Auctour seyth," *Medium Aevum*, 12 (1943) 25-39, explores the ways in which medieval notions of fiction and history mingle and overlap one another in poetry. See also B. W. O'Dwyer, "St. Bernard as Historian: The Life of St. Malachy of Armagh," *Journal of Religious History*, 10 (1978), 141: "Bernard [of Clairvaux] did not have a historical mind; his was a metaphysical mind in the sense of being open to the eternal beyond the factual."

[18]See Hay, *Annalists and Historians*; R. G. Collingwood, *The Idea of History* (Oxford, 1946), pp. 46-56; Southern, "Aspects of the European Tradition of Historical Writing," p. 173; and Ray, "Medieval Historiography Through the Twelfth Century," pp. 40, 57, 58.

[19]Southern, "Aspects of the European Tradition of Historical Writing," p. 181; Ray, "Medieval Historiography Through the Twelfth Century," p. 42; B. Guenée, "Y a-t-il une historiographie médiévale," *Revue Historique*, 258 (1977), 264. See also E. Auerbach, *Mimesis: The Representation of Reality in Western Literature*, trans. Willard R. Trask (New York, 1957), p. 178 (quoted on p. 133 here). The best discussion of the interpenetration of theology and history is M-D Chenu, *La Théologie au Douzième Siècle* (Paris, 1957), ch. 3, trans. J. Taylor and L. K. Little as ch. 5 in *Nature, Man and Society in the Twelfth Century* (Chicago and London, 1968). See also B. Guenée, *Histoire et Culture Historique dans l'Occident Médieval* (Paris, 1980), pp. 29-33.

[20]Ward, "Classical Rhetoric and the Writing of History," p. 3, n. 16, and p. 5, n. 44; Ray, "Medieval Historiography Through the Twelfth Century," p. 52; Ray, "Bede the Exegete as Historian," in *Famulus Christi. Essays in Commemoration of the 13th Centenary of the Birth of the Venerable Bede*, ed. G. Bonner (London, 1976), pp. 128 f.; Ray, "Bede's *Vera Lex Historiae*," *Speculum*, 55, 1 (1980), 4; and Sayers, "The Beginnings and Early Development of Old French Historiography," pp. 36-39.

[21]Ward, "Classical Rhetoric and the Writing of History," p. 3.

[22]Ray, "Medieval Historiography Through the Twelfth Century," pp. 38-39; Gabrielle M. Spiegel, "Genealogy: Form and Function in Medieval Historical Narrative," *History and Theory*, 22 (1983), 50.

[23]D. W. T. Vessey, "William of Tyre and the Art of Historiography," *Mediaeval Studies*, 25 (1973), 433-55; Sayers, "The Beginnings and Early Development of Old French Historiography, pp. 107 ff.; and Ward, "The Date of the Commentary on Cicero's *De inventione* by Thierry of

151

Chartres," *Viator*, 3 (1972), 247 ff. and literature there cited. Ancient historical prefaces are analyzed in Tore Janson, *Latin Prose Prefaces* (Stockholm, 1964), pp. 64 ff. It will be clear to any reader of Janson's discussion that the authors surveyed here were familiar with the exordial topic lore of antiquity, particularly the apology for stylistic rusticity and its implications for historical truth. Such consciousness, like the contemporary northern French precocity in the use of the cursus in literary Latin (T. Janson, *Prose Rhythm in Medieval Latin from the 9th to the 13th Century* [Stockholm, 1975], pp. 72 ff.) is an illustration of the heightened rhetorical sensitivity from which the urge to rewrite the earlier, cruder, crusading chronicles itself springs (on this, see the discussion later in this chapter). Useful also on the exordial stylistic apology is Guenée, *Histoire et Culture Historique*, pp. 214-20.

[24]Ray, "Medieval Historiography Through the Twelfth Century," p. 41.

[25]Gervase of Canterbury's distinction is discussed in: V. H. Galbraith, *Historical Research in Medieval England* (London, 1951), pp. 1-3; *The Anglo-Saxon Chronicle*, trans. G. N. Garmonsway (London, 1953), p. xviii; and Ray, "Medieval Historiography Through the Twelfth Century," p. 49. The best discussion is probably P. Wiseman, *Clio's Cosmetics: Three Studies in Greco-Roman Literature* (Leicester, 1979), chs. 1-4. For Cicero's views see *De oratore*, 2.12.51 ff.

[26]As, for example, in the *Historia Vizelacensis Monasterii*.

[27]Ray, "Medieval Historiography Through the Twelfth Century," p. 41. Imperial historians, from Einhard and Widukind of Corvey to Otto of Freising and Rahewin, allow the overriding necessity of displaying the theme of *Romanum imperium* in German history to affect the "veracity" of their narratives; thus Einhard uses Suetonius and plays down the papal coronation of 800 A.D., Widukind ignores the papal coronation of 962 A.D., and Rahewin includes large slabs of text from imperial historians in his work:

> Rahewin's final description and assessment of Frederick is drawn in part from Einhard's description of Charlemagne (*Gesta* 4.lxxxvi), not merely because Einhard was a respected and readily available source, but because in Rahewin's estimation, and doubtless that of Frederick himself, the Emperor was the heir to Charlemagne's Empire and his successor. In accordance with the plan laid down by Otto, Rahewin has the task of showing the successful re-establishment of the rights and functions of the Emperor. With the account of the second diet of Roncaglia and the "downfall of the people of Milan," Rahewin is able to bring Frederick's political ventures to an appropriately successful conclusion (from

an unpublished study by Patrick Cook, cartoonist for the *National Times*, Australia). One could add that even Rahewin's inclusion of portions of Jordanes' picture of Attila the Hun in his portrait of Frederick is less the result of a failing of *inventio* than a desire to suggest Barbarossa's dominating proportions: he combines the best of famous Roman and barbarian rulers.

Another structuring factor may be mentioned here, that of "lignage": see Spiegel, "Genealogy: Form and Function in Medieval Historical Narrative," pp. 43-53.

[28]*HP*: "praetermissas . . . hystorias" (p. 1) and "que ad pontificalem hystoriam" (p. 3).

[29]Interesting because the beginning or inspiration of John's *sermo* (*HP*, p. 4) will be God the son *qui in principio erat Verbum*; thus, the inspiration of history as *sermo* is *verbum*.

[30]*HP*, sect. 15, p. 41.

[31]*HP*, p. 3

[32]Ray, "Bede the Exegete as Historian," p. 131. See also R. Barthes, "The Discourse of History," trans. S. Bann, in *Comparative Criticism: A Yearbook*, ed. E. S. Shaffer (Cambridge, 1981), p. 12: what the historian talks about, "collections" of "units of content," are the "signifieds" of the historical discourse, not the referents, to which the signifieds refer.

[33]*HP*: "favore cardinalium quos ad . . ." (p. 49); "minimum habens de fastu Romano" (p. 55); "in genere suo rapax" (p. 75 and sects. 38 and 39); "corruperat curiam" (p. 81).

[34]Sect. 23 (Louis VII and Eleanor) is at first sight anomalous, but I group it with "the papacy and society" because of Eugenius' personal interest (sect. 29). Sect. 28 is also anomalous but concerns Sicily, a particular interest of the pope's (see sects. 32-34); consequently, I have grouped it with "relations with secular princes." Sect. 46 is difficult to group, as it is incomplete (2 lines); I have put it under "relations with secular princes."

[35]S. Chodorow, *Christian Political Theory and Church Politics in the Mid-Twelfth Century: The Ecclesiology of Gratian's Decretum* (Berkeley, 1972). See Robert L. Benson's review for cautionary comments on Chodorow's book (*Speculum*, 50 [1975], pp. 97-106).

[36]*Five Books on Consideration: Advice to a Pope*, trans. J. D. Anderson and E. T. Kennan, Cistercian Fathers Series, 37 (Kalamazoo, MI, 1976). See also E. Kennan, "The *De consideratione* of St. Bernard of Clairvaux and the Papacy in the Mid-Twelfth Century: A Review of Scholarship," *Traditio*, 23 (1967), 73-115.

[37]See H. Liebeschütz, *Medieval Humanism in the Life and Writings of John of Salisbury* (London, 1950).

[38]For example, *HP*, pp. 12-13; "familiari colloquio" (p. 61); "non potuit lacrimas continere" (p. 81). John stresses Eugenius' conception of the value of personal morality and uprightness in other ways also, e.g., chap. 45. Ray in "Bede the Exegete as Historian" states that" *sermo humilis* thrives on concrete words, circumstantial details, dramatic episodes, and familiar situations" (p. 136).

[39]*HP*: "hiis presens interfui" (p. 82). Cf. "quod vidi loquor" (p. 17): John is anxious here to correct the record of Gilbert of Poitiers' trial.

[40]On Frederick's epistle to Otto and Otto's expansion of it, see P. Brezzi, "Le fonti dei Gesta Friderici imperatoris," *Istituto Storico Italiano per il medio evo e Archivio Muratoriano, Bullettino*, 75 (1963), 110.

[41]*Ad Herennium* 4.15.21, and Waitz, pp. 12-14.1.

[42]See Koch, in *Geschichtsdenken und Geschichtsbild im MA*, ed. W. Lammers (Darmstadt, 1961), p. 330; and K. F. Morrison, "Otto of Freising's Quest for the Hermeneutic Circle," *Speculum*, 55, 2 (1980), 221 ff. On Otto's theoretical historical principles see F. P. Pickering, "Historical Thought and Moral Codes in Medieval Epic," in *The Epic in Medieval Society, Aesthetic and Moral Values*, ed. Harold Scholler (Tübingen, 1977), pp. 12, 13; Leopold Grill, "Bildung und Wissenschaft im Leben Bischof Ottos von Freising," *Analecta Cisterciensia*, 14 (1958), 316 ff.; and Classen, *"Res Gestae,"* pp. 400-03.

[43]C. Halm, *Rhetores Latini Minores* (Leipzig, 1863), pp. 202.8, 487.6, 521.36. See also W. Ryding, *Structure in Medieval Narrative* (Mouton, 1971), p. 69 on the legitimacy of digressions.

[44]The phrase *de hoc hactenus* elsewhere (Waitz 43.10) concludes a letter digression. The Gilbert de Poitiers digression occupies Waitz pp. 67-88 (Mierow, pp. 82-101).

[45]"Parataxis" and "hypotaxis" are defined in Partner, *Serious Entertainments*, p. 197. See also E. Vinaver, *The Rise of Romance* (Oxford, 1971), chs. 1-2; Auerbach, *Mimesis*, pp. 61-66, 86-106; Sayers, "The Beginnings and Early Development of Old French Historiography," pp. 390 ff., 407, 409. Partner speaks of the prevalence of paratactic prose in the twelfth century "in spite of well-known classical models (p. 199) . . . the essential point is simply the universality of episodic, non-developmental serial organization—Auerbach's 'parataxis' without the philosophic implications" (p. 202). I am not sure this generalization applies to texts other than the type studied in Partner's book.

[46]*Gesta Friderici I imperatoris in Lombardia auctore cive mediolanensi (Annales mediolanenses maiores)*, ed. O. Holder-Egger (Hannover, 1892), pp. 14-16. See also the remarks of H. A. Myers, "The Modification of the Augustinian-Orosian Theory of History in the Treatment of Empire by Vernacular Historians of Medieval Germany," Diss. Brandeis 1965, pp. 312 ff.

[47]See, for example, *Ottonis Episcopi Frisingensis Chronica; Sive,*

Historia de Duabus Civitatibus, ed. A. Hofmeister (Hannover and Leipzig, 1912), p. 320. (Henceforth cited as Hofmeister.)

⁴⁸*Recueil des Historiens des Croisades, Historiens Occidentaux*, 5 vols. (Paris, 1866), 3: 327A. (Henceforth cited as *HC*.) Compare Otto's use of *stilus* (Waitz 54.4) or William of Malmesbury's "traxi stilum per latebrosissimas historias . . ." (*Gesta Pontificum Anglorum*, p. 4). There is much of value on Otto's conception of what he was doing in W. Lammers, "Weltgeschichte und Zeitgeschichte bei Otto von Freising," in *Die Zeit der Staufer*, Katalog der Ausstellung, Stuttgart, 1977 (Stuttgart, 1979), pp. 77-90.

⁴⁹Hugh of St. Victor, *Didascalicon*, 6.3; and Guibert of Nogent on preaching, in *PL* 156:25D. See J. B. Allen, *The Friar as Critic* (Nashville, 1971), pp. 10 ff. for the literal and spiritual senses and on Hugh of St. Victor's sense of the letter. On the latter, see also G. A. Zinn, "*Historia fundamentum est*: The Role of History in the Contemplative Life According to Hugh of St. Victor," in *Contemporary Reflections on the Medieval Christian Tradition*, ed. G. H. Shriver (Durham, NC, 1974), pp. 138 ff., esp. p. 143.

⁵⁰Geoffrey of Monmouth is also attracted by this affectation: see the variant version of *Historia regum Britanniae*, ed. J. Hammer (Cambridge, MA, 1951), p. 22.

⁵¹Bede, *Opera Historica*, ed. C. Plummer (Oxford, 1896), 1:5.2. (Hereafter cited as Plummer.)

⁵²Stubbs 1:51: "historia panegyrico prosequitur stilo" and "adeo est amplior laus ista in Oswaldo quam ut nostra oratione indigeat cumulari" (1:52).

⁵³Plummer, 1:5.

⁵⁴Note William's use of "veraciores litterae" (Stubbs 1:161) and his description of himself as "homine litterato" (Stubbs 2:357). Also: "quam si meis texuissem litteris" (Stubbs 1:203).

⁵⁵On the *De oratore* and historiography see Sayers, "The Beginnings and Early Development of Old French Historiography," pp. 18 ff.; H. F. North, "Rhetoric and Historiography," *Quarterly Journal of Speech*, 42 (1956), 234-42; Ward, "Artificiosa Eloquentia in the Middle Ages," Diss. Toronto 1972, 1.398-407; and Wiseman, *Clio's Cosmetics*, pt. 1.

⁵⁶See: R. Mortier, *Les Textes de la chanson de Roland*, 10 vols. (Paris, 1940-44) and on the circumstances, B. Sholod, *Charlemagne in Spain: The Cultural Legacy of Roncesvalles* (Geneva, 1966), p. 141; on the process of textual reworking to produce "truth" and "splendidness" in the *Chansons* and similar literature, Stephen G. Nichols, Jr., "The Interaction of Life and Literature in the *Peregrinationes ad Loca Sancta* and the *Chanson de Geste*," *Speculum*, 44 (1969), 53; and, on pre-existing *materia* in medieval poetics, Douglas Kelly, "The Scope of the Treatment of Composition in the Twelfth / Thirteenth Century Arts of Poetry," *Speculum*, 41 (1966), 261-78.

[57]R. M. Thomson, "Two Versions of a Saint's Life from St. Edmund's Abbey: Changing Currents in Twelfth Century Monastic Style," *Revue Bénédictine*, 84 (1974), 384-408.

[58]For an event, see Ailred of Rievaulx who rewrites Richard of Hexham's account of the Battle of the Standard on the model of crusade historiography (*Chronicles of the Reigns of Stephen, Henry II and Richard I*, ed. R. Howlett, vol. 3, pp. 179-99). On later reworkings of aspects of the crusades see M. R. Morgan, *The Chronicle of Ernoul and the Continuators of William of Tyre* (Oxford, 1973). Sayers discusses vernacular reworkings of other crusade histories ("The Beginnings and Early Development of Old French Historiography," pp. 7 ff.). For a person, see R. Ray, "Orderic Vitalis and William of Poitiers: A Monastic Reinterpretation of William the Conqueror," *Revue Belge de philologie et d'histoire*, 50 (1972), 1116-27. Partner notes the emphasis in medieval historiography on recasting "received materials into a magnified, elaborated, more impressive form" (*Serious Entertainments*, p. 206). A good example is that of Adam of Bremen: see Anders Piltz, *The World of Medieval Learning*, trans. D. Jones (Oxford, 1981), p. 35.

[59]R. W. Southern, *St. Anselm and His Biographer* (Cambridge, 1966), pp. 43 ff.

[60]Ward, "Classical Rhetoric and the Writing of History."

[61]See R. Somerville, *Decreta Claromontensia*, vol. 1 of *The Councils of Urban II*, Annuarium Historiae Conciliorum, supp. 1 (Amsterdam, 1972), pp. 3-6; his "The Council of Clermont and the First Crusade" in *Mélanges G. Fransen*, *Studia Gratiana*, 20 (Rome, 1976), pp. 323-27; R. Rohricht, *Geschichte des ersten Kreuzzuges* (Innsbruck, 1901), pp. 18-21 (the conventional account); A. Fliche, "Les origines de l'action de la Papauté en vue de la croisade," *Revue d'histoire Ecclésiastique*, 34 (1938), 765-75; and his "Urbain II et la Croisade," *Revue d'histoire de l'église de France*, 14 (1927), 289-306. See also Rene Crozet, "Le voyage d'Urbain II et ses négociations avec le clergé de France (1095-96)," *Revue Historique*, 179 (1937), 271-310; his "Le voyage d'Urbain II en France (1095-96) et son importance au point de vue archéologique," *Annales du Midi*, 49 (1937), 42-69; J. Richard, "La Papauté et la direction de la première croisade," in his *Orient et Occident au Moyen Âge: contacts et relations XIIᵉ-XVᵉ s.* (London, 1976), pp. 49-58; C. Erdmann, *Die Enstehung des Kreuzzugsgedankens* (Darmstadt, 1974), pp. 304-05, 364 ff. (*der Kreuzpredigt von Clermont*). Bernard McGinn presents a conventional faith in the basic sources for Clermont ("The Piety of the First Crusaders," *Essays on Medieval Civilization*, ed. Bede Lackner and K. Philp, The Walter Prescott Webb Memorial Lectures [Univ. of Texas, 1978], pp. 44-47). By contrast, J. H. and L. L. Hill are more critical of the sources ("Contemporary Accounts and the Later Reputation of Adhemar, Bishop of Puy," *Mediaevalia et Humanistica*, 9 [1955], 30-38). C. J. Hefele mentions some minor matters of ecclesiastical administration and

discipline that Urban dealt with at the Council (pp. 403-06) and discusses the crusade element in a massive digression (pp. 406 ff.); his discussion of the sources for the pope's speech begins p. 419; p. 420, n. 2 cites R. Crégut, *Le Concile de Clermont en 1095 et la première croisade* (Clermont, 1895), with useful physical details of the Council (*Histoire des conciles*, trans. H. Leclercq, 12 vols. [Paris, 1912], 5/1:397 ff.). Crégut, it seems, anticipated Munro [see n. 72 below] in creating a synthetic text of the Pope's speech. The primarily ecclesiastical reform motive for and context of Urban's French journey of 1095-96 and his church councils is discussed by Alfons Becker, *Papst Urban II 1088-99, MGH, Schriften* 19.1 (Stuttgart, 1964), Teil I, "Herkunft und kirchliche Laufbahn. Der Papst und die lateinische Christenheit," pp. 213 ff. For his view of Clermont, whereby Canon 2 ("quicumque pro sola devotione non pro honoris. . . . ") is felt to accompany naturally the crusade preaching which the Pope entered upon at the conclusion of the Council, see pp. 222-23. Becker sees Orderic Vitalis' emphasis upon the crusades as an example of concord between *sacerdotium et regnum, clericalis ordo et laicalis . . . episcopus* (Adhemar) *et comes* (Raymond), *Moysem et Aaron. . . .* as basically a figment of Orderic's inspired imagination, just as William of Malmesbury's cynical interpretation of Urban's real motive for preaching the crusade (pp. 215-16) is a hindsight witness to the travesty of Urban's original ideas that the crusades became. I shall refer to the notion of "concord" again in connection with Baudry of Bourgeuil's crusade account. Becker admits that, although the original emphasis of Urban's visit to southern France was church reform, the issue of the crusade soon swamped it in the popular view (pp. 216-17). My research assistant, Ms. Sharon Davidson, who has looked at Crozet's articles and some of the evidence used, writes from Paris:

> although all the evidence is perfectly compatible with the hypothesis that Urban came to France to preach the crusade, it is by no means a necessary hypothesis. Virtually everything Urban did there can be explained equally well by the general policy of building the monastic orders at the expense of the secular clergy, increasing the prestige, power, and direct dependence on the Papacy of the Cluniac order, and gaining support from the nobility for the excommunication of Philip I. If the crusade was a major part of the papal visit it is very strange that there is not more mention of it in the sources.

Urban's activity in France after Piacenza consisted of visits to Cluniac monasteries, consecration of altars (some to the Holy Cross), and the blessing of monasteries in connection with grants of lands, liberties, etc. (see Hefele, p. 397, esp. n. 2). The few specific instances of crusade preaching in the sources Crozet cites (principally for Limoges, Angers,

Nîmes) need much closer analysis than is currently available before firm conclusions can be based on them. See R. Somerville, "The Council of Clermont (1095) and Latin Christian Society," *Archivum Historiae Pontificiae*, 12 (1974), 57-58, where some "hints" that Urban intended to raise crusade matters at Clermont are discussed (esp. p. 58, n. 14); and H. E. J. Cowdrey, "Pope Urban II's Preaching of the First Crusade," *History*, 55 (1970), p. 181.

[62]*MGH, Scriptores* 5 (Hannover, 1844), p. 462.

[63]*MGH, Scriptores* 5.463-64; Somerville, *Decreta Claromontensia*, p. 100; Erdmann, *Die Enstehung des Kreuzzugsgedankens*, pp. 301 ff., 363 ff; and Hefele, *Histoire des conciles*, 388 ff.

[64]Anna Comnena, *Alexiad*, trans. E. R. A. Sewter (Penguin Books, 1969), p. 308.

[65]P. Labbe and G. Cossart, *Sacrosancta Concilia*, 23 vols. (Venice, 1728-33), 10.821-26.

[66]A. Hatem, *Les poèmes épiques des croisades: genèse—historicité—localisation: essai sur l'activité littéraire dans les colonies franques de Syrie au Moyen Âge* (Paris, 1932), p. 68, n. 175. For Clermont and Philip I's adultery see G. Duby, *Le Chevalier, La Femme et le Prêtre* (Paris, 1981), pp. 7 ff.

[67]Somerville, *Decreta Claromontensia*, App. 3, pp. 142-50.

[68]Somerville has two versions for item 60, but canon two in item 3, version H (p. 143) is the same reference as canon two in item 60, version H (p. 150). It should be pointed out that the conciliar decrees by no means cover all the business conducted at the Council. Somerville (*Archivum Historiae Pontificiae*, pp. 84-90) documents twenty-nine matters of ecclesiastical administration and jurisdiction dealt with at the Council, many of which would have arisen out of Urban's dealings with southern French churches and monasteries in the months immediately preceding Clermont and many of which had long histories before Clermont. None, it is hardly necessary to say, had anything to do with crusade. See also Somerville, "The Councils of Pope Calixtus II: Reims 1119," *Proceedings of the 5th International Congress of Medieval Canon Law, Salamanca 21-25 September, 1976* (Vatican City, 1980), p. 46: "the canons from Clermont survive mainly in summaries, and there is no reason to think that the extant texts cover everything that occurred." I am grateful to Professor Somerville for providing me with copies of his many articles and for discussing a number of matters with me personally.

[69]Somerville, *Decreta Claromontensia*, pp. 74, 108.

[70]Somerville, *Decreta Claromontensia*, p. 124. For some of the language of this canon forming an "addition" (presumably, therefore, of later date) "stuck into" this same version of the canons, see Somerville, "The Council of Clermont and the First Crusade," p. 328, n. 12.

[71]The "oldest text of the canons of the Council of Clermont"—MS.

BL Cotton Claudius E V (Schafer Williams, "Concilium Claromontanum 1095: A New Text," *Studia Gratiana*, 13 [1967], 38-39; see also Somerville, *Decreta Claromontensia*, p. 69)—has only item 3 as translated above. I must thank Roger Ray for his efforts to obtain a copy of this article for me.

[72]Somerville, "The Council of Clermont and the First Crusade," p. 328; D. C. Munro, "The Speech of Pope Urban II at Clermont, 1095," *American Historical Review*, 11 (1906), 234-35; and Cowdrey, "Pope Urban II's Preaching of the First Crusade," pp. 185-87.

[73]For text and translation see *Gesta Francorum et aliorum Hierosolimitanorum*, ed. and trans. Rosalind Hill, Nelsons Medieval Texts Series (London, 1962). (Henceforth cited as *Gesta*.) See also *Peter Tudebode, Historia de Hierosolymitano itinere*, trans. J. H. and L. L. Hill, Memoirs of the American Philosophical Society, 101 (Philadelphia, 1974), p. 11.

[74]Fulcher, *Historia Hierosolymitana*, ed. H. Hagenmeyer (Heidelberg, 1913); *Fulcher of Chartres: A History of the Expedition to Jerusalem 1095-1127*, ed. H. S. Fink, trans. F. R. Ryan (New York, 1973), p. 20. (Henceforth cited as Fink.) I have also used the text in *HC* 3:311-485.

[75]*HC* 3:231-309. See also *Raymond d'Aguilers: Historia Francorum Qui Ceperunt Iherusalem*, trans. J. H. and L. L. Hill, Memoirs of the American Philosophical Society, 71 (Philadelphia, 1968).

[76]*HC* 3:1-229; and *Peter Tudebode*, trans. J. H. and L. L. Hill. I have derived my principal information about the crusade chroniclers from materials cited in notes 68-75, along with Cowdrey, "Pope Urban II's Preaching of the First Crusade," 177 ff.; S. Runciman, *A History of the Crusades* (Penguin Books, 1951), vol. 1, App. 1; *The First Crusade: The Accounts of Eye-Witnesses and Participants*, ed. A. Krey (Princeton, 1921; Gloucester, MA, 1958); *The First Crusade: The Chronicle of Fulcher of Chartres and Other Source Materials*, ed. E. Peters (Philadelphia, 1971). On the use of Fulcher by later writers, see Hagenmeyer, *Historia Hierosolymitana*, pp. 71-91. There are far more extant chroniclers of the first crusade than those surveyed here, of course, but my intention has been to discuss the most elaborate of the chroniclers and those most used by modern historians. Lesser accounts of Clermont, principally fragmentary, can be found in *HC* 5.354, 356, 363, 380 ff., and 393 ff. See also the *Gesta Andegavensium Peregrinorum*, p. 345: "venit Andegavim papa romanus Urbanus, et admonuit gentem nostram ut irent Jerusalem, expugnaturi gentilem populum. . . ." I learn from *The Bulletin of the Society for the Study of the Crusades and the Latin East*, 1 (1981), 11, that Dr. John France (Swansea) has the following work in progress: "The Textual Relationship Between All the Accounts of the First Crusade."

[77]Fink, p. 21; Hagenmeyer, *Historia Hierosolymitana*, p. 71.

[78]Fink, p. 9.

[79]*HC* 4:274. On Albert and his sources see *Peter Tudebode*, pp. 10-11.

Runciman dates Albert's writing as sometime after about the year 1130 (*A History of the Crusades*, 1.331). Hefele rejects the notion of Peter the Hermit as the primary organizing spirit of the first crusade, because Albert of Aix and William of Tyre are inferior sources (*Histoire des conciles*, 1:424-25).

[80]See citations in n. 25 above. For an interesting example of the traditional prefatory disavowal of philosophy and rhetoric in favor of plain language, see Landulf Senior in B. Stock, *The Implications of Literacy: Written Language and Models of Interpretation in the Eleventh and Twelfth Centuries* (Princeton, 1983), p. 74.

[81]Hammer, *Historia regum Britanniae*: "nam si in ampullosis dictionibus paginam illevissem, taedium legentibus ingererem, dum magis in exponendis verbis quam in historia intelligenda ipsos commorari oporteret" (p. 22). Geoffrey parodies the relationship between the high and the humble style by describing his source, Walter, as "vir in oratoria arte atque in exoticis historiis eruditus" and his own efforts as "tametsi infra alienos hortulos phalerata verba non collegerim agresti tamen stilo propriisque calamis contentus."

[82]On William see: D. W. T. Vessey, "William of Tyre and the Art of Historiography"; A. C. Krey, "William of Tyre," *Speculum*, 16 (1941), 149-66; R. B. C. Huygens, "Guillaume de Tyr Étudiant: Un Chapitre (XIX, 12) de son 'Histoire' Retrouvé," *Latomus*, 21 (1962), 811-29; D. W. T. Vessey, "William of Tyre: Apology and Apocalypse"; *Hommages à A. Boutemy*, Collection *Latomus* 145 (Brussels, 1976), pp. 390-403; R. H. C. Davis, "William of Tyre," in *Relations between East and West in the Middle Ages*, ed. D. Baker (Edinburgh, 1973), and R. C. Schwinges, *Kreuzzugsideologie und Toleranz: Studien zu Wilhelm von Tyrus* (Stuttgart, 1977). On William of Malmesbury see: R. M. Thomson, "William of Malmesbury as Historian and Man of Letters," *Journal of Ecclesiastical History*, 29 (1978), 387-413; and J. Haahr, "The Concept of Kingship in William of Malmesbury's *Gesta Regum* and *Historia Novella*," *Mediaeval Studies*, 38 (1976), 351 ff. On Ordericus Vitalis see: Ray, "Orderic Vitalis and William of Poitiers," and his "Orderic Vitalis and His Readers," *Studia Monastica*, 14 (1972), 15-33. See also: "Orderic Vitalis on Henry I: Theocratic Ideology and Didactic Narrative," in *Contemporary Reflections on the Medieval Christian Tradition*, ed. G. H. Shriver (Durham, NC, 1974), pp. 119-34. Henry of Huntingdon considers his crusade mini-chronicle to be a justifiable digression but provides no account of Clermont, since it does not concern his particular interest: "ob cuius rei magnitudinem digrediendi veniam a lectore postulo; nec enim si voluero, tam miranda Dei magnalia tacere vel coactus potero, cum nec absit causa, Normannorum ducis occasio" (*Historia Anglorum*, ed. T. Arnold, Rolls Series 74 [London, 1879], p. 219).

[83]William: "qui postea apostolicae sedis legatione functus"; Fulcher: "qui postea vice fungens apostolica."

[84]William's "praesentibus ex Dei nomine praecipio, absentibus mando" equals Fulcher's "praesentibus dico, absentibus mando." William must have approved of the *colores* here: isocolon, homoeoptoton, asyndeton, antithesis.

[85]William: "absolutionem criminum"; Fulcher: "remissio peccatorum."

[86]Runciman gives c. 1122 as the date for Robert (*A History of the Crusades*, 1:330); other writers say c. 1107. On Guibert see: J. Chaurand, "La conception de l'histoire de Guibert de Nogent (1053-1124)," *Cahiers de Civilization Médiévale*, 8 (1965), 381-95; and *Self and Society in Medieval France: The Memoirs of Abbot Guibert of Nogent (1064?-c. 1125)* ed. J. F. Benton, trans. C. C. Swinton Bland (New York, 1970).

[87]See n. 45 above and Southern, "Aspects of the European Tradition of Historical Writing," pp. 180-81. For a good analysis of classicism in twelfth century prose style, see Janet Martin, "Classicism and Style in Latin Literature," *Renaissance and Renewal in the Twelfth Century*. On parataxis, see H. C. Gotoff, *Cicero's Elegant Style: An Analysis of the Pro Archia* (Urbana, IL, 1979), p. 68. It must be emphasized that carefully contrived periodicity replaces a factual, chronological, historical ordering of sentence units with a specifically rhetorical / linguistic one. This opposition stresses the priority of language in the discourse of the rhetor-humanists of the Middle Ages and the Renaissance.

[88]Marc Bloch, *Feudal Society*, trans. L. A. Manyon, (London, 1961), p. 78.

[89]Auerbach, *Mimesis*, p. 178.

[90]Sayers, "The Beginnings and Early Development of Old French Historiography," p. 444.

[91]H. J. Chaytor, *From Script to Print* (London, 1966), p. 48. See also Vinaver, *The Rise of Romance*, chs. 1-2; and Franz H. Bäuml, "Varieties and Consequences of Medieval Literacy and Illiteracy," *Speculum*, 55 (1980), 263 on differences between the vernacular and Latin.

[92]M. Richter, "A Socio-linguistic Approach to the Latin Middle Ages," *Studies in Church History*, 11 (1975), 76. Richter has shown how Latin as a clerical monopoly reinforced the caste status of the clergy, helping it elevate, mythologize, and ritualize its own divinity and supremacy, to demarcate the spheres of the two swords. Clerical success here was marked: the clergy succeeded in overawing and "divinizing" the "liturgical" monarch of the pre-twelfth century period, and thereafter it sought to tie the burgeoning secular world together in an endless series of bulls, *diplomata*, letters, interdicts, judicial delegations, provisions, *decreta*, etc. The mystique of church and papacy was sustained by and epitomized in the monopoly of a sacred, relatively little-understood language, and with the evaporation of that monopoly, as has often been observed, the mystique diminished.

[93]I assume Scaglione's definition of "the periodic style," *The Classical Theory of Composition from its Origins to the Present* (Chapel Hill, NC, 1972), pp. 28-30, 31 ff. See also Auerbach, *Mimesis*, p. 77; and Gotoff, *Cicero's Elegant Style*, pp. 49, 67-69.

[94]*Ioannis Saresberiensis episcopi Carnotensis Metalogicon*, ed. C. C. J. Webb (Oxford, 1929), p. 55. (Hereafter referred to as Webb.) *PL* 199 854 D.

[95]*Ad Herennium* 1.8.13. See also Ryding, *Structure in Medieval Narrative*.

[96]*PL* 854 B, Webb, p. 54. See Scaglione, *The Classical Theory of Composition*, p. 29: John's words refer to rhetorical embellishment in general, rather than, presumably, to periodicity as such, but they do reveal an awareness of some of the key features of the Latin *periodus, ambitus, circumductus*, or *oratio vincta atque contexta* as contrasted with *oratio soluta*. For a good analysis of the difference between the periodic sentence structure associated with classical and, more particularly, Ciceronian prose and the heightened rhetorical patterning of medieval elevated prose style, see Martin, "Classicism and Style in Latin Literature."

[97]Cf. John of Salisbury, *Metalogicon* 1.24, *PL* 855 B, Webb, p. 56 ("vestigia imitari") with Guibert's phrase here ("nudo vestigio").

[98]Cf. William of Tyre, in Vessey, "William of Tyre and the Art of Historiography," p. 443.

[99]Horace, *Ars Poetica* 97; and see quotation in n. 81 above.

[100]N. Struever, *The Language of History in the Renaissance* (Princeton, 1970), pp. 32 ff., 81.

[101]*HC* 4:130I. For a summary of Guibert's remarks on Eastern heresy see Rosalind Hill, "Pure Air and Portentous Heresy," *Studies in Church History*, 13 (1976), 135-40.

[102]Cf. the figure of *tricolon abundans*; see Gotoff, *Cicero's Elegant Style*: "the principle of the expanding tricolon plays against isocolon and syntactic symmetry by giving added volume to succeeding members" (p. 99); the noun "Jerusalem" and its successive adjectives form an elaborate instance of *hyperbaton* (discussed by Gottoff, p. 100 and passim) when natural pairs of words are separated to insure complete interweaving and full suspension until final resolution.

[103]Baudry seems to decry a contemporary fashion for versified history. Jeanette M. A. Beer, "Epic Imitation," in *Charlemagne et L'Épopée Romane*, Bibliothéque de la Faculté de Philosophie et Lettres de l'Université de Liége, Fasc. 225, 2 vols. (Paris, 1978) states: "Chronicling in vernacular prose was the late twelfth century's antidote to fabulous *chansons* in rhyme. Some chronicling patrons commissioned prose specifically to distinguish between history and the *chansons de geste*. They claimed that prose was the vehicle of truth, verse the vehicle of fancy" (p. 415). Cf. Myers, "The Modification of the Augustinian-Orosian Theory of History," pp. 317 ff. and 419 (n. 150).

[104]On the place of readings from accounts of the crusades in church and monastic services see n. 16 above; *Peter Tudebode*, p. 12; and *Raymond d'Aguilers*, pp. 10-11. Note Ray's remark: Orderic Vitalis' preference for Baudry as a basis for his crusade rewrite can be explained by the fact that it was "closer to the ambiance of the daily monastic *lectiones*," ("Orderic Vitalis and William of Poitiers, 1125-26"). Once grasped, this point explains many of the peculiarities, in terms of modern notions of history, of twelfth century learned historiography.

[105]Perhaps the same motive underlies some versions of the *Song of Roland*. Later (p. 732) Robert makes reference to the route Charlemagne used to Constantinople!

[106]Compare the content of the papal letters, Somerville, "The Council of Clermont and the First Crusade," p. 330 and above n. 72.

[107]Luke 9:23, 14:27; Matthew 10:38, 16:24; Mark 8:34; *Gesta*, p. 1.

[108]Baudry, *HC* 4:16D. Bernold of St. Blasien calls Urban at Piacenza "primus legislator Moyses populum Dei in campestribus legalibus praeceptis Deo iubente instituit" (*MGH, Scriptores* 5.462). On the exegetical significance of Moses and Aaron see Hugh of St. Victor, *Didascalicon* 6.3. See also citations in n. 61 above. Robert's addition of a prologue to the "acephalous history" is not uncommon medieval practice. Prologues come and go in different MSS. of the same work. A curious example is Madeleine Tyssens, "Le prologue de la *Vie de St. Alexis* dans le MS de Hildesheim," in *Studi in onore di Italo Siciliano* (Florence, 1966), pp. 1165-77.

[109]*Peter Tudebode*, p. 93; Guibert, *HC* 4:210.

[110]Fink, *Fulcher of Chartres*, p. 107, and his "Fulcher of Chartres, Historian of the Latin Kingdom of Jerusalem," *Studies in Medieval Culture*, 5 (1975), 57. See also Hagenmeyer, *Historia Hierosolymitana*, p. 259; and his *Epistulae et Chartae ad Historiam Primi Belli Sacri Spectantes, die Kreuzzugsbriefe aus de Jahren 1088-1100* (Innsbruck, 1901), pp. 97-98. On the strength of some verbal similarities, Hagenmeyer argues a close relationship between the writer of the letter and the writer of the *Gesta Francorum* (pp. 96-97, 354). I would prefer to see a close relationship in general between the propaganda letters, which are in the nature of dictaminal / historical exercises, and the general drift of the crusade histories. There is, for example, overlap between Robert of Rheims' version of Urban's speech at Clermont and the spurious letter discussed in E. Joranson, "The Problem of the Spurious Letter of Emperor Alexius to the Count of Flanders," *American Historical Review*, 55 (1950), 811-32. Special purpose re-writing, based on the primary accounts of the first crusade, seems to have been an early propaganda priority (Joranson, pp. 828 ff.). There is room, perhaps, for a close examination of the MS. context of all appearances of the unusual letter Fulcher (?) inserted into his History.

[111]Fink, *Fulcher of Chartres*, p. 111; Hagenmeyer, *Historia Hiero-*

solymitana, p. 259. The letter proposes a specifically papal solution to the problem of rulership in Jerusalem. It is carefully linked to the Clermont speech and would have been quite inappropriate after the events of 1099 A.D. Note the words "qui hanc viam incepisti et sermonibus tuis. . ." and "viam Jesu Christi a nobis inceptam et a te praedicatam perficias" (p. 264).

[112]On the Fulcher text the later rewriters used, see Fink, *Fulcher of Chartres*, pp. 20 ff., 46 ff.

[113]Fulcher, 1.32 in Fink, *Fulcher of Chartres*, p. 128 (see *HC* 3:364: "principatum Iherosolymitanum rexit . . . consensu omnium"); 1.30.1, Fink, p. 124; and 2.6.1, Fink, p. 148. Fulcher, 1.30.2 has the election of a patriarch deferred "until they had inquired from the Roman Pope whom he wished to place in authority." Thus Fulcher covers up for the tension indicated in Raymond; see Fink, p. 124, n. 3.

[114]*Peter Tudebode*, p. 120.

[115]*Gesta*, p. 92.

[116]*Raymond d'Aguilers*, pp. 66 ff., 128-30.

[117]*HC* 3:301; *Raymond d'Aguilers*, pp. 9, 129. Albert of Aix avoids use of the term "king": "dominium urbis et custodiam Dominici sepulchri . . . urbis principatum . . . ductorem ac principem atque praeceptorem Christiani exercitus" (*HC* 4:485-86). J. Riley-Smith, "The Title of Godfrey of Bouillon," *Bulletin of the Institute of Historical Research*, 52 (1979), 83-87, reviews some of this evidence but shows an arbitrary tendency to accept chroniclers' statements as directly factual. So also does J. C. Andressohn, *The Ancestry and Life of Godfrey of Bouillon* (Bloomington, IN, 1947), pp. 104 ff.

[118]Sayers, "The Beginnings and Early Development of Old French Historiography," pp. 359 ff.

[119]Mierow, pp. 146, 234; *HP*, p. 84; Stubbs 1:36-37 (using *epanaphora*, *homoeoptoton*, *interrogatio*, etc.); and *Chronicles of the Reigns of Stephen, Henry II and Richard I*, pp. 185 ff.

[120]*Gesta*, pp. 53-56; also pp. 9, 18-19, 22, 24-25, 30, 33-34, 36, 46, 50, 64, and so on.

[121]*Raymond d'Aguilers*, pp. 122-24, for example.

[122]Sayers, "The Beginnings and Early Development of Old French Historiography," pp. 284, 297, 359 ff. On William of Newburgh's "frequent use of dialogue," see Partner, *Serious Entertainments*, p. 207. Auerbach, *Mimesis*, comments most interestingly on the contrasting use of direct speech in "primitive" and "rhetorical" historians, pp. 34, 40, 75-77.

[123]Sayers, "The Beginnings and Early Development of Old French Historiography," pp. 359 ff.; and see, for example, the dialogue between Karbuqa and his mother in *Gesta*, pp. 53 ff.

[124]Streuver, *The Language of History in the Renaissance*, pp. 123, 127-28.

[125]Otto of Freising, *Gesta* 3.xvi(xv)-xviii(xvii) and 2.xxix(xxi)-xxx. See also Wiseman, *Clio's Cosmetics*, pp. 28-30.

[126]Odo of Deuil, *De profectione Ludovici VII in orientem*, ed. and trans. V. Berry (New York, 1948), pp. 104, 129-33. Speeches are often set singly as vivid summaries of a position; see, for example, pp. 79, 99. See also Baudry, *HC* 4:83.

[127]Otto, *Gesta* 2.xxv.

[128]On such "eternal verities" see Vessey, "William of Tyre: Apology and Apocalypse," and Ray, "Orderic Vitalis on Henry I: Theocratic Ideology and Didactic Narrative," 128 ff.

[129]Streuver, *The Language of History in the Renaissance*, pp. 118 ff.

[130]See *Crisis in the Humanities*, ed. J. H. Plumb (Penguin Books, 1964), pp. 24-44; G. Connell-Smith and H. A. Lloyd, *The Relevance of History* (London, 1972); G. S. Jones in *Ideology in Social Science*, ed. R. Blackburn (Glasgow, 1978), ch. 6; and A. Megill, "Foucault, Structuralism and the Ends of History, *Journal of Modern History*, 51 (1979), 500-03.

[131]Odo, *De profectione Ludovici VII*, pp. 4-5; Ray, "Orderic Vitalis and William of Poitiers," p. 1119.

[132]Odo, *De profectione Ludovici VII*, pp. 4-5.

[133]The errors involved in supposing that *sermo humilis* was intended to reflect what we call "fact" are well put by Ray, "Medieval Historiography Through the Twelfth Century," p. 50.

THE SENSE OF TIME IN WESTERN HISTORICAL NARRATIVES FROM EUSEBIUS TO MACHIAVELLI

DONALD J. WILCOX

The Renaissance Narrative of Change

From Petrarch to Guicciardini, few themes more fascinated Renaissance thinkers than the meaning of change. They perceived changes that had escaped the notice of previous centuries, changes such as the fall of the Roman Empire and the coming of the Dark Ages. They also saw clearly and precisely more recent changes, especially the calamitous collapse of Italian culture in the wake of the Spanish and French invasions at the beginning of the sixteenth century.[1] The explicit concern for change among Renaissance writers during the invasions is particularly striking. In the *Prince*, Machiavelli chose the most volatile and changeable of states, a new principate, to discuss his ideas about politics and statecraft. Guicciardini opened his *History of Italy* on a theme of overwhelming change, calling human affairs unstable, like a sea whipped by the winds.[2]

Many elements of Renaissance culture combined to produce this insight into change. In part it can be traced to the growth of historical consciousness during the period. Starting with Petrarch's letters to the ancients, Renaissance humanists, realizing that classical authors were not abstract authorities but actual persons living in a specific time, sought to discover the meaning of classical texts by identifying their historical context. By the fifteenth century they had produced a body of scholarship which defined the nature of specific times with greater and greater precision.[3]

Within this tradition of scholarship the Florentine humanists of the fifteenth century made a particularly important contribution. Leonardo Bruni and his successors turned their attention to Florence's own past and explained the political realities which lay behind the important changes of Florentine history. Identifying the psychological vigor produced by republican institutions, they argued that the secret of Florence's greatness lay in its constitution. Changes in the constitution could explain and tie together the many changes through which Florence had passed since it had become an independent city.[4]

To master fully the problem of change, however, Renaissance writers needed more than a scholarly tradition to perceive it and a theoretical apparatus to explain it. They also needed a means of narrating it. Neither theory nor scholarship sufficed to give dynamic reality to events themselves as they unfolded into a meaningful story. Such a narrative, in which events were intrinsically interrelated, was also a major achievement of the Renaissance, but a truly dynamic narrative did not emerge until the early sixteenth century. Machiavelli achieved such a narrative in his *Florentine Histories*, written between 1520 and 1524.

The *Florentine Histories* are particularly instructive because he used earlier historians with whom his narrative can be compared. In the introduction to his work Machiavelli acknowledged the humanists who preceded him in writing histories of the city, Leonardo Bruni and Poggio Bracciolini.[5] He did, in fact, owe much to these earlier historians, as well as to the vernacular chroniclers of Florence.[6] But Machiavelli began his account with the barbarian invasions, and Bruni and Poggio, who started with the founding of Florence, could offer him little help there. Instead, he relied on the *Decades* of Flavio Biondo, both as a source of facts and as a model for organization. Biondo, writing from 1439 to 1442, more than half a century before the *Florentine Histories*, surveyed the history of the Middle Ages starting with the invasion of Rome by the Goths in 410. His history is noted for its antiquarian research, and many generations of historians mined its pages for details of the past.[7]

The fall of Rome was a change of particular importance both to Biondo and to Machiavelli, and a comparison of the two accounts is helpful in illuminating how Machiavelli used events to express important changes. Biondo offered his readers both a theory to explain the change and a scholarly description of the invasions themselves, but he failed to organize his account so that the reader could see a connection between the theory and the scholarship. He cited in his introduction three possible reasons for the success of the barbarian invasions: oppression by the emperors after they had transferred the capital to Constantinople; the Fates, which determine that all empires die after a certain time; and the persecution of the Christians.[8] This list of causes is not wholly consistent. The first suggests the kind of pragmatic political analysis so dear to the hearts of the Florentine humanists. The second evokes the cyclical view of history so common among classical writers, while the third is a specifically Christian interpretation suggesting the vengeance of a personal God concerned with the Christian collectivity. The inconsistency among these explanations is typical of Biondo's general approach to history and is partly due to the complexity of historical traditions influencing Renaissance writers.[9]

The inconsistencies hardly matter, however, for when Biondo actually narrated the barbarian invasions, he paid little attention to any of these general causes. Instead, he simply noted that whatever the cause, the fall of Rome began with the Goths. He detailed their origins, wanderings, and battles, concluding with a summary of the state of Rome at the death of Theodosius, after the first wave of barbarian invasions. At no time in this account did Biondo try to explain how even a single invasion was directly linked to any of the three general causes he identified in his introduction. He wrote without assuming that these two parts of his work had any intrinsic connection.

Machiavelli, by contrast, integrated the didactic, explanatory element of his history with the narrative order by focusing on particular events and using these to convey his general explanation. Beginning with the increase in population of the German tribes, Machiavelli led his readers through an increasingly complex network of events, each explained without sacrificing its uniqueness, until they understood how the fall of Rome could have happened. He described how the German tribes handled the problem of overpopulation, then talked about the political change—moving the capital to Constantinople—that left the western empire open to the migrations of the Germans. Only after narrating these actual events did he describe the general situation.

> Indeed to destroy such an empire, founded on the blood
> of so many virtuous men, required no less foolishness
> in the princes or disloyalty in the ministers than force

and obstinacy in those who attacked it, since not only
a single people but many joined together to ruin it.[10]

Machiavelli did not intend this assessment as a comprehensive
psychological theory for the fall; it was simply a means of leading
the reader into the following passage which discussed the various
tribes which participated in the invasions.

Machiavelli's narrative is less static and more expressive of
change partly because he avoided strict chronological and geographic order in favor of a thematic narrative. Biondo, in discussing the Visigothic invasion, traced in some detail the route
of Alaric moving towards the sack of Rome. Machiavelli concentrated instead on the schemes of Stilicho, whose mistreatment of
the Visigoths provided an example of how an unjust government
can lead to revolt. To draw our attention to that theme, Machiavelli had to convey the exact relation between Alaric's sack of
Rome and Stilicho's devious policy. Thus, Machiavelli ignored the
geographic details in Biondo, saying simply, "the Visigoths, de-
prived of their provisions, created Alaric their king to be better
organized to avenge their injuries, and, having attacked the empire, after many events lay waste to Italy, seized Rome, and sacked
the city."[11] At the beginning of the following chapter Machiavelli
selected details from several different sections of Biondo's work,
where he found the events in strict chronological order, and rearranged them thematically to give a general picture of the dis-
orders which afflicted the west as the emperors turned their
attention more and more to the east. Biondo had also mentioned
the theme that absentee government never functions well, but
Machiavelli's organization threw it into relief and tied it explicitly
to the shifting events of the invasions.

The *Florentine Histories* convey a sense of time deeper, richer,
and more pervasive than mere chronological order; they convey
a sense that gives structure to the whole while resisting all efforts
at precise definition or systematized expression. This dynamic
picture of the past contrasts with Biondo's static description of
a series of events that illustrate general principles, a philosophy
teaching by examples.

What, then, did Machiavelli add to his narrative? It will be
argued here that Machiavelli created a dynamic narrative by
blending a number of elements from the previous tradition of
western historical writing, including the civic humanism of the
Florentine historians, the Augustinian notion of personal reality,

170

and the narrative techniques of Tacitus. He encountered these three elements in a variety of sources. He was an early admirer of Tacitus and read the civic humanists as sources for his own history of Florence. His exposure to the Augustinian notion of personal reality was more indirect. He came in contact with the tradition of medieval historiography in two ways: through the Florentine vernacular chronicles and, indirectly, through his humanist sources who relied on Orosius and other medieval writers for their material on long-past events. But these medieval historians and chroniclers did not write narratives in which personal realities play a central role.

In a broader sense, Augustinian theology had, by the time of the Renaissance, become a major element in the way experience was perceived. Recent scholarship has focused on personality as a key element of the Augustinian tradition that deeply influenced Renaissance humanists, particularly those in Florence. The Augustinian tradition saw man not as an objectifiable part of the order of nature but as the mysterious creation of a personal God. As William Bouwsma has said, "Augustinian humanism saw man, not as a system of objectively distinguishable, discrete faculties reflecting ontological distinctions in the cosmos, but as a mysterious and organic unity."[12] References to Augustinian ideas in the pages that follow should be understood in this context.

The following sections will illustrate the static nature of medieval historical narratives and analyze Machiavelli's use of his sources and models in an attempt to clarify the nature of his achievement.

Medieval Narratives of Change

Medieval narratives lacked the dynamic quality of Machiavelli's work. Events in medieval histories took on meaning as illustrations of abstract categories but not through any inherent traits. Because of their dependence on abstract categories, medieval historians did not narrate complex events leading to a single result without sacrificing chronological order. This section will examine the conceptual models historians used to interrelate events and the limitations these models imposed on their works.

Medieval narratives were based on several theoretical models for change. G. W. Trompf has shown that these had both biblical and classical roots and manifested two basic patterns.[13] One model

was linear, chronologically organized, and most commonly represented by age theory, which divided human history into a limited number of periods showing the progress of God's plan from
creation to the apocalypse. The other model was reciprocal; it
emphasized the vicissitudes of fortune in a manner similar to
classical writers. Both models related particular events to general, self-subsistent categories rather than to one another. Because of this abstract reference, the events did not have the internal
relationship which characterized Machiavelli's narrative.

To say that medieval historians related events to abstract
categories seems, on the face of it, an obvious generalization
about the medieval tradition. Certainly the medieval historians'
assumptions about divine intervention in history are too patent
to require comment. Yet, the issue goes beyond the divine intervention which all medieval historians assumed as part of the pattern of history. Divine intervention alone need not have prevented
medieval historians from developing effective techniques for narrating change. A dynamic narrative can as easily be present in a
religious history as in a secular one. God can be incorporated
into the historical process in ways that do not diminish the inherent connections between the actual events.

Consider the climactic scene in Augustine's *Confessions*. He
introduced the events leading to his conversion by describing a
period of personal anguish and despair. The events flow naturally
and are interrelated; we recognize his human reactions and motives. He left the house because he felt it more proper to weep
alone. He heard the voice of the child and wondered whether it
could have originated from a natural source like a child's game.
He interpreted the phrase *tolle et lege* as an injunction to open
the scriptures and read the first passage he encountered because
he had just read of St. Anthony's doing that. Since he had recently
been studying St. Paul, he turned to that apostle and read the
first passage his eyes fell upon. Only then did he describe the
change. "Instantly, in truth, at the end of this sentence, as if
before a peaceful light streaming into my heart, all the dark shad-
ows of doubt fled away."[14]

God explicitly intervened as a direct cause of events only
once in this chapter, when Augustine interpreted the child's voice
as a divine command, and even then the writer alluded to the
events in his own life which predisposed him to think so. He
narrated all of the events as necessary parts of the change, each
dependent on the ones that came before and each contributing an

essential element to the final result. None served only to illustrate a general causative principle. Implicit was the view, of course, that the entire sequence of events was caused by God and was part of His will for Augustine, but this aspect alone did not determine the narrative's structure. The events are related simultaneously to one another and to the transcendent reality which gives meaning to them all.

In describing his own personal development, Augustine could narrate meaningful change by grounding it in the visible reality of his own body, the development and change of which formed a continuing background to the spiritual changes. In the scene just described, all spiritual changes were expressed as changes in physical position or perception. Readers can see his conversion as a temporal event because they have no doubts about Augustine's movements into the garden and his hearing of the voice. Augustine, the biographer, could thus make use of the physical unity of the subject to narrate personal religious history. When he came to narrate general events as a historian, describing the movements of groups and institutions, Augustine was not so successful in presenting a convincing picture of change. Although he developed a theoretical model that explained the reality and direction of historical change by showing the differing fates of the two cities, his *City of God* did not attempt a narrative picture of history. Instead, he concentrated on particular conceptual and historical problems associated with this model.

Divine intervention alone is not, then, a sufficient explanation for the lack of a dynamic narrative among medieval historians. Nor are the two orders—chronological for the linear model and moral for the reciprocal one—such simple alternatives as they may seem in giving structure to medieval narratives. Medieval historians blended these in many imaginative ways to produce vigorous and memorable stories, but none managed to separate events from the abstract concepts which gave them meaning.

At first the problems of using chronological order to convey the meaning of the past were overwhelming. The historians' concern to locate historical events in chronological relation to the Incarnation did not lead to any sense of the general significance of temporal relations. Eusebius, who was in so many ways the father of Christian historiography, separated chronological studies from an inquiry into the meaning of events. He was preoccupied with chronology not only in his *Chronological Tables*, which listed in parallel columns the events of human history, but in his

173

Ecclesiastical History, which included as one of his major topics the succession of bishops from the Holy Apostles to his own time.

Eusebius' preoccupation with chronology did not lead him to assess the significance of the order of events; the order existed for its own sake and led to no inquiry into its meaning. The fact that he let the chronology stand alone is most apparent toward the end of the *Ecclesiastical History*, where he summed up his preceding narrative. After a brief digression on Dionysius of Alexandria, he announced that he would now describe the events of his own time so that those who came afterwards would know about them. The importance of the topic might have led him to assess some general characteristics of these events, but he did not. In fact, he devoted the passage primarily to a catalogue of bishops and emperors down to the year 305, to which he added some letters describing the lives and doctrines of heretical movements and a work on the celebration of Easter.[15] His most explicit summation is found at the end of Book 7, where he introduced the persecutions of Diocletian. Eschewing deeper intentions, he said simply, "we have described the subject [*upothesin*] of the successions from the birth of our Savior to the destruction of our churches in 305 years."[16]

Medieval historians did not use chronological order to give meaning to specific events. Instead, they employed reciprocal models to explain events as the just punishment or reward of a personal God. Eusebius' other chief topics, especially the calamities suffered by the Jews after the Crucifixion and the persecutions of the Christians before the conversion of Constantine, take on meaning through these retributive themes. Eusebius thought that the sufferings of these two groups had completely different meanings, that the Jews were being punished while the Christians were being tried in preparation for ultimate victory. Although the historian made this distinction clear in his direct statements, his actual narrative did not show that pattern so plainly. In Book 4, for instance, he described the differing fates of the Jews and the Christians during the reign of Trajan: "Thus indeed the teaching and the church of our Savior flourished and daily grew and progressed, while truly the misfortunes of the Jews grew as disaster succeeded disaster" (4.2). He did go on to list a series of reverses suffered by the Jews in different parts of the east, though not in any progressive order. But the brief passage preceding the quotation did not show a progressive growth of the church and teaching of the Christians. Eusebius was content to list the succession

174

of the Bishops of Alexandria and Rome. Neither his account of the Christians nor that of the Jews illustrated the progressive pattern he described in his abstract statement.

Later on, when he narrated the Great Persecution, he again failed to offer a detailed illustration of complex divine judgement. On that occasion he seemed more aware of the shortcomings of his account, for he noted that he would not describe the misfortunes of the Christians or detail their quarrels and cruelty to one another before the persecutions. Instead he would record just enough to satisfy divine judgement (8.2). He described the actual persecutions as an episodic series of unrelated martyrdoms in various parts of the empire.

The disjunction between his chronological and retributive themes lent an episodic quality to his account of major events. Even the conversion of the Empire to Christianity, which is the major event of the work, was broken up into episodic sections which expressed Eusebius' major retributive themes at the expense of chronological clarity. Persecutors of Christianity, like Galerius or Maximin Daia, suffered the torment of hideous diseases (8.16 and 9.10), while Constantine was victorious because of his piety (9.9). Eusebius constantly reminded the readers of the retribution that resulted from each event. What does not emerge from the narrative is a picture of the complex process by which particular political and personal factors led to the final result. Some have attacked Eusebius for this failing by saying that he was overly concerned to exalt his benefactor, Constantine.[17] Partisanship alone, however, was not the decisive factor. Eusebius lacked the conviction that the particular events leading to the conversion had a meaning in relation to one another. Therefore, he felt each important event had to be an explicit illustration of God's punishment or reward. For example, Eusebius did not care why the infantry which Licinius trusted so fully let him down when he met Maximin Daia in battle; it was enough to say that Licinius had been hostile and treacherous to the Christians and that God had deserted him.[18]

Nevertheless, Eusebius was concerned with the chronological order of events leading to the conversion. He began Book 9, which described the victory of Christianity in the east, with Maximin's renewed persecution and the outbreak of famine and pestilence (as God punished the cities of the east for attacking the Christians) and ended it with the death of Maximin and the cessation of persecution. This order remains an abstract and fixed sequence, lacking the dynamic quality that might give depth and background. Eusebius even mentioned Maximin's death three times when narrating the three separate events which led to his final defeat. Each event thus manifested a clear and distinct significance which could be understood without taking into account any other part of the narrative. Neither of Eusebius' goals—the demonstration that history represented the retributive judgement of God and the establishment of the chronological order—required the sense of time found in Machiavelli's narrative. Both goals located events in relation to fixed realities: one a transcendent moral order that used events as illustrations, and the other a simple chronological sequence which was as static and unchanging as a numerical series.

Other historians of the early Middle Ages also had difficulties integrating these twin themes of chronology and retributive justice into a single narrative. They could not present individual events as reflecting both the order of God's plan for history and the moral order of virtue and vice. Orosius, for instance, who shared Eusebius' interest in these issues, often found he could not use events to convey chronological and moral order. His narrative of Hannibal's failure to capture Rome can serve as an example. He described Hannibal's progress through Italy and the defeat of the Roman armies as a series of military encounters, culminating in the salvation of Rome by a sudden hailstorm which prevented the rival armies from engaging outside the gates of the city. In the order of the narrative, he stressed the vicissitudes of fortune without any other meaning emerging from the sequence of events. He even quoted Hannibal's observation that he could have taken Rome twice, but on one occasion he lacked the desire, while on the second he lacked the power.[19] This observation leads readers to see unpatterned alternation of fortune in the events. To incorporate the incident into his thesis of patterned temporal change, Orosius added a section explaining that God saved Rome for her future faith in Christ just as he had punished her with Hannibal for her present unbelief. This retributive theme is buttressed, however, not by reference to any events surrounding Hannibal's invasion, but by citing a drought in Orosius's own times, which was relieved by Christian prayers after pagan ones had failed.[20] Orosius viewed the overall chronological order as a thing in itself whose meaning could be demonstrated by events from any point in the sequence. He sacrificed the peculiar importance of Hannibal's actual invasion to a clearer description of the abstract meaning of the general sequence of time from creation to his own day.

In quoting from Hannibal, Orosius actually undermined the meaning of the chronological sequence by invoking the notion of unpatterned alternation. On other occasions, he showed himself willing to use classical explanatory devices which blurred the divine pattern even of religious events. In recounting the fate of Sodom, Orosius explained its decay by the fertility of its land, which brought abundance. This abundance was the cause of its ruin, since it produced luxury, and luxury gave rise to disgraceful passions.[21] Orosius' source for this explanation of the sin of Sodom is certainly not biblical. In Genesis, Sodom was already deep in sin when the story began, while Wisdom gave no historical background to the city's reputation.[22] Augustine simply observed that Sodom was fertile, drawing his information from the reference in Genesis to its being the paradise of God.[23] The most likely source of Orosius' interpretation is Sallust, whom he much admired and who was widely influential among medieval historians in general.[24] Sallust, among all classical historians, was clearest in tracing moral corruption to an increase in wealth and the accompanying luxury. Orosius' explanation, however, does not fit clearly into his linear model, for he did not see an overall pattern in the alternation of wealth and poverty in human history.

Even Orosius' most distinctive contribution to historical theory, his notion of successive empires, was not well integrated into his narrative. Trompf has pointed out that he based these successive empires on the assumption that there were recurrent patterns in history that gradually made clear God's intentions.[25] He applied this assumption to the persecutions of the Christians from Nero to Diocletian. At the end of Book 6 he analyzed the persecutions from a theoretical standpoint and explained their significance as punishment for sins. He also promised to set forth in the following book the persecutions themselves and the punishment that was visited on the persecutors.[26] In Book 7 he did, indeed, record the sufferings of the Christians and the wretched fates of those who had led the persecutions, but put no general order on this story until he came to the Great Persecution of Diocletian. Then, he reviewed the whole story of the persecutions, saying that the ten persecutions from Nero to Diocletian were like the ten plagues of Egypt. Just as the Egyptians lost their first born as the tenth plague, so the tenth persecution resulted in the destruction of the pagan gods themselves and the conversion of the empire to Christianity. So convinced was Orosius of this pattern that he believed another persecution would follow to parallel the pursuit of the Israelites into the Red Sea.[27]

He used this elaborate theoretical discussion of the connection between the plagues and the persecutions as an introduction to the reign of Constantine. When he came to that period, however, the model was forgotten, and he narrated Constantine's rise to power and the defeat of his rivals, alternating descriptions of military victories with descriptions of God's punishment of the persecutors. This narrative is less repetitious than Eusebius', but it is no more successful at integrating the themes of military and political change with that of God's vengeance. He explained Licinius' death, for instance, solely by Constantine's political machinations, without mentioning the issue of divine punishment. The positive aspect of Constantine's conversion, the favor he received from God, received much less attention than Eusebius devoted to it. One might expect Orosius, lacking Eusebius' immediate interest in flattery, to be less effusive, but he ignored Constantine's good fortune completely and passed directly from the death of Licinius to a narrative of the Arian heresy and of Constantine's brutal attacks on his own family (6.28).

In effect, Orosius' concern to narrate history as a series of disasters overcame his search for meaning in the linear pattern of historical events. According to his theory, this meaning is found in the beneficial effects of the gradual spread of Christianity. Yet, his inability to bring together chronological and retributive themes in a single narrative forced Orosius to concentrate on the disasters which emerged, even from the conversion of the empire. He did, on occasion, note the decline in evil in the world since the conversion of Constantine,[28] and he did have a theoretical explanation of this process, but he could not express it through the narrative of particular events. In his narrative, such issues were subordinated to the abstract chronological order and the theme of God's retributive justice.

More is involved here than the fact that these writers did not explain the theological significance of the survival of Rome or the conversion of Constantine. To integrate such events into the divine plan is a challenge for any writer, and failure should occasion no surprise. The striking feature of these narratives is that the events were given order only by reference to abstractions; they had no specific internal relationship. They lacked, therefore, any intrinsic meaning dependent upon the temporal sequence in which they occurred. This feature of medieval histories emerges even more clearly when we examine how historians of that period narrated events not explicitly conceived as part of the divine plan.

An excellent example of such a narrative is found in the writings of Gregory of Tours. Gregory, although he set forth as his principal goal the establishment of the proper chronological sequence of events from the beginning of the world to his own time, did not see a clear order in this sequence. In the general preface to his *History of the Franks*, he observed ingenuously, "many things are happening, some good and some bad,"[29] and he began the second book by noting that the order in which he presented events followed the mixed and confused manner in which they occurred, blending the virtues of the saints with the butchery of peoples.[30]

Lacking a sense that the chronological order of events had a significance of its own, he gave his events meaning through the theme of the retributive justice of God. Sometimes the reasons for the punishments were clear, such as Athanaric's expulsion from his kingdom because he tortured Christians[31] or the loss of the fortress at Vollore because of an earlier offense by its priest against St. Quintinianus (3.13). At other times he was less careful to integrate conventional social and political virtues into his retributive model. Clovis, in particular, enjoyed God's favor despite his part in some of the most brutal stories in the work. In one particularly striking passage, Gregory recounted how Clovis induced Sigibert's son to assassinate his father and then seized his kingdom and killed the son for committing parricide. Commenting on Clovis' success, Gregory observed, "day in and day out God submitted the enemies of Clovis to his dominion and increased his power, for he walked before him with an upright heart and did what was pleasing in his sight" (2.40). Even the Old Testament with its accounts of crafty but religiously correct kings could not provide an adequate model for Gregory's seeming blindness to ordinary political virtues.[32] The retributive aspect of history was even robbed of specific moral content.

As an example of the peculiarities which these features introduced into his narrative, consider the passage in Book 3, in which he tried to explain how the citizens of Verdun became so prosperous. He told how Desideratus, the Bishop of Verdun, had asked King Theudebert for a loan, which Theudebert had granted out of compassion. From this, Gregory commented, the citizens became rich and remained so in his own day.[33] Had he stopped

179

there he would have explained to his readers the historical origin of a contemporary phenomenon. Instead, he complicated the event by recounting a later conversation between Desideratus and Theudebert in which the king rejected the bishop's offer to return the money. Gregory commented on this, "by demanding nothing in the way of repayment he made the aforesaid citizens rich."[34]

It is hard for the modern reader to tell exactly what point Gregory was trying to make here. He was certainly stressing the charity of King Theudebert—a virtue conspicuously lacking in his predecessor, Theuderic, who plundered the diocese of Verdun and imprisoned Desideratus. Perhaps he also meant to point out that the citizens of Verdun did not ask for charity, since the bishop, when requesting the loan, specifically said he would pay it back with interest. What is clear is that Gregory did not perceive, in the wealth of Verdun, a series of events related in time and producing a single result out of partial ones. He narrated the story in separate parts, much as Eusebius narrated the conversion of the Empire. Gregory did not tell his readers whether the citizens of Verdun got rich by using the money, keeping the loan, or both. Instead, he gave the reader a single result (their wealth), a combination of factors (the loan and its forgiveness), but no interrelationship among the factors to understand how they produced the result.

Underlying the narratives of these early historians, then, was an assumption that the reality of events was static. Events took on meaning through entities abstracted from history in general. One of the abstract entities was the chronological sequence which hypothesized divine meaning for every discrete event, but this abstraction was not implemented in the narrative to give particular events real individual meaning. The example from Gregory of Tours suggests that the static quality of medieval narratives was more than simply an inability to relate specific events to God's plan; it was an inherent tendency to ignore the meaning of complex chronological relationships.

Several medieval historians succeeded in narrating complex events leading to a single result. Bede and Otto of Freising spring to mind as historians interested in using their narratives to convey their sense of the dual nature of the historical process. A close analysis of their narratives, however, reveals that they accomplished their purpose only by breaking chronological continuity, by confusing the chronological order, or by other practices which

180

displayed their indifference to the intrinsic temporal connections among the events they narrated.

Among Bede's central themes was the spread of Christianity in Britain. He saw this change as both intellectual and spiritual, and he sought to interrelate the factors of learning and piety in his narrative. His description of the conversion of the monks of Iona, a major example of this theme, shows his willingness to break up the chronological sequence to integrate these particular themes. When he first mentioned Iona he noted that Columba, who founded it, instilled piety in his followers.[35] This piety was marred, however, by their celebrating Easter at the wrong date, and Bede felt it was important to interrupt the chronological narrative to tell the reader that 150 years later the monks of Iona were finally brought to full Catholicism by the efforts of Bishop Egbert. Bede took some pains to show that this final conversion was effected by an increase in knowledge. The monks, he said, were pious Christians who celebrated Easter on Sunday, but since they were *barbari et rustici*, they lacked the knowledge to calculate the correct Sunday. Since they did not fail in the grace of charity, they deserved to learn the truth, and Egbert, a man of both piety and learning, was able to teach it to them.

Much later in the book, Bede returned to the subject in its proper chronological place. He again narrated the conversion of the monks of Iona to the canonical rite of Easter, but this time he impressed on his readers its significance within God's general plan for the English. He observed,

> it is clear that this happened by a wonderful dispensation of divine mercy, since that race had willingly and ungrudgingly taken pains to communicate its own knowledge and understanding of God to the English nation; and now, through the English nation, they are brought to a more perfect way of life in matters wherein they were lacking (5.22).

Bede here adopted the theme of retributive justice which played such an important part in earlier historiography. To underline his point, he noted that the Britons, who did not try to convert the English, remained themselves unconverted to the canonical date and tonsure which were the signs of full membership in the Catholic Church. In this version, Bede expressed in a narrative of particular events two important themes—God's justice in history, and human progress through learning and piety. Furthermore, he brought these themes to his readers' attention without sacrificing the implicit interrelation of the several events. The conversion was not only a reward for the monks' piety and, thus, an example of divine justice; it was also a natural result of their instruction and learning, which removed specific obstacles to observing the proper date.

In describing the conversion of the monks of Iona, Bede showed himself willing to break chronological order to make a point, relying for clarity on geographical and racial continuity. He put this chronological flexibility to conceptual as well as organizational uses, as is particularly evident in his treatment of the end of Roman power in Britain. Bede wished to present certain important moral lessons, but before doing so he called his readers' attention to his organizational categories. He began by detailing the geographical and racial elements that contributed to the invasions. First he described the geographical boundaries of Roman Britain, fixing these as clearly as he could in his readers' minds by noting that an earthwork, whose traces could be observed in his own day, formed the northern border of the Roman occupation. He also described the estuaries that cut deeply into the island from east to west and separated the land of the Picts from the rest of Britain. When he discussed the wall the Romans built to help keep the invaders out, he again reminded his readers that it could be seen in their own time. The origins and eventual places of settlement for the Angles, Saxons, and Jutes were all clearly described. These tribal and geographical units provided a framework within which Britain changed its polity from that of a Roman colony to the kingdoms found in his day (1.11-16).

Bede portrayed the invasions as an example of God's retributive justice; they were divine punishment for the sins of the Britons. In focusing on the latter, he paid scant attention to the issue of Roman decline. He remarked simply that

> Rome was taken by the Goths in the eleven hundred and sixty fourth year after its foundation; after this the Romans ceased to rule in Britain, almost four hundred and seventy years after Gaius Julius Caesar had come to the island (1.11).

Like other medieval historians, Bede failed to see the intellectual and cultural significance of Roman decline. As far as he was concerned, the changes that occurred after the departure of the legions were solely military. As to the fall of Rome itself, he ascribed this to the murder of the emperor by a personal enemy, feeling no need to draw any larger lesson out of it (1.21).

Bede obviously wished to emphasize that the invasions were direct punishment for the Britons' luxurious and sinful behavior. In keeping with this goal, he gave only the briefest attention to the fact that their lack of military prowess made the Britons an easy prey for invaders (1.12). Not content to make this retributive point abstractly, he described in detail the historical process by which the Britons lapsed into wicked ways. After the Romans left, he said, some Britons, trusting in God's help, hid in mountains, caves, and forests, and gradually drove the Picts and Scots away until the raids ceased. But their troubles were not over:

> After the enemy's depredations had ceased, there was so great an abundance of corn in the island as had never before been known. With this affluence came an increase of luxury, followed by every kind of foul crime, in particular cruelty and hatred of truth and love of lying increased. . . . They cast off Christ's easy yoke and thrust themselves under the burden of drunkenness, hatred, quarreling, strife, and envy and other similar crimes (1.14).

For this they were punished by a plague, but when disease failed to correct them, worse was to follow.

> For this reason a still more terrible retribution soon afterwards overtook this sinful people for their fearful crimes. They consulted as to what they should do and where they should seek help to prevent or repel the fierce and very frequent attacks of the northern nations; all, including their king Vortigern, agreed that they should call the Saxon peoples to their aid from across the seas. As events plainly showed this was ordained by the will of God so that evil might fall upon these miscreants (1.14).

Bede filled his account of the ensuing conquest of the island with references to the Old Testament and with vivid descriptions of pillage.[36]

Bede constructed his narrative to teach an important lesson, that history showed a pattern of divine judgement, but he did so at the price of chronological confusion. Important questions are left unanswered. When and why did the raids from the north begin again, necessitating the fateful invitation to the Saxons, Angles, and Jutes? Bede had previously told us that the Britons had recovered their military prowess and stopped the raids. Perhaps the internal quarrels he alluded to reopened the way for the Picts. Bede did not say so, though he easily could have explained it in a simple phrase. Probably the question arose neither in his own mind nor that of his readers. Obviously, his lesson was not blunted by lack of a clear chronological sequence, as its clarity would apparently have suffered had the geographical and racial origins of the invaders been left ambiguous. The latter were more important to eighth-century perceptions of change than a clear chronological order. Bede gave the invasions reality and meaning not by explaining how the events themselves unfolded in chronological relation to one another, but by explaining how they reflected the judgement of God. He dramatized this judgement by expatiating on the wickedness of the Britons and by describing in sharp and concrete words the suffering visited upon them. The impact of the lesson depended on the drama, not on the chronological order.

These examples have demonstrated Bede's interest in complex secular events as well as complex religious ones. He was also concerned to interrelate the religious and secular dimensions of events, but as the following example will show, he accomplished this only at the expense of their inherent chronological relationship. When he discussed Bishop Wilfrid's conversion of the people around the monastery at Bosanham, he said that the Bishop's preaching saved them not only from eternal damnation but also from a cruel death in this world, for on the very day of their baptism a rain fell that broke three years of drought, which had been years of terrible famine—a famine that Bede described in lurid detail. By this miracle the people came to understand how God had granted them both material and spiritual blessings.

Here Bede recorded a simple miracle, demonstrating the connection between the spiritual and physical worlds that formed the heart of his historical theory. The story could stand by itself were he not also interested in explaining why the people were receptive to the bishop's preaching even before the rain fell. In doing so, he recounted another story that raised chronological problems. According to Bede, the people accepted the bishop's ministry because he had taught them to fish, first by offering them part of his own catch and then showing them how to make use of the plentiful supply of fish in the local waters. "By this good turn the bishop won the hearts of all, and they had greater hope of heavenly blessings from the preaching of one by whose aid they had gained temporal blessings."[37] The exact chronological relation between the fishing, the famine, and the conversion cannot be easily determined from this account. Possibly Bede's vivid description of emaciated and starving people throwing themselves off cliffs belongs to the period before they learned to fish, not to that immediately preceding their baptism; possibly the fishing had become poor in the period just before baptism. In either case, strict chronological order would probably have blunted the miracle that constituted Bede's main point in the story.

In a historian less concerned about credibility, such problems as these could be blamed on carelessness or indifference. Bede, however, was determined to convince his reader of his accuracy. In the preface he discussed his sources and presented various arguments to show that he could be trusted.[38] Furthermore, he could easily have avoided the problem of temporal sequence by ignoring the historical background of the miraculous examples of God's justice. Orosius had simply stated that Sodom fell into luxury as a necessary consequence of the fertility of its soil; the historical process by which it happened did not interest him. Bede was too aware of the historical context to dismiss it so easily. He saw that events, even miraculous ones, happened against a background of other real events. Furthermore, he knew that historical events had a chronological sequence which could be determined, but that chronological sequence did not provide the events with an intrinsic significance. Unlike Machiavelli, he did not feel that the historian could derive meaning from a careful examination of the chronological order. Instead, meaning came from the relation of specific events to abstract, transcendent verities. Thus, when Bede broke chronological sequence to narrate important themes, he felt free to ignore the implied temporal order to make his point. His preconceptions of historical reality did not depend on orderly development in time of one event into another.

Of all the historians of the period none had a more clearly articulated model for significant historical change than Otto of Freising.[39] He drew from St. Augustine a developmental relationship between the City of God and the City of Man. He looked beyond the simple interest in the earthly city's miseries that had so preoccupied Orosius. For Otto, particular events of history were meaningful not only because they were related to transcendent reality and moral values, but also because they were the unfolding of actual political, ecclesiastical, spiritual, or intellectual trends.

When Otto narrated complex political events, this model did not emerge so clearly. He did use secular categories which expressed growth and change, but these categories did not help him organize the details of the narrative. For example, when recounting how Pope Nicholas excommunicated Lothar for remarrying, he considered the event to reveal the growth of ecclesiastical power at the expense of the state. "Observe now that as the state declined the church became so powerful that it even judged kings."[40] To perceive such general trends without specific reference to transcendent moral or intellectual categories is certainly a major achievement.

Like his predecessors, however, Otto had difficulty organizing his story to support his conclusion. The statement just quoted is preceded by a narrative that seems to have other goals. First, Otto tried to make the event vivid and unforgettable. To this end, he described in detail how the king subverted Archbishop Gunther, how the queen was charged with incest, and how a new queen was chosen and ceremoniously crowned. Then Otto invoked the theme of retributive justice by describing how the churchmen who cooperated with Lothar came to disgrace. Evidence of the growth of ecclesiastical power is missing from the narrative. Instead, Otto pointed to its result: "In consequence of this [Lothar's excommunication] the gravest danger threatened him personally and his whole kingdom."[41] But he followed this statement by no concrete examples. Only when Otto returned to Lothar's affairs in the next chapter did he describe him as paying for his sins. Even so, his retribution was non-political and personal, for his army succumbed to heat and spider bites in Italy, and the king himself died of disease (6.4). Thus, Otto chose for his narrative dramatic details that were memorable and convincing, and he endowed them with meaning by invoking retributive justice. It was only when he stated a general conclusion that he made manifest the clarity with which he saw historical development in political change.

Otto treated larger historical trends in a similar fashion. Describing the growth of the Frankish kingdom, he observed that

by this time the peoples that before had inhabited provinces of the Romans—not kingdoms—were learning to
choose kings. Now they were learning to break loose
from the power of the Romans and to stand in the authority set up by their own discretion (4.32).

Once again, the supporting evidence is hardly apparent in the
narrative. The generalization is preceded by an anecdotal listing
of the early leaders of the Franks in which we read about Clo-
dion's long hair and Salagustus' law. It is followed by a list of the
geographical movements of the Franks and chronological roster
of successive leaders down to Clovis. The use of chronological
and geographical categories as organizing principles is identical
to the practice of earlier historians.

At times Otto tried to use chronological sequence directly to
explain the meaning of the events. When he described Pepin's
coronation, he dated it from the Incarnation and found it significant as the beginning of both the Carolingian dynasty and the
Roman popes' authority to change kingdoms (5.23). These two
developments, however, are obscured by the actual narrative. In
the preceding chapter, Otto described in some detail an earlier
ceremony in which Pepin had assumed the kingship by the authority of Pope Zachary. The modern reader is left confused as
to when the pontifical authority actually asserted itself. The confusion might easily have been avoided if Otto had narrated the
two events as contributing to a single result, but this he did not
do. In addition, Otto had little interest in tying these two developments together with a third that had occupied most of the narrative up to this point, namely, the Lombard invasions of Italy,
which led the popes to ally themselves with the Carolingians.
When Otto discussed the significance of Pope Stephen's coronation of Pepin, he made no reference to the Lombards, and only
a fleeting allusion is found in the preceding chapter which was
concerned with the earlier assumption of royal power. Not until
Chapter 25 did he describe Pepin's campaign against them, even
though that campaign was an essential factor in his alliance with
the pope. Otto did not seem to feel that the historian's task com-
pelled him to narrate such specific political interrelationships.

Otto was far more successful with intellectual progress than
political change. He described the actual events to show specific
intellectual trends. By comparison, Gregory of Tours, who also
felt that changes in intellectual capacity were an important part

187

of the historical process,[42] was singularly ineffective in giving concrete examples of the intellectual decline which he saw as part of his own times. When he described King Chilperic, whose unorthodox view of the Trinity might have provided him with a fine opportunity to demonstrate how decadence led to intellectual and spiritual decline, he was most interested in reassuring the reader that he and his fellow bishops effectively resisted the king's ideas (5.44). The entire passage on Chilperic's intellectual activities is anecdotal and provides no picture of their general significance.[43]

Otto, by contrast, did present intellectual progress as part of the actual events of his narrative. At the beginning of the work he explained Ninus' ability to conquer his empire by the fact that men were simple and rustic and had no training in warfare.[44] Since growth in intellectual capacity was so important to Otto, he was especially interested in particular intellectual achievements. In those sections of the work where he quoted from another source, such as Eusebius or Orosius, he frequently added only a discussion of intellectual events that they had omitted or insufficiently treated.[45] This notion of intellectual growth was not simply an abstract theory; it took on concrete meaning in the narrative. In Book 2, he discussed at length the growth of Greek philosophy, both analyzing the achievements and relating them to one another. He identified, for instance, Aristotle's contribution to the syllogism. Aristotle did not invent it, but he did give it a strict rule so that it was no longer made in a haphazard manner. To prove this, Otto quoted and analyzed a syllogism from Plato's writings, showing that it was not in the proper form set out in Aristotle's *Prior Analytics* (2.8).

Not all medieval historians were so concerned with models for change as the ones discussed here. Some, like the crusade chroniclers Joinville and Villehardouin, simply described events which they themselves participated in. The events took on order as illustrations of God's retributive justice, which tended to reinforce the moral values of their own social class.[46] The absence of an external chronological model did not strengthen the internal relationships among the events, however. Instead, these narratives often failed to relate specific events to general themes, even when the general themes were stated elsewhere in the work.

Joinville, for example, told of one complex battle in which the Christians suffered casualties from pursuing their enemy too far. Before the battle, the Templars had been assigned the vanguard, and the Count of Artois had agreed to follow with his men. Once the stream was crossed, however, the count attacked, to the annoyance of the Templars who insisted that he retreat. The count did not respond because the knight holding his reins was deaf. Not being able to hear the Templar's protests, he pushed on, shouting "After them! After them!" At this, the Templars attacked as well, and in the ensuing melee two hundred and eighty Templars were killed as well as the count himself. An important engagement, then, was lost as a result of the deafness of a single man. A modern reader might conclude that there were tactical lessons that could be learned from the event. It might, for instance, illustrate the importance of a unified command. Joinville often recorded his own conversations with King Louis in which he complained of the fragmented command as a source of weakness in the crusader army. Yet he failed to use this vivid battle scene to illustrate his general theme. The scene stood by itself, a rich and colorful incident in which a variety of particulars lead to a single result, but without any obvious larger significance.[47]

Despite the variety of conceptual models available to them, medieval historians did not present the events of their narratives as if they were inherently related in any temporal sense. The events took on meaning only through relation to abstract categories. Without a notion that the temporal relation of events has an inherent meaning, these historians could describe time only in a theoretical sense. Machiavelli's narrative of real political change, found in his *Florentine Histories*, stands, then, as a radical departure from the traditions of medieval historiography. The next sections will examine the nature of Machiavelli's achievement by contrasting his narrative with those of his immediate sources and models.

Machiavelli and the Florentine Historians

Two major perspectives on the ideas in Machiavelli's *Florentine Histories* have emerged in the past decade. They have greatly illuminated the work and made it easier to see its distinctive contribution to Machiavelli's intellectual development, but they do not provide answers to the questions about his view of change posed here.

The first perspective looks at the theory of historical corruption presented explicitly in the introductory chapters of Books 2 to 6 of the work. Felix Gilbert has brilliantly analyzed these in an essay for *Studies on Machiavelli*.[48] Gilbert focuses on the cyclical theory that held prominent place in his *Discourses* and lay at the root of his conviction that the study of history was useful. This cyclical theory, drawn largely from classical writers like Polybius, led Machiavelli to look for answers to the problems of Florentine political life in a comparison with ancient institutions.

As valuable as this observation is, there are reasons to believe that cyclical theory does not explain the most distinctive features of Machiavelli's narrative. Gilbert himself notes the recent discoveries of Eugenia Levi, which indicate that Machiavelli completed the narrative parts of the first six books before writing the introductions. Since these introductory chapters, which contain the explicit discussions of corruption and decay, are additions to an already completed text, they are unlikely to have served as organizing principles for the narrative itself. Furthermore, the cyclical theory of history has proved difficult to incorporate into any historical narrative. Arnaldo Momigliano has observed that no historian of the ancient world produced an actual history based on the cyclical recurrence of births and deaths.[49] Trompf has stressed the ambiguities and complexities of Polybius' cyclical theory and the difficulties he encountered in writing a narrative to support it. To illustrate Machiavelli's adaptation of this theory, Trompf refers more often to the *Discourses* than to Machiavelli's narrative works.

A second perspective on the *Florentine Histories* looks at Machiavelli's political biases and shows how he structured the narrative to bring out particular factional and constitutional issues that were important in his own day. The most recent and persuasive study of this type is that of Mark Phillips.[50] Referring to the expulsion of the Duke of Athens from Florence, Phillips describes Machiavelli's use of his sources in the following terms:

> Machiavelli accepted the constitutional framework Bruni had created but within it he restored the scene of violence Bruni expunged. Yet for all the sensuality of his description he established a sense of order absent from Villani's vivid narration. . . . He joined the general to the particular by putting universal considerations to work to understand and dramatize the particulars of the Florentine situation.[51]

Phillips explains Machiavelli's interest in the tangible elements of Florentine history by his personal relationship to the city and suggests that Machiavelli constructed his narrative from the chroniclers who wrote during the fourteenth and fifteenth centuries.

The present investigation takes a point of view that lies between the general theories stressed by Gilbert and the particular political issues to which Phillips draws attention. It seeks to clarify Machiavelli's distinctive understanding of the way in which historical events are interrelated and how these relationships give rise to historical meaning. Bruni's influence on Machiavelli was decisive in precisely this area. Machiavelli took from Bruni his political interests, not simply the rhetorical form he admitted to.[52] Both writers are fundamentally concerned with the exercise of power and the effect of various types of political decisions. By analyzing such matters, they sought to imbue their works with practical and moral value, which was an important goal of humanist history. In pursuit of these aims, both men looked to the same classical models, particularly Polybius and Tacitus.[53]

The similarity in political interests is clear not only in the accounts of such major events as the fall of Walter of Brienne or the Ciompi revolt, where Machiavelli might be expected to use a standard history like Bruni's. Machiavelli's dependence is also evident in the minor details, where he could easily have used chronicle sources if those had been his basic reference. Where the chronicles narrated the career of Corso Donati or the reforms following the death of Manfred as a complex variety of personal, familial, and political elements, Machiavelli followed Bruni in describing them as political actions.[54] Even where he supplemented Bruni's account with details from the chronicles, he was guided by the earlier historian's political interests and narrative order.[55]

More important, a vital part of Machiavelli's history lay in the observation of psychological and political abstractions, which were absent from the chronicles but formed the substance of Bruni's historical insight.[56] Machiavelli's borrowing went beyond a general use of such psychological categories as envy, hatred, fear, suspicion, ambition, discontent, or that elusive term *virtus*. He adopted the same abstractions Bruni used to explain the events of Florence's past. Where Bruni saw hatred, so did Machiavelli; where Bruni found fear, Machiavelli found it as well.[57]

In narrating the behavior of Walter of Brienne before his overthrow in 1343, Machiavelli stressed the fear and indignation he inspired in the Florentines, despite their initial support of his *signoria*. After Walter committed two unusually cruel and senseless acts, the dominant emotion of the Florentine citizens was hatred; Machiavelli no longer mentioned fear. The hatred, in turn, inspired the specific conspiracies that led to Walter's expulsion from the city. Thus, his overthrow was caused by a change in the psychological attitude of the citizens from fear to hatred.[58] Machiavelli's interest in this change will not surprise a reader familiar with his other works, since he stressed in the *Prince* that the ruler should be feared but not hated. That generalization, however, is not the original source of this particular interpretation. Rather, Machiavelli based his explanation of Walter's overthrow on a similar change narrated by Bruni, who said, "Since the situation seemed intolerable and the evils grew daily, hatred now overcame fear, and first there were various quarrels among the citizens, then conspiracies followed, indeed many at a time so that they were ignorant of each other."[59] The fact that hatred overcame fear at the moment effective resistance to Walter began is not found in the chronicle sources, which described Walter's acts and the outbreak of violence without reference to general psychological states.[60]

Bruni and Machiavelli agreed on another major event of Florentine history, the Ciompi revolt. Bruni emphasized the spread of discontent through all classes of Florentine society, beginning with the Guelfs, who misused the laws to attack their political enemies, continuing with Salvestro de' Medici, who tried to have the laws annulled by mobilizing popular pressure, and finally spreading to the lowest orders of society who tried to gain entrance to Florentine political life. Bruni drew from this revolt the practical lesson that discontent, once started, cannot be controlled if it induces a class to break the law.[61]

Machiavelli saw the revolt in precisely the same terms and drew the same lesson from it. His account in Book 3 concentrated on the spread of enmity through the various elements of Florentine life, noting that at each stage there was a growth of suspicion and discontent. He described the revival of the anti-Ghibelline laws and said, "everyone lived in such great suspicion and each feared ruin through either party."[62] After recounting Salvestro de' Medici's futile attempts to stop the popular uprising which he himself had stirred up, Machiavelli warned, "let no one create a change in a city thinking he can stop it when he wishes or guide it according to his own intentions."[63] For both Bruni and Machiavelli, changes in the attitude of the Florentine people were the key to understanding the origin, course, and aftermath of the revolt. They made their narratives didactic by telling us how these changes occurred and why they were important.

Machiavelli not only followed Bruni's psychological interpretation of the revolt, but he agreed that Florence's political institutions would not have survived without Michele di Lando, the lower class leader who moderated the extremist elements within the Ciompi and eventually led the forces of order in a successful counterrevolt. Bruni said of di Lando that only his *virtus* and constancy saved Florence from destruction. Machiavelli echoed "the tumult was put down only through the virtue of the Gonfaloniere, who in soul, prudence, and goodness was greater than any other citizen and deserves to be numbered among the few who have benefited their fatherland."[64] This view is a major departure from the chroniclers di Stefani and Gino Capponi, who either played down di Lando or regarded him as a rabble-rouser.[65]

From the foregoing discussion, it is clear that Machiavelli drew on Bruni as a major source of facts for his *Florentine Histories*. Today we regard the psychological and political elements he took from Bruni not as facts but as judgements which the historian made on the facts. This is, however, a post-Rankean distinction which Machiavelli did not make so clearly. To his eyes, Bruni's abstractions were simply facts. Machiavelli's interest in these facts is easy to understand, for they formed the basis of his own political theory, which saw distinctive patterns of behavior in political life. These patterns arose from common psychological attitudes, together with specific situations or institutions that affected these attitudes.

Bruni and Machiavelli differed not in the facts but in the way they presented them. Bruni used direct statements. In the foregoing examples he inserted into his narrative phrases such as "hatred now overcame fear," "sedition among the chief citizens must be avoided," or "because of liberty the city grew." Machiavelli, in additon to such direct statements, described actual events which gave life to Bruni's abstractions. For the details of these events, he could not rely on Bruni's narrative but had to go back to the chronicles which Bruni himself had used as sources.

Machiavelli gave a disingenuous explanation of why he consulted the chronicle sources. He went beyond the humanists, he said, to find materials on domestic affairs, which Bruni and Poggio had slighted.[66] In fact, as the foregoing analysis has indicated, Machiavelli relied on Bruni for his treatment of domestic affairs.[67] Since Machiavelli's explicit statement about his sources cannot be trusted, his narrative itself must be investigated for a clearer picture of exactly what he took from his chronicle sources that he could not find in Bruni.

Machiavelli went to the chronicles for details of a sensory rather than intellectual nature that gave his narrative a tangible quality. Neither Bruni nor the chroniclers used details in this way. Bruni tried to eliminate tangible elements in order to emphasize the abstract constituents of historical change. The chroniclers, who tended to refer the intangible dimensions of history directly to God without analyzing them in secular terms, employed sensory details in their accounts, because those were the most obvious elements of the past. In adding details to Bruni's abstract account, Machiavelli followed in the footsteps of the Florentine humanist historians who succeeded Bruni, while at the same time he resolved some of the problems in these later works. Both Poggio Bracciolini, in his history of Florence, and Angelo Poliziano, in his account of the Pazzi conspiracy, included elements foreign to Bruni's political analysis, but their results were not conceptually coherent.[68] Bartolomeo Scala, the last of the humanist historians of Florence, wrote a more scholarly history than his predecessors, and he included sensory details largely for antiquarian reasons.[69] Machiavelli shared neither of these attitudes of the later humanists; he sought as rigorously analytical a perspective on the past as Bruni did.[70] The details he added were placed firmly in the service of developing and reinforcing his analysis.

Machiavelli used the details to convey historical change. He wed the political analysis borrowed from Bruni to specific, tangible details and created a new style of writing, one which focused on the human personality. Individual behavior played a greater role in his history than it did in the chronicles or the humanist histories. The personalities of such characters as Corso Donati, Walter of Brienne, and Michele di Lando became decisive. He even stressed the individual roles of many less important people. In narrating the events leading up to the execution of Giorgio Scali, for instance, he made the personal initiative of the Captain of the People a key factor, while the chronicle source noted only that Giorgio's behavior aroused general opposition.[71]

Despite Machiavelli's interest in analysis, individual behavior remained the final cause of historical events. At the height of the Ciompi revolt, when the Palace of the Signoria was under siege by the rioters, two of the leaders of the original movement to abolish the anti-Ghibelline laws, Tommaso Strozzi and Benedetto Alberti, advised the Signoria to abandon the palace to the Ciompi. Machiavelli said they did this "moved either by their own ambition, desiring to remain lords of the palace, or because they believed that action would be best" (3.15). His source, Capponi, suggested no personal motives in the event, saying only that the two were sent down to negotiate with the mob and returned with that advice.[72] Bruni ignored the event, apparently feeling that it added nothing to his abstract explanation of the revolt as a spreading of discontent. Machiavelli used psychological abstractions so that they clarified the decision to leave the palace without diminishing the significance of the particular events which led to that decision. To do this, he offered two quite different motives, one suggesting selfish ambition and the other responsible judgement. By not settling on a single motive, he made the abandonment of the palace and, hence, the victory of the Ciompi the result of personal factors rather than fixed character traits like ambition or astuteness. Motives were suggested, but the decision could not be fully explained in precise abstract terms. Machiavelli showed his readers that a reality whose dimensions were inherently imprecise and dynamic lay behind the political process.

In part, Machiavelli incorporated individuals into his narrative by the simple device of finding the right detail to leave us with a strong impression of their personalities.[73] He told us that Walter of Brienne had a long scraggly beard[74] and that Michele di Lando entered the Palace of the Signoria with bare feet.[75] He was so determined to incorporate personal elements into his narrative that he occasionally added them even when his chronicle source had none. The chronicler Gino Capponi described the first riot of the Ciompi revolt as a time when anyone who had suffered wrong could use the disturbance as a pretext for vengeance.[76] Machiavelli seemed dissatisfied with such a general account, for he dramatized the scene by adding a voice inciting people to riot and a gonfalon in the hand of the rioter.[77]

Some of Machiavelli's practices in treating individuals went beyond pure literary technique and involved new concepts. He emphasized the personal element of history, partly by modifying the notion of fixed character. Bruni, as well as most classical historians, frequently identified individuals by assigning them abstract characteristics such as political acumen, ambition, or military skill. Bruni seldom used these characteristics to explain events; more often he used them didactically to help the individuals in his story serve as examples of virtue and vice. Machiavelli did give the individuals fixed characters which did not change during the course of their lives, but he altered Bruni's practice in subtle yet important ways that changed the function of these characterizations. Essentially, Machiavelli ascribed general, often quite traditional, virtues and vices to people but presented their specific actions in such a way that these characteristics took on a special meaning.

Machiavelli's special use of character traits within a personal context is clearly seen in his treatment of the chief protagonist of the Ciompi revolt, Michele di Lando. After his account of the revolt, Machiavelli described Michele's character in a general way, singling out prudence and goodness or kindness as his prevailing traits.[78] This seems straightforward enough, but Michele's actions, as Machiavelli described them in the preceding section, were not those traditionally associated with the virtues of prudence and kindness.

When Michele entered the Palace of the Signoria and took command of the revolt, his first act was to direct his followers to go in search of an unpopular law officer named Nuto. In the chronicle sources, this did not appear as an act of kindness or goodness. Gino Capponi marvelled at the ferocity and cruelty of the mob which wrought a terrible vengeance on this hated official, hanging him by his feet and tearing him to pieces. Machiavelli thought the act kind and prudent only in the specific context in which it was committed, since Michele used the opportunity to begin his rule with justice. Having sated the peoples' appetite for vengeance by means of a horrible sacrifice, he ordered them to cease all burning, rioting, and destruction of property (3.16). Machiavelli's determination to show the particular nature of Michele's goodness is all the more evident when we take into account the fact that he had to distort his source in order to attribute the act to Michele. The chroniclers all portrayed the death of Nuto as a spontaneous act of mob violence; Machiavelli, by showing it to be the result of an individual's act, gave specific substance to Michele's personality.

Later, a deputation from the Ciompi came to Michele in the palace to make certain demands on the government. They pressed their point with threats that so infuriated Michele that he drew his sword, severely wounded several petitioners, and imprisoned the rest. The action enraged the Ciompi, and they turned against Michele and attacked the Signoria. The chronicler, di Stefani,

196

regarded this episode as an example of Michele's spirited character rather than an indication of prudence.[79] Machiavelli thought di Lando's behavior an example of both prudence and sagacity, because it showed that he was aware of the importance of his political position and capable of taking action to preserve it.[80] Thus, it was prudent only in the particular context in which it occurred; in another it might be rash and foolhardy.

For Machiavelli, Michele di Lando's significance lay both in his character and in the specific acts which expressed his personality. Just as the actions themselves had no significance without the character that inspired them, the character was meaningless without the specific, concrete acts that manifested it. Michele thus effected change as a person, not as a purely physical mechanism causing unrelated and discontinuous acts or as a collection of abstract traits independent of a physical body.

Ascribing the classical virtues of prudence and sagacity to a man of the lower classes, a wool comber, leads us to a second way in which Machiavelli's treatment of personality differed conceptually from that of his predecessors. For him, personal realities transcended social and political categories; all individuals were real, whatever their social class. Among classical writers, the traditional virtues were the property of the upper classes; the lower classes were less human because they lacked them. As a result, classical historians were notoriously deficient in their treatment of lower class movements. Even when they dramatized lower class feelings, they saw them as fundamentally different from their own. For example, as Erich Auerbach has noted, Tacitus, at the beginning of his *Annals*, described a mutiny in the army in Germany.[81] He included an oration in which a common soldier talked movingly about the wrongs his comrades suffered and the grievances they had against their officers. Yet, these grievances were concerned exclusively with matters of food and clothing. Absent from the speech is any sense of the larger moral or political considerations that Tacitus found in revolts led by members of the Roman upper class and that modern scholars have found in the mutinies of the early empire.

Humanist historians shared this insensitivity to the motives of classes below their own. They felt the rules governing political behavior among the ruling classes did not explain these motives. Even Leonardo Bruni, nearly unique in his praise of Michele di Lando, was thoroughly contemptuous of the Ciompi. He saw them as a band of common looters and rioters, and he praised di

Lando only for keeping them under control.[82] Bruni did not see that the Ciompi might calculate their political interest in ways similar to those used by the members of the wool guild.

Machiavelli's handling of the Ciompi was strikingly different from that of his sources. Where Bruni and the chroniclers often described the Ciompi as uncontrollably violent, closer to animals than men, Machiavelli ascribed to them appropriate strategic and tactical considerations. When disturbances broke out again after being quieted the first time, Capponi said, "the people wanted to disgorge some of the poison that remained in their bodies."[83] Machiavelli made clear that the members of the Florentine upper classes themselves were responsible for the outbreak and that the poor had specific reasons for their discontent.[84] In many cases where Capponi gave no motive for acts of violence, Machiavelli told the reader that they were committed for tactical reasons. He noted, for instance, that the mob burned Lapo di Castiglionchio's house for injuries they had received from the Guelfs, with whom Lapo was identified. Capponi, by simply narrating the burning without explanation, made it look like a senseless act of violence. Further on, Machiavelli explained that the rioters opened the prisons "to have company that would accompany them with a greater thirst to rob the goods of others" (3.10). Again Capponi was silent on the motive. In some cases, Machiavelli changed the material found in his source to make the actions of the mob more comprehensible. Where Capponi gave a list of buildings burned by the rampaging mob, Machiavelli singled out the palace of the wool guild and described the action as a burning of the records of the guild rather than their palace. Since he had already mentioned that these records maintained the dependence of the Ciompi on the masters of the wool guild, the action took on a significance that it did not have in the original source (3.14).

In explaining the second outbreak of violence, Machiavelli mixed general character traits with specific historical experience, just as he did with the personality of Michele di Lando. He began by discussing the variety of motives among the lower classes. Many were afraid that they would be punished for the fires and looting of the night before. To this fear was added the hatred of the wool guild. Machiavelli did not see this hatred as an abstract trait of the rioters but as one derived from experience. He rehearsed the injustices of the guild system, showing how the wool workers had been subject to the guilds and oppressed by them since the thirteenth century. He wanted his readers to see that the Ciompi's feelings grew out of concrete historical events and that they were acting on basic but inprecise and unfocused human desires.

Nowhere is Machiavelli's insight into the Ciompi clearer than in the oration which an unidentified leader of the wool workers delivered to incite his followers to continue the uprising (3.13). In one sense it dramatized and made concrete Bruni's thesis that the revolt was caused by the spread of discontent through the various classes in Florence. Machiavelli included all of the elements found in his other orations: the blending of moral and practical considerations, the detailed analysis of the strengths and weaknesses of the Ciompi's position, and the tactical advantages of continued revolt. The oration demonstrated clearly that the Ciompi were not blind animals fundamentally different from the other classes in Florence. Their tactics were rational and included an awareness of specific objectives that, for Machiavelli, characterized all human political conduct.

Understanding the Ciompi should not be confused with sympathy, however. Machiavelli thought the Ciompi's behavior threatened the bases of Florentine political life and no more approved their behavior than did Bruni. He simply saw that their actions were those of human persons in a particular historical context and did not arise out of abstract characteristics which set the Ciompi absolutely apart from other Florentines.

Behind the political analysis and narrative order Machiavelli took from his humanist predecessor lay a new approach to personality. Machiavelli saw that political analysis of abstract categories did not fully explain historical events. They were also a product of concrete personal decisions that arose out of a variety of motives which were not wholly consistent. Machiavelli showed the reader a historical reality which was unpredictable but comprehensible, a reality whose most direct manifestation was the individual person.

The personal element in Machiavelli's history is part of a larger aspect of Renaissance thought, one which has been increasingly appreciated by scholars over the past decade. Charles Trinkaus, in his *In Our Image and Likeness*, has shown how pervasive was the concern for religious questions among Renaissance humanists and how deeply they drew on Augustine in grappling with basic human problems.[85] William Bouwsma's stress on the personal aspect of the Augustinian tradition, noted earlier, also helps put Machiavelli's achievement in a clearer context. He represents an important stage in the secularization of the Augustinian belief in the "integral unity of the personality."[86] Machiavelli presented the person as a vital and essential unit creating history and affected by it in meaningful ways.

Medieval Treatment of Personality

Individuals served a variety of functions in medieval histories. They illustrated specific virtues and vices, much as they did in classical histories. They were part of the retributive justice of God as He worked out his plan for human history. Individuals were even used for anecdotal material to enhance the entertainment value of the work and draw the readers' attention to the more serious purposes of the narratives. None of these functions demanded that the person be presented as an integrated unit, acting directly on historical events and being acted upon by them in turn. Yet to modern readers it is precisely such interaction that is implied in the doctrine of the Incarnation with its insistence on an integrated personal reality. This section will explore the uses to which medieval historians put individual behavior, to show that such an implication is not found in their works.

Just as the general theory of God's plan for history did not produce a dynamic narrative of events, so the specific doctrine of the Incarnation—despite the example of Augustine's *Confessions*—did not produce a dynamic picture of the individual's interaction with his environment. All of the historians discussed here displayed a knowledge of the basic theological concepts underlying this doctrine. Even such an unreflective writer as Gregory of Tours included discussions of the resurrection of the body and the Incarnation, while Otto of Freising incorporated elaborate essays on the persons of the Trinity from both nominalist and realist perspectives.[87] Yet, the static quality of medieval narratives extended even to the treatment of individuals, whose dynamic reality they theoretically understood.

An analogy in twentieth century thought may help modern readers see that this separation between theory and practice in medieval histories is not surprising. The theory of relativity has certainly introduced profound changes into our notion of time, changes which may ultimately prove to be as decisive in the formation of historical consciousness as was the rise of Christianity. Historians seldom have to confront the significance of these changes in their own works, but if the changes had explicit religious, cultural, and social significance, a situation might easily arise where no historian could be credible until demonstrating an understanding of Einsteinian time. Faced with such a situation, most historians might respond much as medieval historians did; they would find ways of showing that they understood the theory but would fall back on earlier conventions to describe actual events.

Especially in the early Middle Ages, historians tended to use individuals in contexts more appropriate to classical conceptions of time and personality. Eusebius and Orosius were explicit in their use of individuals for general lessons. Eusebius said in his preface that one of his subjects was the heroism with which men faced torture and death to defend their faith. Heroism appeared in his work as an abstract virtue, illustrated by representative examples. He began the Great Persecution, for instance, by describing the death of one martyr, saying he would leave it to his readers to infer from this case what happened in the others. The account is a short but grisly tale of torture and death in which the martyr's name is not even disclosed until the end. Even then, Eusebius stressed the exemplary function of the incident by saying that his name was Peter and his martyrdom was worthy of the name he bore.[88]

Orosius had little interest in explaining how particular people influenced the disasters he recorded as his main theme. Instead, he focused on character traits whose moral significance he wished to bring to his readers' attention. He considered Jugurtha interesting only because of his fickle and insufferable character and mentioned Marius only to give an example of his astuteness, which led to Jugurtha's defeat.[89] Philip and Alexander of Macedon combined to form examples of the effects of bravery and spirit, with Orosius' assurance that the deeds of Philip would have sufficed as examples had Alexander not succeeded him (3.16).

That Eusebius and Orosius, with their overriding concern for general patterns, ignored individual behavior is hardly surprising. More astonishing is the fact that Gregory of Tours, whose vivid and unforgettable anecdotes have often been cited as the beginning of personalized narrative,[90] subordinated individuals to general considerations. Not only did he reinforce moral lessons by ignoring the differences between individuals, but he commonly explained the details for which he is so well known by referring to abstract causes having no obvious relevance to the details themselves.[91]

Gregory's willingness to sacrifice the individual's integrity to didactic or religious considerations cannot be fully explained by the indifference to motives which has so often been noted.[92] He was curiously undisturbed by inconsistencies between individuals and their assigned character. While Machiavelli used this disparity to individualize persons, Gregory was simply trying to make individuals serve different general functions. For instance, he used Queen Clotilda both as an example of otherworldliness and of disastrous feminine involvement in politics. Queen Clotilda entered the story as a fierce political manipulator, who agreed to the execution of her grandsons rather than have them lose their rights to the throne. Gregory felt, in general, that women caused bloodshed when they intervened in politics, and he described the queen to illustrate this theme. Later on in the same section, however, Gregory praised the queen as an example of piety, humility, and indifference to political power. There he concluded by noting that she earned the respect of all because of these traits and moved forward to heavenly grace by humility.[93] The modern reader might wonder if the queen learned her humility from her political defeats, but Gregory offered no sense of development which might support this interpretation. The two parts of the narrative stand alone, serving as examples of two different themes.

The more detailed and complex Gregory's treatment of individuals, the more obvious it is that he did not integrate behavior and character into a single reality. In the passage on Parthenus, an advisor of King Theudebert, he showed his readers a series of unrelated traits, each with its own moral function. The story began after Theudebert's death when the mob sought vengeance on Parthenus for his activities as tax collector during the king's life. The terrified Parthenus convinced the bishops to escort him to Trier. On the way he had a nightmare in which his wife and her lover, both of whom he had murdered years earlier, appeared and demanded that he repent. Parthenus' flight from the mob is forgotten as we learn the details of the old murders and how Parthenus confessed to the bishops after his dream. When we return to the original story, we find ourselves in Trier watching the people break into the church where Parthenus was hiding in a chest of vestments. We are told how they dragged him forth and stoned him to death, but Gregory felt no need to tell how Parthenus' homicidal jealousy years earlier was related to his tax collecting. Gregory did not even indicate that Parthenus' conduct in that profession was particularly rapacious. The two facts stand alone, the homicide providing the sin and the tax collection providing the punishment. Without further comment on his public career, Gregory added to this tale that Parthenus was a glutton, ate aloes to give himself an appetite, and farted in public without any consideration for those around him (3.36). Gregory used Parthenus' life and death to warn the reader against a variety of unrelated vices, from oppressive government (which is not even specifically attributed to Parthenus), through uxoricide, to gluttony and poor manners. He did not seem to care whether these could be related in one individual or how they brought about his punishment. Parthenus was portrayed not as a person but as a series of isolated vices.

The details of Parthenus' life would be difficult for anyone to integrate, but even when Gregory was working with more coherent material he avoided presenting a unified picture of personality. In narrating the death of Avius, Gregory first reminded readers that Avius had earlier murdered two men in order to commit adultery. Then, he recounted how Avius chanced to meet Childeric, the Saxon, and, after an exchange of insults, was killed. Gregory saw a clear lesson in this: "Thus the divine majesty avenged the innocent blood which [Avius] had spilled with his own hand" (7.3). To a modern reader, Avius' temper seems to be the issue, both in the murder of two men and in his rash exchange of insults with Childeric. But Gregory was not interested in that personal trait. When he first mentioned the murders, Avius was not even named as the murderer, despite the gory detail with which the assault was described (6.13). Gregory subordinated Avius' personality to the general principle of God's vengeance on those who shed innocent blood.

Where Augustine had used bodily details to stress the unity of his own personality, Gregory used them to entertain. Physical details are certainly prominent in the work. We see Guntram Boso's corpse, unable to fall to the ground after he is killed, because so many spears have pierced it. We hear the outraged voices of the mob searching through the church for Parthenus. These details entertain us and stimulate our interest, but they serve no larger purpose. Physical description, moral lessons, and divine intervention remain separate concerns for Gregory and leave his narrative without true personal dimensions.

Because of his preoccupation with the conversion of England, Bede focused more strongly on the personal element of history than did Gregory. Conversion in the Augustinian tradition is a personal experience that involves not only the intellect but the body and the will. Furthermore, Bede had the example of Augustine's *Confessions* to structure his narrative. The personal elements in Bede's descriptions of important conversions do not, however, convey a unified sense of personal reality. Instead, Bede stressed the abstract traits which dominated earlier historians' treatment of persons. An examination of the most important event in the book, the conversion of King Ethelbert by Augustine of Canterbury, will illustrate this point.

In describing the two major events in the conversion—Pope Gregory's decision to send Augustine to England and Augustine's conversion of King Ethelbert—Bede was more interested in showing the workings of divine Providence than in portraying the particular events that manifest those workings. Bede had anecdotes which might show Gregory's decision as an outgrowth of his personality or of specific historical events. He could easily have used the Pope's famous encounter with the Angles in the slave market at Rome to show what brought the matter to his attention. But this anecdote is included only much later in the work, when Bede concluded his account of Gregory's death with a brief biography.[94] Instead Bede told the reader simply that Gregory sent Augustine under the inspiration of God. He omitted speculation on the particular factors influencing that decision, including instead the Pope's words of encouragement to the missionaries as they departed (1.23).

The king's conversion itself was described in general terms which give the reader no sense of how the personalities interacted. Bede began with a description of Augustine's behavior after the king gave him permission to preach in Kent. After stressing the abstract virtues of purity and piety which Augustine and his followers displayed, he narrated the conversion in the following terms: "At last the king, as well as others, believed and was baptized, being attracted by the pure life of the saints and by their most precious promises, whose truth they confirmed by performing many miracles" (1.26). By generalizing the missionaries' behavior, Bede portrayed the king's conversion as a response to abstract virtues to which God's direct intervention had exposed him. The personalities of Pope Gregory and of Augustine did not determine the event.[95]

Bede subordinated individuals to abstract character traits partly as a means of fulfilling the moral and didactic purpose of the work.[96] He often introduced individuals primarily to illustrate

204

the value of their salient characteristic. When he narrated the life and murder of Oswin, he was little concerned with the political or religious significance of the murder but used Oswin's humility didactically, concluding his account,

> among all the other graces of virtue and modesty with which, if I may say so, he was blessed in a special manner, his humility is said to have been the greatest, as a single example is enough to prove.[97]

The reader is expected to forget Oswin's unfortunate end, narrated in the preceding passage. The two parts of Oswin's life are separate, not elements of a single reality.

As a final example of Bede's use of individuals, consider his treatment of the death of King Sigbert:

> For a long time the instruction of the people in the heavenly life prospered day by day in the kingdom, to the joy of the king and the whole nation; but it then happened that the king was murdered at the instigation of the enemy of all good men, by his own kinsmen. It was two brothers who perpetrated the crime. When they were asked why they did it, they could make no reply except that they were angry with the king and hated him because he was too ready to pardon his enemies, calmly forgiving them for the wrongs they had done him as soon as they asked his pardon. Such was the crime for which he met his death, that he had devoutly observed the Gospel precepts. But nevertheless, by this innocent death, a real offense was punished in accordance with the prophecy of the man of God. For one of the *gesiths* who murdered him was unlawfully married, a marriage which the bishop had been unable to prevent or correct. So he excommunicated him and ordered all who would listen to him not to enter the man's house nor take food with him. But the king disregarded this command and accepted an invitation of the *gesith* to dine at his house. As the king was coming away, the bishop met him. When the king saw him, he leapt from his horse, and fell trembling at the bishop's feet, asking his pardon. The bishop, who was also on horseback, alighted too. In his anger he touched the prostrate king with his staff which he was holding in his hand and exercising his episcopal authority, he uttered these words, "I declare to you that because you were unwilling to avoid the house of this

man who is lost and damned, you will meet your death
in this very house." Yet we may be sure that the death
of this religious king was such that not only atoned for
his offense but even increased his merit; for it came
about as a result of his piety and his observance of
Christ's command.[98]

Bede offered two moral lessons in this passage. First, he held
the virtues of King Sigbert up for emulation. The king's willingness to forgive brought him atonement for his sins and the rewards
of heaven, a theme Bede developed throughout his history by
frequent references to the saints and martyrs. But Bede also
wanted to teach the dangers of disobeying the commands of the
church. The king was killed *iuxta praedictum viri dei*, for his real
fault was to ignore the church's ban of excommunication. Bede
wove into the narrative both the king's punishment and his reward
to present the same event as an example of both virtue and vice.

For Bede, Sigbert's death was an instance of the twofold
direction of the course of history. A principal theme of the work
is the growth of the English church, the conversion of the four
nations, and their unification in Catholic worship. Thus, he began
his account of the king's death by noting the real significance of
his life, that it represented an advance in the spread of the Gospel.
This victory was not won without a struggle, however. He identified the death of the king as part of the Devil's power over
human history when he said *instigante omnium bonorum inimico*.
Bede was not content with this direct statement of significance.
He made it part of his narrative by noting the murderers' lack of
an acceptable motive, implying that their conduct could be adequately explained only as the work of the Devil.

These examples show that Bede's basic conceptions of historical reality did not require an integrated personality. Sigbert's
life and death illustrated particular moral lessons as well as the
general pattern of history. Scholars have identified several themes
in Bede's writings: the didactic value of history, the parallels between Old Testament times and his own, and the absence of becoming as a basic category of history.[99] None of these implied the
concept of an integrated human personality. In fact, Bede used
the individuals to illustrate a number of these aspects of history
at the expense of their own basic reality.

Classical models were not decisive among medieval historians in either promoting or hindering the development of a narrative technique that presented a unified personality interacting

in concrete ways with historical events. The influence of classical models is clearest in the most famous biography of the early Middle Ages, Einhard's *Life of Charlemagne*. Einhard's dependence on Suetonius has long stood as a common example of the uncritical use of the classics during this period. Helmut Beuman has observed that Einhard's preface contains not a single original idea.[100] Since Suetonius was indifferent to the coherence of the personalities of his subjects, one might expect that Einhard's individuals would be less convincing than Bede's, but such is not the case. He presented Charlemagne as an individual with coherent, well-defined, and interrelated traits.

Einhard's success arose partly from the stated purpose of the book. He wanted to preserve great deeds for the instruction of the future, but more than that he had a sense of personal obligation to Charlemagne, who was a benefactor and friend. Thus, unlike Suetonius, who mined Augustus' life for examples of unusual cruelty as well as of clemency,[101] Einhard did not use the events of Charlemagne's life to illustrate common vices of rulers. He suppressed the vices or, when he could not ignore them, attributed them to others. For example, after describing the cruel and bloody suppression of a revolt in Germany, he claimed,

> it was believed that the cause and origin of these conspiracies was the cruelty of Queen Fastrada and that they conspired against the king because he seemed to acquiesce in his wife's cruelty though it was against his usual kindness and gentleness.[102]

Einhard intended simply to de-emphasize negative traits of Charlemagne, but the effect was to present a more coherent set of character traits than he found in his model.

Einhard convincingly related Charlemagne's virtues to the particular events of his reign. Early in the book Einhard discussed the King's continuance of his father's wars in Aquitaine. According to Einhard, Charlemagne began the war thinking that his brother would come to his aid and that it would soon be over. Even though his brother refused to help and he had to undertake it alone, he pressed on, refusing to abandon a task once begun. In the end, he won by "perseverance and continued effort."[103] Einhard was not content with this general observation; he went on to offer a specific example of the character trait, describing Charlemagne's pursuit of Hunold over the Garonne and into Gascony. This description, introduced by the simple connective *nam et* illustrates the *perseverantia et jugitate* which just preceded it and helps convince the reader that Charlemagne's policy in the war and the source of his victory really lay in his prudent character. Einhard used steadfastness to explain Charlemagne's success throughout his career. His constancy conquered the Saxons in the face of their vacillation and perfidy (pg. 7).

Charlemagne's enemies displayed the vices Einhard wished to warn his readers about. These vices, like Charlemagne's virtues, are constant characteristics which cause behavior and influence general events. War broke out in Bavaria because of the pride and folly of Duke Tassilo.[104] These characteristics were mobilized into specific action by his wife who urged him on because, as King Desiderius' daughter, she wished to avenge her father's defeat and exile at Charlemagne's hands. Einhard described Tassilo's refusal to carry out Charlemagne's orders as the arrogance that spurred the king to war, leading to Tassilo's defeat and submission. Einhard's treatment of personality here contrasted with that of Gregory of Tours. Unlike Gregory, Einhard explored the historical background within which character traits produced specific behavior.

Charlemagne's personality, then, had a coherence found in neither Suetonius' biographies nor the works of earlier medieval historians. Yet, even in Einhard's work the individual's reality depends wholly on abstract and constant states of character. These abstract states gave meaning to both the individuals and the general events of the story, but they were not themselves affected by either. Einhard treated Tassilo's arrogance just as he treated the Saxon's fickleness. Both were abstract traits that struggled with Charlemagne's constancy and perseverance. Neither individuals nor groups had a reality of their own; they simply expressed abstract characteristics.

Thus, Einhard's conscious imitation of classical models had a paradoxical quality. Suetonius led him to minimize divine intervention and leave aside the larger questions of direction and pattern in history, which were of such concern to earlier medieval historians. Instead, he focused on the protagonist and his enemies in ways that gave them coherent personalities explicitly related to specific historical events. On the other hand, Einhard brought from the classical models a preoccupation with identifying the abstract charcteristics of his subjects. He treated these character traits as the fundamental, unchangeable stuff of history, determining the course of both individual behavior and military or political events.

Otto of Freising had a theoretical sense of real personality that distinguished him from these earlier historians, yet his narrative did not always illustrate his theory. The disparity between narrative and theory that often characterized his description of general events also dominated his treatment of individuals. He seemed even more self-conscious of using abstractions to express his interpretations of individuals. Although he often stated in *The Two Cities* that he preferred a story to explicit moral and philosophical judgements, he began his biography of Frederick I by referring to philosophy as a higher form of expression, drawing attention to his frequent use of philosophical digressions to make clear his meaning in the subsequent narrative.[105]

An example from this biography will illustrate the disunity between Otto's philosophical statements and his narrative. Early in that work he explained that the Saxon rebellion arose not so much from the instability of the Saxons as from the arrogance of Emperor Henry IV. Einhard might have left the arrogance as an abstract cause of the revolt, but Otto felt the need to explain how it was tied to the actual events. To give historical meaning to Henry's arrogance, Otto quoted a remark the youthful Henry made about the cowardice of his subjects, a remark which

> did not vanish as soon as it had been uttered—as words usually do—but taking root in the minds of many, germinated so effectively that in a short time the whole province was aroused against him, and uniting in one body, supplied to countless peoples and tribes death-dealing potions.[106]

Otto thus gave Henry's arrogance an historical context, showing that it produced specific actions which had unusual and predictable results. The narrative gives full weight to the combination of abstract and concrete elements in Henry's personality.

To this account, however, Otto added some lengthy philosophical comments which did little to clarify the meaning of Henry's early career. Rather than philosophize on how God displays his providence through the actions of particular men, he turned instead to the theme which dominated all his works: the inevitable rise and fall of human events. The digression on this theme is much longer than the actual narrative of Henry's early career. It is drawn largely from Boethius and concerns the inevitable decay which accompanies the composite nature of human beings. Otto concluded with a general admonition not to become too elated when experiencing good fortune, because we must inevitably fall again into misfortune. The main point Otto wished to draw from Henry's personality, thus, concerns the necessary vicissitudes of life, a point he felt could be made more convincing by philosophical argument than by pure narrative.

At other times, Otto displayed an explicit understanding of the reality of individuals as part of the historical process, even though he did not organize his narrative to bring the point out. His explanation of Pilate's punishment illustrates the ambivalence of his treatment of personality. Otto clearly saw that God used Caligula to punish Pilate, for he wrote that that Roman emperor treated Pilate so badly that he killed himself with his own sword. Otto commented on the significance of Caligula's behavior,

> behold the most just and mysterious judgements of God: He avenges himself on his foes through the instrumentality of a most sinful man and, without bestirring himself at all, triumphs over his enemies by the efforts and frenzy of the citizens of the world.[107]

Otto's statement reveals a complex theoretical perspective. He not only saw history as a union of unchanging and changing realities but realized that the most important manifestation of this union is found in the acts of individuals who do not themselves embody abstract virtues. This perspective is similar to that found in many passages of Augustine's *Confessions*. Augustine showed how, in particular stages of his life, his evil motives caused behavior which, in turn, led to good, because they prepared him for a subsequent stage of development. As a student of rhetoric, for instance, he first read Cicero's *Hortensius* because he wanted to further his worldly ambitions by learning how to write and speak more effectively. From Cicero he learned to love wisdom, which launched him on a course of philosophical study that brought him to neo-Platonism and eventual conversion. Like Otto, Augustine discoursed at some length on the theoretical significance of his having used *Hortensius* for purposes other than that originally intended.[108] Augustine, however, also made his point descriptively by integrating it into a detailed account of his own motives and actions. Readers of the *Confessions* follow Augustine as he first learned to speak in order the better to implement his desires, as he was beaten to study, and as he grew into a young man. His career ambitions emerged from this early need to speak and thereby get what he wanted in life. Thus, they had a specific historical background which could be used to explain his interest in Cicero.

Otto did not possess this wealth of personal information about his subjects and, thus, could not make his point so effectively. But he did possess details which could have strengthened his point. He cited, for instance, examples of Caligula's cruelty, but they were narrated in another section of the work, after he had finished with Pilate. Caligula's specific cruelty to Pilate thus remained an abstract trait unconnected with a larger pattern of personality. Secondly, Otto blunted the point of his story by admitting that some say Pilate did not commit suicide but drowned in the Rhone. Otto did not seem concerned that this version, which is incorporated into the narrative on an equal basis with the first, negated his point that God uses the wicked of the world to implement his will. He appeared satisfied that the statement had theoretical validity and did not need the narrative to support it.

On other occasions, Otto subordinated the narrative of personal realities to the conventional purpose of exemplifying praiseworthy or blameworthy conduct. He attributed the fall of the Roman monarchy to a combination of general causes (the oppressive tyranny of Tarquin) and individual ones (his rape of Lucretia).[109] In the narrative that followed, he did not explore the relationship between the two or show how the particular act crystallized discontent into open revolt. After a brief reference to the combination as *causa iustissima* of his expulsion, Otto devoted most of the section to Lucretia's chastity, which her suicide eloquently proved, and included some verses in praise of it. He was clearly more interested in using the event to display exemplary virtue than to illuminate the role of individuals in historical change.

The degree to which Otto both succeeded and failed to portray integrated personalities can be illustrated by comparing his treatment of the apostate emperor Julian with that of his principal source, Orosius. Julian presented problems for all Christian historians. How was one to explain the temporary success of his apostasy, or fit his reign into the retributive pattern of history, or justify the study of philosophy after he had used pagan philosophy to attack Christianity? For Orosius, these were three separate

211

problems. He explained Julian's success by attributing it to cunning rather than force; God's retributive justice appeared in Julian's death; and philosophy was justified by describing how Christian teachers piously gave up their professions rather than comply with Julian's edict requiring professors of the liberal arts to abjure Christianity.[110] Otto, by contrast, integrated these themes into a portrayal of Julian's life which included both its good and bad features and pointed out the ways in which Julian misused philosophy. Adding anecdotes from other medieval historians,[111] he praised Julian for his modesty and cultivation of philosophy but blamed him for practicing magic, which was an aberration from wisdom. He adopted Orosius' basic premise that Julian succeeded by stratagems rather than force, but, instead of the unadorned statement that God punished Julian with death, Otto introduced the theme of divine judgment by suggesting that Julian's fatal spear wound was a response to the prayers of St. Basil.[112]

Otto thus integrated the events of Julian's life into a biography which supported his belief in the virtue of philosophy by noting Julian's specific misuses of it. What Otto did not do is adduce historical motives for Julian's behavior. He might easily have expanded Orosius' reference to deviousness to make an Augustinian point about the importance of will in determining the value of intellectual activity. Otto actually used this theme in discussing heresies and other aspects of philosophy. It would have been appropriate here, had he been interested in portraying Julian as an integrated personality, for events could then be organized to show that Julian's interest in knowledge and wisdom brought him to grief because it was not accompanied by a good will and was thus directed to the wrong objectives. Otto focused, however, on the abstract virtue of wisdom and not the person who embodied it. His basic historical realities remained abstract, even though his abstractions acknowledged the reality of concrete changes.

The crusading chroniclers experienced problems describing individuals that parallel their difficulty in recounting general changes. Individuals remain separated from the general events of the narrative even when the writer felt that they were important causative elements. Villehardouin, for instance, opened his chronicle with Foulque de Nouilly's preaching of the crusade. We read of his early efforts, that his fame spread to Rome, that the pope requested him to preach a crusade and then dispatched a cardinal to proclaim an indulgence. But when Villehardouin came

to state why people went on crusade, Foulque was forgotten.[113]
On other occasions, he used abstract characteristics as exemplary
virtues without tying them explicitly to any specific behavior. He
characterized the Doge of Venice as wise and prudent,[114] but he
did not tell his readers what was wise about the Doge's words,
even though Villehardouin himself was present as part of the
crusaders' embassy and quoted some of the Doge's speech. Perhaps the fact that the Doge aided the crusaders was sufficient
reason to call him wise and prudent.

Psychological states were also included in the narrative, but
they were no more tied to specific events or causes than these
intellectual and spiritual traits. Villehardouin said that the Duke
of Burgundy would not go on the crusade because "such was his
will that he refused" (p. 21). The men on the fleet broke their
word simply because they feared the great danger involved in the
enterprise (p. 27). Elsewhere, abstract psychological states linked
events that had no obvious connection with one another. The
Emperor Isaac, hearing that his son was deposed, "had such a
great fear and took sick and died shortly" (p. 115). No other part
of the chronicle suggests that Villehardouin had a sophisticated
conceptual scheme that associated fear with physical sickness.
After the conquest, when the crusaders began to divide up their
lands, the *convoitise del monde*, which had done such evil did not
leave them in peace, but each began to do evil in his land, so that
the Greeks began to hate them (p. 160). Here he joined two psychological states to one another without the concrete details that
abounded in most of the chronicle. These examples suggest the
lack of a coherent theoretical framework for interpreting the role
of individuals in the historical process. Unlike Otto of Freising
and Bede, who were directly influenced by Augustine, Villehardouin had no theory for comprehending the emotional and intellectual complexities underlying human conduct. He recognized
simple psychological states and narrated them, insofar as they
helped interrelate the events he observed. They did not create a
systematic picture, however.

Joinville's failure to integrate the personality of his protagonist, King Louis, is even more obvious. He placed anecdotes
about Louis' life and rule in a separate section at the beginning,
because by the separation his readers would be better instructed
in the king's exemplary virtues.[115] More than that, he abandoned
chronological order in the section where he anecdotally described
Louis' acts during the period between the two crusades, as if

Louis' non-military life had no temporal development but was interesting only insofar as it cast light on the king's unchanging character (pp. 331-44).

Placing anecdotes and sayings in a separate section is a normal part of the form of classical biography. Even Machiavelli adopted this practice in his biography of Castruccio Castracani, written shortly before the *Florentine Histories*. Joinville accentuated the division by using the anecdotes almost exclusively to illustrate the king's exemplary virtues, such as temperance in eating, drinking, and speaking. In the chronological part of the work, anecdotes served a different purpose. For instance, Joinville told, in the narrative of the crusade, how the king selected for his army a cleric who had killed three bandits. Though the chronicler might easily have used this story to reveal a number of positive attributes about Louis' character, he emphasized instead how he came to learn of the story. The virtues and traits that would have been stressed had the story been included in either of the two anecdotal sections are ignored.

The crusading chronicles, like the vernacular chronicles which the humanists used as sources, include a wealth of detail out of which a dynamic narrative could be constructed, a narrative that would show how individuals act on events and are influenced by them. But the chroniclers used details differently. Some illustrated virtues which nevertheless remained abstract characteristics; others had no obvious purpose beyond entertainment;[116] still others appear to have been included only because the chronicler was himself a participant in the events.

Two salient features underlie medieval narratives of individual behavior. First, medieval historians did not generally assume a unity to individuals' actions beyond that afforded by their individual bodies. Intellectual, spiritual, and psychological traits were usually presented as part of general realities transcending the individuals rather than as part of a personal unity. Even Otto of Freising, who understood the theoretical unity of personality, did not take full advantage of this theory in practice. Instead, he felt constrained to expound the theory in philosophical digressions. Second, medieval historians did not use concrete details to show how individuals interacted with their environment. To convey a sense of interaction, they had recourse to the same retributive and chronological devices that informed their accounts of general changes. Both of these features, the lack of personal integrity and the absence of concrete interrelationship between the individual and the environment, make medieval descriptions of individuals less dynamic than those found in Machiavelli's histories.

Narrative Technique and the Description of Change

No theory would suffice to produce the dynamic quality of Machiavelli's historical narrative. To assert that time is real—even to explain the source of its reality—does not of itself enable a historian to describe actual events in an inherent temporal relationship. Medieval historians, possessing a theory that time expressed the purposes of God in moving toward a definite end, nonetheless related events to one another through abstract categories of retributive justice or chronological sequence.

This is not to say that theory plays no part. The concepts Machiavelli took from the civic humanists had many advantages. Many of the narrative problems besetting medieval historians arose from their preoccupation with establishing a proper chronological sequence in relation to the birth of Christ, the central event of human history. The psychological framework the humanist historians adopted gradually liberated them from that concern, as they abandoned strict adherence to the annalistic form in the course of the fifteenth century. Machiavelli could give meaning to the specific events of his narrative by referring to the psychological and institutional context within which they occurred.

In addition, these psychological concepts were not as independent from historical events as the intellectual character traits which the earlier historians used. Ambition or fear needed some sort of object before it could be understood, while character traits like arrogance or perseverance could more easily be grasped through an abstract definition. To say that fear caused a war raised questions in the readers' minds about the particular things the combatants were afraid of. To say that it was begun by arrogance might also raise these questions, but not necessarily, since arrogance could be defined as simply a sense of superiority without any reference to a specific object. Because of this dependence on actual events, any attempt to narrate a history based on these psychological realities should produce a more dynamic picture than one which regarded the intellectual and moral traits as more important.

But neither of these theoretical advantages fully explains the quality of Machiavelli's narrative. His achievement has undeni-

215

able literary and rhetorical dimensions, and to understand it, his narrative technique needs to be analyzed.[117] Questions must be posed about what techniques he commonly used to describe the actions of individuals, what models were available on which he might have based those techniques, and in what way he modified the models.

Considerable evidence points to Tacitus as the most likely inspiration for Machiavelli's narrative technique. Tacitus was more flexible in his organization and adhered less rigidly to annalistic form than either Livy or Bruni. Even in his *Annals*, Tacitus sought to organize thematically, using the year by year progression only for an underlying order. He was more conceptual and analytical than Livy, and he answered political questions with more attention to the characteristics of powerful individuals than did Bruni. Tacitus approached historical generalizations in a more ambiguous and suggestive manner than did Polybius. Furthermore, his ironic and bitter tone should have appealed to Machiavelli. Sallust would be a possible rival for Machiavelli's attention, but his general history of Rome did not survive, and the existing monographs were not so useful to Machiavelli in constructing a general narrative of Florentine history.

Students of Machiavelli have found his affinities with Tacitus tantalizing. From the seventeenth century, when Amelot de la Houssaye translated the *Prince* with appropriate citations from Tacitus,[118] to the twentieth, when Toffanin argued that Machiavelli was a Tacitean thinker,[119] scholars have felt that Tacitus exercised a definitive influence. Yet, the precise nature of this influence continues to elude us. Machiavelli himself offered little help, and his comments on his humanist predecessors have to be interpreted with great circumspection, if not outright skepticism. His failure to acknowledge a great debt has led many scholars to conclude that he was more directly influenced by other writers. Recently, J. H. Whitfield has argued that Machiavelli took few examples from Tacitus, that the intellectual similarities are too vague and general to be meaningful, and that he made far more use of Livy.[120]

Machiavelli certainly made more direct use of Tacitus than did his late medieval predecessors. Otto of Freising's citations came not from Tacitus but from Orosius.[121] Moreover, Machiavelli, especially in the *Discourses*, used Tacitus as both a source of examples and an authority for political interpretations. The most recent student of Tacitus' influence has argued that Machiavelli relied on Tacitus to support his republican ideas.[122] While Machiavelli mentioned or quoted Tacitus several times in the *Discourses*, in the *Florentine Histories* he cited him only once, as an authority on the origin of Florence's name.[123] Faced with the problem of identifying affinities which transcend the explicit use of Tacitus' words, historians have either denied the influence or, like Toffanin, have resorted to vague assertions of mystical affinity.[124] In fact, Machiavelli's work contains a number of characteristically Tacitean devices, and their presence can hardly be accidental. In particular, we can identify several important techniques of portraying individual character and at least one distinctive method of explaining historical events.

Tacitus clearly differed from early Roman historians like Livy and Sallust in portraying individuals. Where they assessed character directly, plainly stating a person's virtues or vices, Tacitus was more indirect.[125] He reported a person's reputation, describing how others saw him or interpreted his actions. Tacitus also avoided the open moralism of other Roman historians, preferring to narrate behavior without explicit comment, allowing values to be conveyed by innuendo. To understand events and motives, Tacitus more often than not offered alternative explanations that were mutually exclusive.[126] These devices gave verissimilitude and an air of impartiality to what was often an eccentric interpretation.[127]

Tacitus used all of these techniques to portray the character of Tiberius. In exposing Tiberius as a calculating autocrat who completed the destruction of republican institutions, Tacitus faced a number of problems. Chief among these was the fact that, in the early part of his reign, Tiberius spoke and acted like a sincere republican. Only later did he seem to realize that republican Rome was irretrievably lost. Tacitus solved this problem by implying that Tiberius was a thoroughly devious ruler whose words and policies meant exactly the opposite of what they appeared to. The aforementioned narrative devices allowed Tacitus to do this quite convincingly.

By giving differing explanations of Tiberius' actions, Tacitus accustomed his reader to the notion that any action could have meanings not immediately apparent. Thus, when Tiberius began his reign by expressing solicitude for the rights of the Senate, Tacitus suggested he was not really sincere but simply trying to find out how people would react to his republican words.[128] Concerning the emperor's speeches to the Senate, Tacitus warned

that he may not have meant them. He noted that Livia and Tiberius did not appear in public to mourn Germanicus, "either
holding it below their majesty to sorrow in the sight of men, or
apprehending that, if all eyes perused their looks, they might find
hypocrisy legible" (3.3). The fact that Tiberius returned to Rome
on hearing that his mother had fallen ill caused Tacitus to speculate that either "the harmony between mother and son was still
genuine, or their hatred concealed" (3.64).

Tacitus certainly wanted to influence his readers' attitudes
toward the emperor, but, at the same time, he did not wish to
compromise his claim to be dispassionate and without rancor.[129]
These two goals, together with simple political prudence, led Tacitus to avoid direct expression of his opinions in favor of suggestive statements. Tiberius was particularly susceptible to innuendo,
because his dour and arrogant manner made him unpopular in
his own time and spawned many unsavory rumors. Where Suetonius used these rumors to form the basis of explicit descriptions
of character, Tacitus let them stand by themselves, forcing the
reader to make his own judgements. Tacitus began by noting the
rumors about the future ruler that were circulating prior to the
death of Augustus. Tiberius was said to be mature in years, expert
in war, but with the old inbred arrogance of the Claudian house
and with hints of a future cruelty.[130] Tacitus employed rumors to
describe the emperor's character throughout his reign. When Tiberius used the *lex majestatis* to punish libel against himself, he
did so, according to Tacitus, because he was upset by some verses
satirizing his cruelty and arrogance (1.72). Without quoting or
even commenting on the verses, the historian managed to give
the impression that they had some foundation in truth. When
Tiberius declined to attend the games, Tacitus reported that some
thought it was due to impatience with crowds, while others claimed
that his native moroseness would appear in a bad light when compared with Augustus' good humor (1.76). Once again Tacitus
managed to convey a vivid impression of Tiberius' weaknesses,
without directly compromising his stance of impartiality.

Tacitus also characterized other figures by repuation. He introduced Germanicus, for example, by discussing other peoples'
attitudes towards him. Livia and Tiberius hated him, but the nation as a whole, which thought he might restore the republic,
viewed him with hope and affection (1.33). Despite his obvious
admiration for Germanicus, Tacitus almost never praised him directly but recounted his good qualities through the mouths of

others. He claimed that Germanicus once put on a disguise and walked around the camp to find out what the soldiers really thought of him, a situation that allowed Tacitus to mention all Germanicus' good qualities as opinions of the soldiers (2.13). At Germanicus' death, Tacitus did not describe his character at length. Instead, he cited the opinion of those who would compare him to Alexander the Great (2.73). Even minor characters are often treated this way. Thus, the prosecutor Fulcinius Trio had a talent, says Tacitus dryly, that was "famous among informers."[131]

Tacitus also presented behavior in ways that subtly led the reader to the desired conclusion while preserving the stance of impartiality. He often introduced individuals by describing their past actions. Percennius, the leader of the Pannonian mutineers, was "in his early days the leader of a claque at the theatres, then a private soldier with an abusive tongue, whose experience of the stage rivalries had taught him the art of inflaming an audience" (1.16). Thus, Tacitus made the soldier's salient characteristics apparent while leaving them unnamed. Further on he described the first prosecutor of libel cases under the *lex majestatis* as follows:

> Indigent, unknown, unresting, first creeping with his private reports into the confidence of his pitiless sovereign, then a terror to the noblest, he acquired the favour of one man, the hatred of all, and set an example, the followers of which passed from beggary to wealth, from being despised to being feared, and crowned at last the ruin of others by their own (1.74).

After this introduction, Tacitus passed directly to a detailed account of the prosecutor's deeds. The man's character traits remained unnamed, but they were clearly implied in this general description of his behavior. Tacitus used the same technique even when describing those he admired. Lucius Piso, for example, whom he considered a fine example of old-fashioned virtue, was defined solely by his attempts to retire and his stubborn efforts to prosecute a friend of Livia's.

Frequently, Tacitus used the device of interpretive innuendo both to reveal a character and to explain a situation. An excellent example is his treatment of Tiberius' practice of prolonging his generals in their commands until death. Tacitus declined to explain this practice directly. Instead, he explored the conflicting

219

rumors it occasioned. Either Tiberius disliked recurring trouble and, thus, kept to a decision once it was made, or he did not like to see too many men enjoying preferment. Tacitus himself seems to have favored the first rumor, since he subsequently observed that Tiberius enjoyed a reputation for shrewd intellect, even though his judgement was considered hesitant. Here, again, the historian avoided stating his own opinion directly. Finally, Tacitus complained that vacillation carried Tiberius so far that he gave provinces to men whom he never allowed to leave Rome. By beginning and ending with concrete acts interpreted by the conflicting rumors they stirred up, Tacitus turned Tiberius' policy, which at first seemed overly rigid, into one of vacillation. Few historians can manipulate their evidence so openly and self-confidently (1.80).

These three techniques—the interest in reputation, the concern for specific details of behavior rather than general moral judgements, and the use of differing explanations for a single action—are basic to Machiavelli's writings. Examples abound in the *Florentine Histories*, as well as in the *Prince*, the *Discourses*, and the *Mandragola*. Machiavelli not only used Tacitean techniques but modified them and thereby drew his reader's attention to a reality different from that of Tacitus. Besides employing the Tacitean technique of describing individuals by their behavior and repuation, Machiavelli made direct assessments of character as did Livy, Sallust, and the humanist historians. This combination of direct assessments with reputation and behavior allowed Machiavelli to express the inherent reality of the protagonists in his narrative.

His practice is clear in his treatment of two major figures in the *Florentine Histories*, Cosimo and Lorenzo de' Medici. Machiavelli began his account of Cosimo in Tacitean fashion, by describing his behavior.

> Cosimo de'Medici, after the death of his father Giovanni, entered into public affairs with more spirit and acted with more zeal and liberality towards his friends than his father had, with the result that those who were relieved by the death of Giovanni, seeing what sort of man Cosimo was, were dismayed.[132]

Tacitus would have been content to mention these reactions to Cosimo's behavior and would have gone on to discuss his reputation, but Machiavelli next injects his own assesssment of the abstract traits of Cosimo's character. "Cosimo was a most prudent man, of serious and gracious presence, completely liberal, completely human."[133] This statement served to give Cosimo an independent character, something Machiavelli obviously thought important to do, recognizing that individuals have a reality beyond their overt acts and public reputation.

Only after thus defining Cosimo did Machiavelli enlarge upon his reputation. He recounted a lengthy speech given by Niccolò da Uzzano to an opponent of the Medici in which Uzzano argues that Cosimo's conspicuous liberality and vigorous policy has so won over the various elements of the city that a campaign to defeat him would encounter the most serious difficulties. The speech not only makes concrete the elements Machiavelli noted in Cosimo's character but also traces the realities of Florentine politics directly to these characteristics, illustrating how individuals influence larger historical situations and events.

The next time Cosimo appeared, he was in prison waiting for his fate to be decided by the Signoria. His jailer proposed to allay his fears of poison by sharing his meals and Cosimo accepted, "offering to be most grateful to him if fortune ever gives him the opportunity" (4.29). Machiavelli did not need to explicitly mention Cosimo's reputation for liberality here, for the earlier characterization, together with Uzzano's speech, helps us interpret the incident. Machiavelli soon made concrete Cosimo's willingness to buy favors. The jailer, wishing to cheer him up, invited one of Cosimo's friends to dinner, leaving the two of them alone for a few minutes. Cosimo seized the opportunity and gave the friend a bribe for the Gonfaloniere of Justice to secure his release. Thus, he escaped execution.

Machiavelli did not comment directly on Cosimo's behavior at this point in the narrative. His opinion was probably divided. On the one hand, he disapproved of bribery as a means of securing political influence, as he made clear in the preface to Book 7 of the *Florentine Histories*. On the other hand, he had great respect for the success of Cosimo's policy. When old Jacopo Pazzi rode though the streets of Florence shouting *Popolo e libertà!* he received no response, "because the first had been made deaf by the fortune and liberality of the Medici" (8.8).

The ideas here are not surprising. Machiavelli, after all, expressed a similar attitude towards liberality in Chapter 16 of the *Prince*. What is striking is how he blended the ideas into his presentation of Cosimo's character. Cosimo took on reality partly from his actual behavior, partly from the attitudes others formed in response to his acts, and partly from the effect those acts had on general political issues. All these facets of individual reality were present in Tacitus' narratives. But Machiavelli gave Cosimo an additional reality peculiarly his own, a character independent from his behavior and reputation. In short, Machiavelli presented Cosimo as a person whose reality had both historical and abstract dimensions.

Machiavelli portrayed Lorenzo with a similar combination of behavior and abstract characterization. In contrast to the liberality of his grandfather, Lorenzo's dominant trait was his ability to create a favorable impression. After the death of his father, Piero, Lorenzo addressed the leading Florentines. In describing the scene, Machiavelli concentrated on his behavior and its effect on others. "Although he was young, Lorenzo spoke with such gravity and modesty that he gave everyone an indication of what he would eventually become" (7.24). An earlier allusion to Lorenzo included a similar combination of actions, reputation, and character. At a tournament, said Machiavelli, "among the young Florentines the most famous was Lorenzo. . . , who won first prize not by influence but by his own valor" (8.12).

In later passages, Machiavelli further illustrated the importance of Lorenzo's ability to create a good impression. During the Pazzi conspiracy, Giovanni Battista, meeting Lorenzo for the first time, was surprised by his affability, "so much so that he admired Lorenzo, finding him another man from that one the conspirators had described, and judging him completely human, wise and most friendly to him" (8.4). Later, Giovanni refused to assassinate Lorenzo, which Machiavelli explained with Tacitean ambiguity. "Either his familiarity with Lorenzo had softened his spirit or some other reason moved him. He said that he would lose his soul if he committed such a crime in a church" (8.5). Whatever else the reader may conclude from this, it is another reminder of that personal charm which Machiavelli wished to stress. Later on, when Lorenzo went to Naples, King Ferdinand was impressed more "with the greatness of his spirit, the cleverness of his mind, and the gravity of his judgement than he had formerly been with his power" (8.19). Thus, according to Machiavelli, Lorenzo's personal qualities were more important to his diplomatic and political success than was his actual power.

Machiavelli, then, combined the Tacitean devices of description through behavior and reputation with direct assessments of character, both giving personal reality to the individuals in his work and connecting them clearly with the larger events. He used the device of alternative explanation to reinforce the personal element in history. He offered alternatives that prevented the readers from creating a systematic picture of events and dispensing with the individual, contingent aspects. In the just mentioned explanation for Giovanni's refusal to assassinate Lorenzo, we cannot interpret the move as a simple effect either of Lorenzo's character or of religious scruples. Machiavelli forced us to consider the personality of Giovanni, in which these motives are combined. Similarly, Machiavelli explained Lorenzo's escape from assassination "either through the conspirators' negligence or by his own spirit."[134]

Machiavelli also used the device of alternative explanations to suggest to the reader that events arose out of states of emotion, out of specific antecedent events, or out of a combination of these. He described the Lucchese hatred for the Florentines as born "from former injuries or from continual fear" (8.14). Galeotto of Faenza's wife hated him "either because of jealousy or because he mistreated her, or because of her evil nature" (8.35). Bernardo Bandini killed Francesco Nori during the Pazzi conspiracy "either because he had long hated him or because Francesco was trying to help Giuliano" (8.6). Early in the work Machiavelli observed that the Florentines quickly divided into supporters of Count Novello "either because of his behavior or because it is natural to the Florentines that every condition saddens them and every incident divides them" (2.25).

The importance Machiavelli ascribed to changing personal factors in his narrative emerged clearly in his version of the first stages of the Pazzi conspiracy. He began with the political and familial considerations underlying the conspiracy, noting Cosimo's decision to marry into the family and Lorenzo's decision to sacrifice the political benefits of that marriage and diminish the wealth of the Pazzi. Then Machiavelli described the emotions engendered by this situation: anger on the part of the Pazzi and fear on the part of the Medici. The conspiracy grew out of these common feelings, but it was sparked by Francesco Pazzi, since "he was more spirited and sensitive than any of the others, so that he decided either to acquire what he lacked or to lose what he had."[135] Thus, Machiavelli traced the conspiracy to a personal act occurring within a general psychological and political context, which in turn was the result of specific personal decisions made by Cosimo and Lorenzo.

Poliziano, the humanist supporter of the Medici, wrote an account of the conspiracy just after it happened in 1478, an account which did not combine personal and general factors as Machiavelli's did. Poliziano's account began with a description of the abstract condition of the city and the moral characteristics of the Pazzi family.[136] Next he listed the conspirators, identifying each by his general character traits. Poliziano mentioned the marriage, which Machiavelli saw as the root of the problem, only briefly, when he assessed the husband's role in the conspiracy (pp. 20-21). Instead of Francesco Pazzi, who assumed a rather passive role, Poliziano blamed the Archbishop of Pisa for originating the plot. The humanist historian gave Francesco the same character traits that Machiavelli ascribed to him[137] but allowed him no specific role in instigating the event. The plot unfolded against a background of fixed character traits which applied to whole families (the Pazzi were distinguished by profligacy and envy) as well as specific individuals.

Machiavelli's emphasis on Francesco's personality contrasts strongly with Tacitus' handling of Sejanus' conspiracy against the Julio-Claudian house. Even though he called Sejanus the *initia et causa* of the disasters that befell Rome in the last part of Sejanus' reign and characterized him fully by noting his origin, past behavior, and mores, Tacitus took pains to diminish Sejanus' personal significance. He found inexplicable Sejanus' influence with the emperor, observing that it could not have been Sejanus' *sollertia*, since Tiberius was more intelligent and ingenious than he. In the end, Tacitus blamed the anger of the gods against Rome.[138] The subsequent narrative gives the reader no clue as to the source of Sejanus' success. He had no distinctive personal traits or patterns of action but was merely an instrument of heaven's wrath.

Even more striking is the comparison between Machiavelli and Sallust. Machiavelli followed this historian in many ways, adopting his practice of introductory prefaces and sympathizing with his complaints about political corruption. Just as Poliziano's account of the Pazzi conspiracy showed many debts to Sallust, Machiavelli must have had the monograph on Catiline's conspiracy in mind as he too wrote of the Pazzi. Yet Sallust, like Tacitus, presented the individual conspirators as passive, blaming the conspiracy on the general state of Roman politics and mores. Although Sallust vividly described Catiline's vigorous body and soul, he saw Catiline's desire to seize the government as something done to him and not a force emanating from his active will.[139] Machiavelli differed from the classical sources in that he granted the individuals a specific and active role in the conspiracy.

This analysis of medieval and Renaissance assumptions about change has proceeded by a comparative method. In studying differences between Machiavelli's narrative and similar narratives in his sources and models, we have found that Machiavelli's ability to describe the inherent relationships among concrete historical events stands in clear contrast to the practice of medieval historians who related events to external, unchanging realities, divine judgement, abstract character, or a rigid chronology. In exposing this contrast, it has been necessary to ignore, or relegate to a secondary position, the immediate issues which dominated the intentions of the authors. But these issues were important. Machiavelli's account of Cosimo and Lorenzo certainly reflected his feelings toward the Medici, who exiled and tortured him in 1512, less than a decade before they commissioned him to write his history. His ambivalence is quite different from the complacency of Poliziano, a comfortable client of the Medici, and is probably similar to the attitude of Tacitus towards the early emperors. Many characteristics of his account must arise from an attempt to show the weakness of Medici rule without offending his patron, the Medici Pope Clement VII. But conscious political intent does not explain all dimensions of Machiavelli's narrative, particularly its striking dynamic quality. Tacitus and Sallust managed to express their political ambivalence without producing such a narrative.

To understand the work of medieval historians it is also important to bear in mind their religious and political concerns. Orosius set out to demonstrate the prevalence of disasters in pre-Christian times, and his decisions about what to include in his history reflected this concern as much as anything. At the same time, his techniques for narrating the events were limited. He could not have described them the way Machiavelli did and probably would not have acknowledged the virtues of Machiavelli's style. An inquiry into the specific conscious intentions of a historian does not expose the differing conceptions of time that underlie his work. These are two separate areas of inquiry; they require different methods and approaches and produce answers which are complementary in scope, not mutually exclusive.

The problem of developing a convincing dynamic narrative

has been treated here as a search for appropriate models for imitation. We have seen that Machiavelli had available a great variety of models, including the civic humanism of Bruni, the Medicean, neo-Platonic humanism of Poliziano, and the scholarly humanism of Biondo, as well as the classical authors and vernacular chronicles. No one of these had all the ingredients found in Machiavelli's narrative. To construct his narrative, he adopted parts of each, taking details from the chronicles, concepts and narrative order from Bruni, and narrative techniques from Tacitus. None of these observations should diminish Machiavelli's creative genius. We might learn from this example that affinity does not always make for similarity. Imitators are not necessarily passive copiers of their models, but are often, like Machiavelli's characters themselves, personal creative realities.

Machiavelli's ability to show the inherent interrelations among concrete events and personalities was radically new and constitutes a turning point in the development of Western historical writing. The Burckhardtian tones of such an assertion should not hide its novelty. The sharp contrast between medieval and Renaissance modes of expression Burckhardt insisted on has become, under the attacks of twentieth-century scholars, a complex continuity. In this particular case, Machiavelli needed Augustinian notions of personality for his result as much as classical narrative techniques. But the search for continuity can obscure distinctive features of an era. As William Bouwsma has recently observed, the notion of the Renaissance is an important part of the drama of Western history, and modern scholarship has lost sight of the depth of its cultural uniqueness.[140] Bouwsma argues that we can maintain this drama without uncritical acceptance of the linear progress that lay behind Burckhardt's work. Machiavelli's complex and dynamic narrative of the past constitutes such a dramatic moment and provides the basis for our own consciousness of modern times.

NOTES

An earlier version of the section entitled "Narrative Technique and the Description of Change" was read at the Conference on Humanism at Duke University in the Fall of 1978. I wish to thank Alan Bernstein and Mark Phillips for reading the manuscript and making many helpful suggestions.

[1]Felix Gilbert, *Machiavelli and Guicciardini* (Princeton, 1965).

[2]For an excellent treatment of this aspect of Guicciardini see Mark Phillips, *Francesco Guicciardini: The Historian's Craft* (Toronto, 1977).

[3]See Eugenio Garin, *Italian Humanism*, trans. Peter Munz (New York, 1965).

[4]See Hans Baron, *The Crisis of the Early Italian Renaissance*, rev. ed. (Princeton, 1966).

[5]Niccolò Machiavelli, *Istorie fiorentini*, vol. 2 of *Tutte le opere di Niccolò Machiavelli*, ed. Francesco and Carlo Cordié, 2nd ed. (Milan, 1960), Proemio. Hereafter cited as *Florentine Histories*.

[6]This matter will be discussed below.

[7]See Denys Hay, "Flavio Biondo in the Middle Ages," *Proceedings of the British Academy*, 45 (1959), 97-128.

[8]Flavio Biondo, *Ab Inclinatione Romanorum Imperii Decades Tres* (Venice, 1483), Bk. 1. Biondo said that the translation of the seat of the empire was only a remote cause, not the beginning of the fall. In general, he was dubious about political causes.

[9]See nn. 48-86 below.

[10]*Florentine Histories*, 1.1.

[11]*Florentine Histories*, 1.1.

[12]"The Two Faces of Humanism: Stoicism and Augustinianism in Renaissance Thought," in *Itinerarium Italicum: The Profile of the Italian Renaissance in the Mirror of its European Transformations, Dedicated to Paul Oscar Kristeller on the Occasion of his 70th Birthday*, ed. Heiko Oberman with Thomas Brady (Leiden, 1975), p. 36. Bouwsma feels that the Augustinian strand is particularly strong in the Florentine civic humanist tradition.

[13]*The Idea of Historical Recurrence in Western Thought: From Antiquity to the Reformation* (Berkeley, 1979). See Roger Ray, "Medieval Historiography through the Twelfth Century: Problems and Progress of Research," *Viator*, 5 (1974), 33-59 for a discussion of the current state of scholarship as the study of medieval historians begins to emerge from the shadow of *Quellenkunde*. See also Beryl Smalley, *Historians in the Middle Ages* (London, 1974) for a recent general treatment of the major historians of the period.

[14]Augustine, *Confessions*, ed. and trans. W. Watts (Cambridge, MA, 1950-51), Bk. 7, Ch. 29.

[15]So strong is the expectation among modern readers that Eusebius saw some expressible general significance in these events that one translator has even rendered the passage "Now let us describe for the benefit of future generations the character of our own" (G. W. Williamson, trans., *The History of the Church from Christ to Constantine* [Baltimore, 1965], p. 313). The use of an abstract term to describe a specific set of temporal

events is anachronistic. Eusebius did not make so specific a promise, saying "kai tēn kath'; ēmas tois metepeita gnōrizein genean opoia tis ēn paradōmen" (*Ecclesiastical History*, 7.26, with Rufinus' translation in *Eusebius Werke*, ed. Edward Schwarz and Theodore Mommsen, vol. 2 [Leipzig, 1903]).

[16]Rufinus even leaves out reference to the *hypothesin*: "Hucusque successiones episcoporum gestaque diversa a domini et nativitate Servatoris nostri ad tempus persecutionis in qua ecclesiae quoque destructae sunt, historiae mandavimus" (*Ecclesiastical History*, 6.32).

[17]See Jacob Burckhardt, *The Age of Constantine the Great*, trans. Moses Hadas (1949; rpt. New York, 1967), p. 283.

[18]*Ecclesiastical History*, 9.10.

[19]Hannibal's comment is found in Livy, *Ab Urbe Condita*, ed. and trans. B. O. Foster (Cambridge, MA, 1951-76), Bk. 26, Ch. 11.

[20]*Historiarum Adversum Paganos Libri VII*, ed. Karl Zangemeister, Corpus Scriptorum Ecclesiasticorum Latinorum, 5 (Vienna, 1882), Bk. 4, Ch. 17. For a recent general treatment of Orosius see Benoit Lacroix, *Orose et ses idées*, Publications de l'Institut d'études medievales, 18 (Montréal, 1965).

[21]*Adversum Paganos*, 1.5.

[22]Genesis 13:10; Wisdom 10:6.

[23]Augustine, *De Civitate Dei contra Paganos*, ed. and trans. Eva Sanford and William Green (Cambridge, MA, 1965), Bk. 21, Ch. 8.

[24]Orosius explained that he would touch only briefly on Jugurtha, because all people, by reason of the fine work of the historians, were sufficiently well-acquainted with his fickle and unbearable character (*Adversum Paganos*, 5.15). Later he observed that the conspiracy of Catiline was well known to all, since Cicero was involved in it and Sallust described it (6.6). See also R. W. Southern, "Aspects of the European Tradition of Historical Writing: The Classical Tradition from Einhard to Geoffrey of Monmouth," *Transactions of the Royal Historical Society*, 20 (1970), 179. Though the historians Southern discusses did not often imitate Sallust's causal principles, it seems that Orosius did so here.

[25]*The Idea of Historical Recurrence*, pp. 222-25.

[26]*Adversum Paganos*, 6.22.

[27]*Adversum Paganos*, 7.26. This insistence on literal parallels is characteristic of Orosius, who also argued that Christ was born in the same year of the Roman Empire and that Abraham was of the reign of Ninus (2.2).

[28]See *Adversum Paganos*, 7.35, where he noted that there were many wars from Maximus to Theodosius but that they occasioned little bloodshed. On other occasions he saw the reverse pattern. Early in the work he said that evils became more complex with time as men became more skilled in wickedness (1.21).

[29]: "Libuit etiam animo ut pro supputatione annorum, ab ipso mundi principio libri primi poneretur initium cuis capitula deorsum subjeci"; and, "Cum nonnullae res gerentur vel rectae vel improbae" (*Historiae Francorum*, vol. 1 of *Gregorii Turonesis Opera*, ed. W. Arndt and B. Krusch, Monumenta Germaniae Historica: Scriptores Rerum Merovingicarum [Hanover, 1885], Preface).

[30]"Prosequentes ordinem temporum mixte confusequae tam virtutes sanctorum quam strages gentium memoramus" (*Historiae Francorum*, vol. 2, Preface).

[31]Gregory explicitly claims that Athanaric felt the weight of God's judgment (*Historiae Francorum*, 2.4).

[32]The most obvious Old Testament reference is to Solomon (1 Kings 3:6), but even David never matched Clovis' behavior. Unlike Eusebius and Orosius, Gregory did not use parallels with the Old Testament to give meaning to his story. His comparisons with Old Testament prototypes were random and literary in intent. As Lothar and Chramm met in battle, he referred to the old king as some new David advancing against Absalom (4.20). He put Solomon's words (Prov. 26:27) in Germanus' mouth to warn Chilperic not to kill his brother (4.51) and described a miracle in Antioch as a re-enactment of Sodom with the hero playing the role of Lot (10.24). He used events from classical antiquity in the same way, comparing drowning troops on the Rhone to Trojans as described by Virgil (4.31). Felix Thürlemann has argued that these are examples of the figurative *topoi* which Gregory used not only as interpretive devices but also to make the narrative more convincing (*Der historische Diskurs bei Gregor von Tours: Topoi und Wirklichkeit* [Bern, 1974]). Whatever the function of these allusions, they certainly do not serve to give an overall meaning to the chronological sequence or to give specific moral content to the retributive aspect of his history.

[33]"At illi negutia exercentes divites per hoc effecti sunt et usque hodie magni habentur" (*Historiae Francorum*, 3.34).

[34]"Et nihil exigens, antedictus cives divites fecit" (*Historiae Francorum*, 3.34).

[35]*Ecclesiastical History of the English People*, ed. Bertram Colgrave and R. A. B. Mynors (Oxford, 1969), 3.4.

[36]"Non illius inpar qui quondam a Chaldaeis succensus Hierosolymorum moenia, immo aedificia cuncta consumsit" (*Ecclesiastical History*, 1.15).

[37]"Et libentius eo praedicante caelestia sperare coeperunt, cuius ministerio temporalia bona sumserunt" (*Ecclesiastical History*, 4.13).

[38]Roger Ray, "Bede, the Exegete as Historian," in *Famulus Christi: Essays in Commemoration of the Thirteenth Centenary of the Birth of the Venerable Bede*, ed. Gerald Bonner (London, 1976), pp. 133-34, has pointed out his great concern for the credibility of his story and the fact that the message of the narrative mattered more to him than the details.

[39]Otto was formerly considered widely influential among medieval historians and typical in expressing the thought of the Middle Ages about universal history. See Felix Fellner, "The 'Two Cities' of Otto of Freising and its Influence on the Catholic Philosophy of History," *Catholic Historical Review*, 20 (1934), 154-74. Modern scholars find Otto less influential and more nearly unique in his approach. See Beryl Smalley, *Historians in the Middle Ages*, for a recent assessment of his significance. R. W. Southern, "Aspects of the European Tradition of Historical Writing: Hugh of St. Victor and the Idea of Historical Development," *Transactions of the Royal Historical Society*, 21 (1971), 159-80, chose Hugh of St. Victor as his example of a developmental historian of the twelfth century.

[40]*Chronica sive Historia de Duabus Civitatibus*, ed. A. Hofmeister, Scriptores Rerum Germanicarum in Usum Scholarum (Hanover and Leipzig, 1912), 2.8. The English passages quoted in the text are taken from *The Two Cities*, trans. Charles Mierow, ed. Austin P. Evans and Charles Knapp (New York, 1928).

[41]*The Two Cities*, 6.3.

[42]"Decedente atque immo potius pereunte ab urbibus gallicanis liberalium cultura litterarum" (*Historiae Francorum*, Preface).

[43]The anecdotal character doubtless reflects Gregory's use of Suetonius as a model.

[44]*The Two Cities*, 1.6. He was sufficiently concerned to convince his reader of this trend that he quoted Eusebius and Cicero in support of his explanation.

[45]See *The Two Cities*, 3.27-35, where he followed Eusebius and Orosius exactly except for mention of the writings of Origen and Cyprian, and 4.13, where he added a discussion of Ambrose's works.

[46]Jean Sire de Joinville, *Histoire de Sainte Louis*, ed. M. Natalis de Wailly (Paris, 1874), Ch. 297, recounted the story of his chastizing seven men for laughing at the funeral of a soldier recently killed in battle and observed that they all died soon after this act of impiety. Geoffroi de Villehardouin, *La conquête de Constantinople*, ed. Emile Bouchet (Paris, 1891) noted that all who declined to follow the army to Venice as they had agreed suffered harm and disgrace (Ch. 117) and that God punished the crusaders who took more than their share of the booty (Ch. 130).

[47]*Histoire de Sainte Louis*, pp. 218-19.

[48]"Machiavelli's 'Istorie fiorentine': An Essay in Interpretation," in *Studies on Machiavelli*, ed. Myron Gilmore (Florence, 1972).

[49]"Time in Ancient Historiography," in *History and the Concept of Time*, Beiheft 6 of *History and Theory: Studies in the Philosophy of History*, 6 (Middletown, CN, 1966), pp. 1-23.

[50]"Machiavelli, Guicciardini, and the Tradition of Vernacular Historiography in Florence," *American Historical Review*, 84 (1979), 86-105.

[51]Phillips, "Machiavelli," p. 94.

[52]He says in the Proemio to the *Florentine Histories* that he read the humanists "per vedere con quali ordini e modi nello scrivere procedevano, acciò che imitando quelli la istoria nostra fusse meglio dai leggenti approvata."

[53]For the political nature of Bruni's history see Donald J. Wilcox, *Development of Florentine Humanist Historiography in the Fifteenth Century* (Cambridge, MA, 1969). The influence of Bruni on Machiavelli is suggested there and is fully discussed in J. G. A. Pocock, *The Machiavellian Moment: Florentine Political Thought and the Atlantic Republican Tradition* (Princeton, 1975). Pocock understands the general similarity between Bruni's political ideas and Machiavelli's but regards Bruni as just one of many Florentines, including Goro Dati and Giovanni Cavalcanti, who resemble Machiavelli. It will be argued here that from no other Florentine writer did Machiavelli appropriate in so detailed a fashion the ideas and interpretations of specific events.

[54]*Florentine Histories*, 2.5. Both men said that Corso Donati forced the priors to become private citizens after having been public officials (*Florentine Histories*, 2.19; Leonardo Bruni, *Historiarum Florentini Populi Libri XII*, ed. E. Santini, in Rerum Italicarum Scriptores, vol. 19, part 3 [Città di Castello; 1934], 4.92), while Villani described his action in concrete terms, saying he drove them out of the Palace of the Signoria (Giovanni Villani, *Cronica* [Florence, 1844-45], 8.49). On the reforms after the death of Manfred see *Florentine Histories*, 2.8 and *Historiarum*, 2.48-49.

[55]Machiavelli drew on Villani to present a fuller account of the elements in the crisis leading to the *signoria* of Walter of Brienne, but he omitted Villani's attack on the personal integrity of those involved and the moralizing judgments in the chronicle. Instead, he selected events which enlarged on the political themes he took from Bruni (*Florentine Histories*, 2.32; *Cronica*, 9.118). Examples of events modeled on Bruni's narrative are the return of the Guelfs after Frederick's death (*Florentine Histories*, 2.4), the establishment of the Guelf domination after Manfred's death (2.7), the order of Giano della Bella's reforms (2.13), the downfall of Corso Donati (2.22-23) the war with Castruccio Castracani (2.26-28), the events preceding the Ciompi revolt (3.2-3), and the reaction to the revolt as far as the exile of Benedetto degli Alberti (3.21-29).

[56]See *Development*, Ch. 2. One example of his use of Bruni's political categories is found early in Book 2, where Machiavelli described the formation of the government of the *primo popolo*. The result of this government, he observed, was to give the Florentines their liberty and greatly increase their power (*Florentine Histories*, 2.6). This attempt to relate power and liberty to changes in polity is taken directly from Bruni, who based his treatment of Florentine foreign affairs on the assumption

that the city's foreign power was a function of its free institutions (*Historiarum*, 2.27-28).

[57]For instance, both writers said that the troubles between the Cerchi and Donati became serious, developing into the feud between the Blacks and the Whites, because of the hatreds and divisions between the citizens (*Florentine Histories*, 2.16; *Historiarum*, 4.88), and both focused on the suspicions that were rife in the city during the feud (*Florentine Histories*, 2.18; *Historiarum* 5.117). Analyzing the war with Castruccio, both stressed the fear of the citizens that determined the city's behavior (*Florentine Histories*, 2.26; *Historiarum*, 4.89), while Villani said it was the internal divisions that caused the behavior (*Cronica*, 9.128). Both noted that at the beginning of the disturbances which led to the revolt of the Ciompi, the *invidia* of the Guelfs against the Eight of the War was a factor in their attempt to misuse the laws against the Gibellines (*Florentine Histories*, 3.7; *Historiarum*, 8.219). At the end of the revolt Machiavelli and Bruni stressed the unhappy and suspicious state of the city (*Florentine Histories*, 3.20; *Historiarum*, 8.230). Both saw that events such as the exile of Benedetto degli Alberti resulted from fear and hatred among the citizens (*Florentine Histories*, 3.22; *Historiarum*, 8.241).

[58]*Florentine Histories*, 2.34-36.

[59]"Superante iam odio metum" (*Historiarum*, 6.164).

[60]*Cronica*, 12.8 and 16; Marchionne di Coppo Stefani, *Cronaca fiorentina*, ed. N. Rodolico, in Rerum Italicarum Scriptores, vol. 30, part 1 (Città di Castello, 1903), rubrics 555-77.

[61]*Historiarum*, 9.223-24.

[62]*Florentine Histories*, 3.4.

[63]*Florentine Histories*, 3.10. See also *Historiarum*, 9.224: "Cavenda vero maxime videntur principia seditionum inter primarios cives."

[64]*Florentine Histories*, 3.17; *Historiarum*, 9.225.

[65]*Cronaca fiorentina*, 796; Gino Capponi, *Tumulto dei Ciompi*, in Rerum Italicarum Scriptores, ed. L. Muratori, vol. 18 (Milan, 1731), col. 1123.

[66]*Florentine Histories*, Proemio.

[67]Machiavelli's dependence on Bruni's narrative order has not often been noted by students of Machiavelli, but Aldo Garosci, *Le 'Istorie fiorentine' del Machiavelli* (Turin, 1973), has studied the similarities of narrative order between the two histories and noted many other events where Machiavelli used Bruni as a source of the order of facts.

[68]On Poggio's use of sensory details, see *Development*, Chs. 5 and 6. On Poliziano, see section of this essay on Narrative Technique.

[69]See *Development*, Ch. 6, and Alison Brown, *Bartolomeo Scala, 1430-1497, Chancellor of Florence: The Humanist as Bureaucrat* (Princeton, 1979).

[70]It is doubtless for this reason that Machiavelli did not use the narrative order or abstract facts of Poggio, despite the fact that Poggio's blending of analysis and narrative of concrete details was closer to Machiavelli's own approach. Machiavelli's failure to use Poggio is clear from analysis of any major event covered by both historians. The outbreak of war between Florence and Filippo Visconti, for example, is narrated in a different order by Machiavelli and given a different explanation from that found in Poggio. While Poggio saw Filippo's constant greed and ambition as the cause of the war, Machiavelli assessed the particular motives of the various combatants. See *Florentine Histories*, 4.3-8; Poggio Bracciolini, *Historia florentina*, ed. J. Recanati, in Rerum Italicarum Scriptores, ed. L. Muratori, vol. 20 (Milan, 1731) Bks. 5-8.

[71]*Florentine Histories*, 3.20. His source is probably *Cronaca fiorentina*, 901.

[72]*Tumulto*, 1122.

[73]Peter Bondanella, *Machiavelli and the Art of Renaissance History* (Detroit, 1973), has discussed this aspect of Machiavelli's historical writing. Disagreeing with Gilbert's observation that Machiavelli created abstract types of character which would illustrate his ideas, Bondanella points out that Machiavelli gave his characters physical details which made them individuals without sacrificing the didactic value of their general character traits. Bondanella sees Machiavelli's accomplishment as a literary one in which he combined the art of portraiture he had already practiced in such works as the *Vita di Castruccio Castracani* with the framework of humanist historiography.

[74]"La barba lunga e rada" (*Florentine Histories*, 2.37). The source of this detail is complex. Machiavelli combined Villani's "barbucino" (*Cronica*, 12.8) and di Stefani's "la barba avea grande" (*Cronaca fiorentina*, 567) to produce a new detail which reinforced his own characterization of the Duke as a man who looked as despicable as he acted.

[75]*Florentine Histories*, 3.16; Capponi supplied the detail, "in scarpette e sanza calze" (*Tumulto*, 1123).

[76]"E chi fusse stato per alcun tempo offeso, poteva ore fare sua vendetta pure che avesse avuto un poco di seguito; e detto andiamo alla casa del tale, era subito fatto perché al mal fare ciascuno era seguittato" (*Tumulto*, 1117).

[77]"Perché bastava solo che una voce nel mezzo della moltitudine 'a casa il tale!' gridasse, o che quello che teneva il gonfalone in mano vi si volgesse" (*Florentine Histories*, 3.14).

[78]"Il quale d'animo, di prudenza e di bontà superò in quel tempo qualunque cittadino, e merita di essere annoverato intra i pochi che abbino beneficata la patria loro; perché se in esso fusse stato animo o maligno o ambizioso la republica al tutto perdeva la sua libertà" (*Florentine Histories*, 3.17).

[79]*Cronaca fiorentina*, 804.

[80]"E venendo poi, nel fine delle parole alle minacce, non potette sopportare Michele tanta arroganza, e ricordandosi più del grado che teneva, che della infima condizione sua, gli parve da frenare con estraordinario modo una estraordinaria insolenza" (*Florentine Histories*, 3.17).

[81]*Mimesis: The Representation of Reality in Western Literature*, trans. W. Trask (Garden City, NJ, 1957), pp. 29-35.

[82]*Historiarum*, 9.224.

[83]*Tumulto*, 1108.

[84]He blames the *ammoniti* for not being willing to wait three years before returning to office (*Florentine Histories*, 3.10).

[85]*In Our Image and Likeness: Humanity and Divinity in Italian Humanist Thought*, 2 vols. (London, 1970). See also his more recent study of Petrarch in this context, *The Poet as Philosopher* (New Haven, 1979).

[86]"The Two Faces of Humanism," p. 36.

[87]*Gesta Friderici I Imperatoris*, ed. G. Waitz, Scriptores Rerum Germanicarum in Usum Scholarum, 46, 2nd ed. (Hanover, 1884), 1.55. Translations taken from *The Deeds of Frederick Barbarossa*, trans. Charles Mierow (New York, 1966).

[88]*Ecclesiastical History*, 8.6.

[89]*Adversum Paganos*, 4.15.

[90]Robert Bossard, *Uber die Entwicklung der Personendarstellung in der mittelalterlichen Geschichtschreibung* (Meilen, 1944), p. 35.

[91]See his treatment of Rausching and Boso, *Historiae Francorum*, 9.8-10; see also the accounts of the wives of Hermanfrid and Sigisimund, *Historiae Francorum*, 3.4.

[92]Erich Auerbach, *Mimesis*, pp. 67-83, has analyzed a long incident, the quarrel between Sicharius and Chramnedindus, showing that the failure to give motives makes the event almost incomprehensible to modern readers. The actors in Gregory's history regularly gave up kingdoms (7.33), refused to help allies (3.11), or murdered subjects (8.36), without a clear indication of motives. This indifference to motives has been variously interpreted. Recently, Charles Radding, "Evolution of Medieval Mentalities: A Cognitive-Structural Approach," *American Historical Review*, 83 (1978), 577-97, has argued that the attention to physical behavior at the expense of intention is not only evidence of a primitive society but is similar to childhood cognitive processes as described by Piaget.

[93]*Historiae Francorum*, 3.18.

[94]*Ecclesiastical History*, 2.1. Bede presented the story as a legend whose authenticity he did not vouch for, but since he did include it in his history he could as easily have done it earlier with the same disclaimer.

[95]The same combination of factors—piety, learning, and effective preaching—is found in Egbert's conversion of the monks of Iona to the

correct date for the celebration of Easter, discussed previously. There, too, Bede was most eager to establish the change as a direct result of divine grace, saying at the beginning of the chapter that the monks were led by divine grace, then describing Egbert's virtues, and reinforcing the notion of divine grace by noting the appropriateness of the conversion as a reward for the missionary zeal the monks had displayed in the past. Egbert, like Augustine of Canterbury, is thus presented as a passive instrument of divine grace operating through general qualities both missionaries embodied and which are not given individual content in the narrative.

[96]It is also partly a rhetorical device. Roger Ray, "Bede the Exegete," has pointed out that in *De Schematibus* Bede discussed *antonomasia*, the use of an epithet in lieu of a proper name, and the practice is common in the *Ecclesiastical History*.

[97]*Ecclesiastical History*, 3.14.

[98]*Ecclesiastical History*, 3.22.

[99]See, for instance, Gerhard Schoebe, "Was gilt im frühen Mittelalter als geschichtliche Wirklichkeit? Ein Versuch zur 'Kirchengeschichte' des Baeda Venerabilis," in *Festschrift Herman Aubin zun 80. Geburtstag*, ed. Otto Brunner et. al., 2 vols. (Wiesbaden, 1965), pp. 625-51.

[100]*Ideengeschichtliche Studien zu Einhard und anderen Geschichtsschreibern des früheren Mittelalters* (Darmstadt, 1969), p. 2.

[101]Suetonius, *De Vita Caesarum*, ed. and trans. J. C. Rolfe (Cambridge, MA, 1964), Bk. 2. Instances of Augustus' cruelty are noted in the conquest of Perugia (Ch. 15) and in his acts as Triumvir (Ch. 27), while his clemency is described in Ch. 51.

[102]Einhard, *Vita Karoli Magni, The Life of Charlemagne*, trans. Evelyn Firchow and Edwin Zeydel (Coral Gables, FL, 1972), Ch. 20.

[103]"Perseverantia et jugitate" (*Life of Charlemagne*, pg. 5).

[104]"Quod superbia simul ac socordia Tassilonis ducis excitavit" (*Life of Charlemagne*, pg. 11).

[105]"Nec si a plana hystorica dictione ad evagandum oportunitate nacta ad altiora velut phylosophica acumina attollatur oratio" (*Gesta Friderici I*, Prologue).

[106]"Quod dictum non secundum naturam generis sui percusso aere mox transiit, sed tam efficaciter in mentibus plurium radicem figens germinavit" (*Gesta Friderici I*, 1.4)

[107]*The Two Cities*, 3.12.

[108]*Confessions*, 3.4.

[109]*The Two Cities*, 2.9.

[110]*Adversum Paganos*, 7.30.

[111]The *Tripartite History*, the chronicle of Frutolf, and Rufinus' continuation of Eusebius.

[112]*The Two Cities*, 4.10.

[113]"Por ce que cil pardons fu si granz, si s'en esmurent mult li cuer des genz et mult s'en croisièrent" (*The Conquest of Constantinople*, 1).

[114]When he is first introduced he is described as "mult sages et mult proz" (*The Conquest of Constantinople*, 12), then when he convinces the Venetian council to help the crusaders he does so "par son sens et par son engin" (15).

[115]*Histoire de Sainte Louis*, p. 19.

[116]For a sensitive analysis of this aspect in an earlier chronicle tradition, see Nancy Partner, *Serious Entertainments: The Writing of History in Twelfth-Century England* (Chicago, 1977).

[117]Bondanella, *Machiavelli and the Renaissance Art of History*, treats both fictional and historical characters, showing Machiavelli's lasting impact through his use of significant detail to portray individuals. Here I am concerned to show how Machiavelli expressed the temporal dimensions of his characters. John Ward, "Classical Rhetoric and the Writing of History in Medieval and Renaissance Culture," *European History and Its Historians*, ed. F. McGregor and N. Wright (Adelaide, Australia, 1977), pp. 1-10, has studied medieval use of classical rhetorical categories, emphasizing theoreticians rather than practicing historians.

[118]*Le Prince*, trans. Amelot de la Houssaye (Amsterdam, 1684).

[119]Giusseppe Toffanin, *Machiavelli e il tacitismo* (1921; rpt. Naples, 1972).

[120]"Livy > Tacitus," *Classical Influences on European Culture, A.D. 1500-1700, Proceedings of an International Conference Held at Kings College, Cambridge, April, 1974*, ed. R. R. Bolgar (Cambridge, 1976), pp. 281-93.

[121]See *The Two Cities*, 1.18, 3.8 and 3.17. On the character of the early Germans he cites only Suetonius and Josephus (2.48).

[122]Kenneth Schellhase, *Tacitus in Renaissance Political Thought* (Chicago, 1976), pp. 66-84.

[123]*Florentine Histories*, 2.1.

[124]Both Schellhase and Whitfield are offended by this approach, since it explains little and often fails to discriminate Tacitus from the entire classical tradition of which he was a part.

[125]The most important general study of Tacitus is still Ronald Syme's *Tacitus* (Oxford, 1958). Herbert Benario, *An Introduction to Tacitus* (Athens, GA, 1975), has also discussed his use of indirect characterization. For an older monographic study, see Friedrich Krohn, *Personendarstellungen bei Tacitus* (Grossschönau in Sachsen, 1934).

[126]This aspect of Tacitus' explanations has been discussed by J. Cousin, "Rhetorique et psychologie chez Tacite," *Revue des études lat-*

ines, 29 (1951) 228-47. Cousin sees this practice in a psychological context as a probing of the unconscious.

[127]Bessie Walker, *The Annals of Tacitus* (Manchester, 1952), has studied the discrepancy between the facts Tacitus provides and the impression he seeks to convey. She has concentrated on the reign of Tiberius, feeling that the discrepancies are less pronounced in later books.

[128]Tacitus, *Ab Excessu Divi Augusti. The Annals*, trans. John Jackson (Cambridge, MA 1931), 1.7.

[129]"Sine ira et studio, quorum causas procul habeo" (*The Annals*, 1.1).

[130]Tacitus introduced this characterization by saying, "pars muto maxima imminentis dominos variis rumoribus differebant" (*The Annals*, 1.4).

[131]"Celebre inter accusatores Trionis ingenium erat avidumque famae malae" (*The Annals*, 2.28).

[132]*Florentine Histories*, 4.26.

[133]"Era Cosimo uomo prudentissimo, di grave e grata presenzia, tutto liberale, tutto umano" (*Florentine Histories*, 4.26).

[134]"O la loro negligenzia o lo animo di Lorenzo" (*Florentine Histories*, 8.6).

[135]"Era costui più animoso e più sensitivo che alcuno degli altri, tanto che deliberò o di acquistare quello che gli mancava o di perdere ciò che gli aveva" (*Florentine Histories*, 8.3).

[136]"Cum is igitur esset eius urbis status" (Angelo Poliziano, *Della congiura dei Pazzi [Coniurationis Commentarium]*, ed. Alessandro Perosa [Padua, 1958], p. 3).

[137]"Cum contumacis homo ingenii esset, magnos sibi spiritus, magnam arrogantiam sumpserat" (*Della congiura dei Pazzi*, p. 14).

[138]"Deum ira in rem Romanam" (*The Annals*, 4.1).

[139]"Hunc . . . lubido maxuma invaserat rei publicae capiundae" (Sallust, *Bellum Catilinae*, ed. and trans. J. C. Rolfe [Cambridge, Mass., 1971], Ch. 5).

[140]"The Renaissance and the Drama of Western History," *American Historical Review*, 84 (1979) 1-15.